The Future of Work Series

Series Editor: Peter Nolan, Director of the ESRC Future of Work Programme and the Montague Burton Professor of Industrial Relations at Leeds University Business School in the UK.

Few subjects could be judged more vital to current policy and academic debates than the prospects for work and employment. *The Future of Work* series provides the much needed evidence and theoretical advances to enhance our understanding of the critical developments most likely to impact on people's working lives.

Titles include:

Julia Brannen, Peter Moss and Ann Mooney
WORKING AND CARING OVER THE TWENTIETH CENTURY
Change and Continuity in Four Generation Families

Geraldine Healy, Edmund Herry, Phil Taylor and William Brown (*editors*)
THE FUTURE OF WORKER REPRESENTATION

Diane Houston (*editor*)
WORK-LIFE BALANCE IN THE 21st CENTURY

Theo Nichols and Surhan Cam
LABOUR IN A GLOBAL WORLD
Case Studies from the White Goods Industry in Africa, South America, East Asia and Europe

Paul Stewart (*editor*)
GLOBALISATION, THE CHANGING NATURE OF EMPLOYMENT AND THE FUTURE OF WORK
The Experience of Work and Organisational Change

Michael White, Stephen Hill, Colin Mills and Deborah Smeaton
MANAGING TO CHANGE?
British Workplaces and the Future of Work

The Future of Work Series
Series Standing Order ISBN 1–4039–1477–X

You can receive future titles in this series as they are published by placing a standing order. Please contact your bookseller or, in case of difficulty, write to us at the address below with your name and address, the title of the series and the ISBN quoted above.

Customer Services Department, Macmillan Distribution Ltd, Houndmills, Basingstoke, Hampshire RG21 6XS, England

Other Books by Theo Nichols:

OWNERSHIP, CONTROL AND IDEOLOGY

WORKERS DIVIDED: A STUDY IN SHOPFLOOR POLITICS (with P. Armstrong)

LIVING WITH CAPITALISM: CLASS RELATIONS IN THE MODERN FACTORY (with H. Beynon)

CAPITAL AND LABOUR: STUDIES IN THE CAPITALIST LABOUR PROCESS

WHITE COLLAR WORKERS, TRADE UNIONS AND CLASS (with P. Armstrong, R. Carter and C. Smith)

THE BRITISH WORKER QUESTION: A NEW LOOK AT WORKERS AND PRODUCTIVITY IN MANUFACTURING

WORK AND OCCUPATION IN MODERN TURKEY (with Erol Kahveci and Nadir Sugur)

THE SOCIOLOGY OF INDUSTRIAL INJURY

GLOBAL MANAGEMENT, LOCAL LABOUR: TURKISH WORKERS AND MODERN INDUSTRY (with Nadir Sugur)

Labour in a Global World

Case Studies from the White Goods Industry in Africa, South America, East Asia and Europe

Theo Nichols and Surhan Cam

First published 2005 by
PALGRAVE MACMILLAN
Houndmills, Basingstoke, Hampshire RG21 6XS and
175 Fifth Avenue, New York, N. Y. 10010
Companies and representatives throughout the world

PALGRAVE MACMILLAN is the global academic imprint of the Palgrave Macmillan division of St. Martin's Press, LLC and of Palgrave Macmillan Ltd. Macmillan® is a registered trademark in the United States, United Kingdom and other countries. Palgrave is a registered trademark in the European Union and other countries.

ISBN-13: 978–1–4039–3979–1   hardback
ISBN-10: 1–4039–3979–9   hardback

This book is printed on paper suitable for recycling and made from fully managed and sustained forest sources.

A catalogue record for this book is available from the British Library.

Library of Congress Cataloging-in-Publication Data
Nichols, Theo
   Labour in a global world: case studies from the white goods industry in Africa, South America, East Asia, and Europe / Theo Nichols and Surham Cam.
      p. cm. – (The future of work series, 1–4039–1477–X)
   Includes bibliographical references and index.
   ISBN 1–4039–3979–9 (cloth)
   1. Electric household appliances industry–Case studies.
2. Household appliances industry–Case studies. 3. Labour market.
4. Industrial organisation. 5. Industrial relations. 6. Globalisation–Economic aspects. I. Title: White goods industry in Africa, South America, East Asia, and Europe. II. Cam, Surhan, 1966– III. Title.
IV. Future of work (Series)

HD9971.5.E542N53 2005
331.7′68383–dc22   2005040246

10   9   8   7   6   5   4   3   2   1
14   13   12   11   10   09   08   07   06   05

Printed and bound in Great Britain by
Antony Rowe Ltd, Chippenham and Eastbourne

Contents

List of Tables

List of Figures

Acknowledgements

This research was conducted as part of the ESRC 'Future of Work' Programme (Award Number L212252072). We are indebted to the Director of
the Programme, Peter Nolan, for his enthusiasm for the project and his
personal support. We are also indebted to Peter Brannen, formerly Director,
ILO London, for his support for a Conference related to the research. Not
least, we are indebted to the School of Social Sciences, Cardiff University,
for further support for Conferences and related research activities.

Our thanks are due to our colleagues Huw Beynon and Peter Fairbrother
at the School of Social Sciences, Cardiff; to Lee Pegler who worked on the
early stage of the project; to Tongqing Feng who helped us with our research
in China; and in particular to Soonok Chun, who collaborated with us in
conducting research in South Korea, which she was unfortunately unable to
report on here because of illness.

Chapter 8 draws in part on an article on Factory Regimes by Nichols et al
in *Work, Employment and Society*, 18 (4). It also draws on some data from
the British Workplace Employment Relations Survey and the help is
acknowledged of the WERS Users Sub-Committee and the Data Archive,
University of Essex for granting access to restricted and unrestrictive data
respectively.

We are grateful to the National Library of Wales, Aberystwyth and to
AB Electrolux for permission to reprint the 1930s Electrolux advertisement
in Chapter 2.

Preface

This book had its origin in an earlier study, *Global Management, Local Labour: Turkish Workers and Modern Industry*, (Nichols and Sugur 2004). As its title suggests, this had been an attempt to investigate the modern corporate sector in one particular developing country, Turkey. Although the book ranged more widely than this, a key objective had been to examine the significance of modern management practices for workers in the developing world. The Turkish study had focused on three industries – automobiles textiles and white goods. After that study had been completed, the opportunity arose to explore further some of the issues with which it had been concerned. With the support of the ESRC, the attempt was made to embark on an explicit comparison between developing and developed economies with particular reference to one of the sectors, white goods, which compared to automobiles and textiles, has been largely ignored by social scientists, and thus to add an interesting comparative dimension to the work which had been conducted before. For this purpose, steps were taken to mount a comparison between the white goods industry in the UK and Australia, on one hand, and Brazil and Turkey on the other.

An ulterior motive that informed this research design was that Nichols had discovered, through contact with Rob Lambert, an Australian academic and labour activist, who had been researching a white goods factory in Australia, that the factory employed, among others, immigrants from Turkey – and not only this, but that some of them had recently returned to Turkey where they had spied, for the Australian management, on the management techniques employed and the organisation of production in one on the very factories that had been the subject of the previous Turkish research. There was something about this which made a comparison that involved among other countries, Turkey and Australia, irresistible.

Unfortunately, a comparison that included the Turkish and Australian factory was not to be. No sooner had the research begun, than the Australian factory was taken over and closed as part of the rationalisation that has swept the Australian industry in recent years. Moreover, it proved extremely difficult to gain access to any other Australian plant. The only prospect held out to us of conducting fieldwork in Australia came from a company that set the date for doing this so far in advance that it would have out-run the life of the project.

The situation in the UK proved to be yet more difficult. After many, many months of trying to gain access, during which some managements refused point blank to even talk to us, and in which, in other cases, promises were made, only to be dashed on the rocks of reorganisation or redundancy programmes or both, we had to face the fact that it was impossible to gain fieldwork access to a single UK factory.

At this point, the project had to undergo a fundamental redesign. It was decided that instead of a 2 + 2 model (comparing the white goods industry in two advanced and two developing countries) we would shift to a 1 + 5 model. We now proposed to look, from the standpoint of the UK, at the industry in Turkey and Brazil, but also in three East Asian countries, China, Taiwan and South Korea. We had close academic ties to colleagues in all these countries and, remarkably, it was easier for us to gain access to factories in each of these countries than it had been to enter a single factory in the UK. The book brings together research in each of these countries, each chapter drawing upon the specific features of each particular social formation and in addition making use of the results of research into at least one specific white goods factory in each country.

The factories were chosen on the basis that they had over 500 workers and played a significant part in the white goods industries of the societies in which they are situated. In each, an approach has been applied that was developed in the earlier study of cars, textiles as well as white goods in the modern sector of the Izmit triangle in Turkey (Nichols and Sugur 2004). Following that study, a central concern has been to examine the industry in each country and, within this, each firm's history, structure and strategy and in particular the implications of managements' knowledge and implementation of management methods for work relations, using both qualitative methods and a systematic interview schedule.

As part of the standard research methodology, recent changes have been investigated in each country, among other things, in policies on the selection of workers; pay; forms of labour and outsourcing; production organisation and new technology; HRM and work relations; trade unionism and collective bargaining. Fifty or more workers were interviewed in each of the factories and information was gathered about their origins and social composition (age, gender, ethnicity, and sometimes religion); their employment history, education and job training; their expectations and aspirations and their experience of work; their knowledge and experience of different management methods; their relations to their trade union and much other information on their lives inside and outside work. In about half a dozen cases in each company further in-depth interviews were also conducted with workers outside the workplace which sought to reconstruct their individual biographies. In addition to making shop floor observations further interviews were also conducted with trade union officials and, where they existed, shop stewards and representatives.

Interviews were also conducted with managers in different functions in each company and with members of relevant trade and industry associations and, in addition, a questionnaire was also completed by circa

50 managers and white collar workers in each company, dealing with such matters as their age, gender, social origin, employment history, career and technical qualifications and the sources and extent of their knowledge of modern management practice. Information on white goods in Turkey was first collected in 1999 and has been subsequently up-dated. Data on Brazil, China, Taiwan and South Korea was mainly collected in 2002, with further monitoring of developments in the plants and national white goods industries thereafter.

The inclusion of a chapter on white goods in Southern Africa marks a partial departure from the methodology outlined above. Early on in the project we had discovered that Andries Bezuidenhout was in process of conducting research into white goods in that region, albeit in a slightly different way. We have collaborated with him throughout and he has played an important part in the several all-country conferences that we have held in Cardiff in order to help the exchange of information and develop our views. We did not find it possible to visit the factories he researched in Southern Africa or to interview managers, trade unionists and workers, as we did in all the other countries (with or without the need translation as was necessary in the given case). Nor did his study provide us with an opportunity to analyse SPSS data of the type that resulted from the systematic interviews conducted in all other countries. However, the inclusion of his work within our research programme has meant that, out of our failures in the UK and Australia, there has resulted what is in effect a 1 + 6 project, which ranges, albeit of course selectively, across four continents – Europe (Turkey); South America (Brazil); East Asia (China, Taiwan and South Korea); and Africa (South Africa).

To conduct research of this type requires a very high level of cooperation between research collaborators who live in different countries, both on an individual basis and as members of a wider team (our four Brazilian colleagues also constituting a team in their own right). We are indebted to all of them. The unfortunate illness of one of those who collaborated in the research project, Soon-ok Chun, whose presence had added much to our research conferences, meant that it was ultimately not possible to provide a separate chapter on South Korea. We have attempted to compensate for this in Chapter 8. A full list of our main international research collaborators follows.

Theo Nichols and Surhan Cam
Cardiff, November 2004

Foreword

Have the forces of globalisation transformed the nature of production, work and employment in the advanced and advancing countries, as many commentators claim? Are the Western economies experiencing the operation of Gresham's Law, according to which bad working practices (eg, low wages and sweated labour) are transmitted internationally and inhibit progressive policy interventions and relatively decent working conditions? Many commentators and policy-makers argue this case but do so from a limited evidence base.

Interpreting the complex changes taking place in the international economy is a challenging task. The controversies in recent years that have outlined a variety of pessimistic and optimistic scenarios have lacked a compelling evidence base. What are the effects of knowledge transfers, new management practices and shifts in patterns of employment for the workers in both advanced and advancing capitalist economies? Few researchers have had the means or the inclination to undertake the detailed empirical research that permits an authoritative assessment of the changes taking place in specific sectors, industries and companies.

This important new book by Professor Theo Nichols, the distinguished international scholar, and Surhan Cam is the latest contribution to the internationally acclaimed Future of Work Series. It addresses head on the issues of change management and the consequences for the organisation and experience of work. Formed on the basis of careful empirical research in six countries, including Brazil, China, Taiwan and Turkey, the conclusions of this authoritative study debunk many of the myths that derive from the stock commentaries on globalisation.

Focusing on the highly internationalised white goods industry, the research reveals the uneven patterns of change in the six countries under scrutiny, the contradictions that flow from the new management practices that have spread throughout the industry, the impact on employment conditions and the responses of workers.

This important book highlights the limits of arm-chair theorising and demonstrates the important insights that can be gained from primary and collaborative international research. It provides a compelling account, to take just two examples, of the experiences of workers in South Korea and the practices of management in Turkey. The lessons for the increasingly ailing UK manufacturing sector and the prospects for other European economies warrant careful consideration. For researchers, practitioners and policy makers grappling with the effects of the new international division of labour, this book will prove to be an essential reference point and spur international research into the management of work and employment.

Peter Nolan
Director, ESRC Future of Work Programme

Notes on International Research Collaborators

Brazil

Angela Maria Carneiro Araújo is Professor, Department of Political Science at the State University of Campinas – SP. She has researched and written on industrial relations, labour and gender relations, and on the restructuring process in different manufacturing sectors in Brazil, including the metal, chemical, garment, white goods and banking industries. She has authored or edited books on various issues, including corporatist unionism in Brazil, labour, gender relations and equity and neocorporatism and neoliberalism in Brazil and the United Kingdom.

Leda Gitahy is Professor, Department of Scientific and Technological Policy, State University of Campinas. She has considerable experience of field research in the car, auto parts and white goods industries. She has published in Brazilian and international journals on the labour process, labour skills, technological changes and labour, subcontracting and supply chains. Her last book was about new management paradigms.

Alessandra Rachid is a Reader, Department of Production Engineering at The Federal University of São Carlos – SP. She has researched production changes, management methods and the labour process in the Brazilian car and white goods industries. She has published in Brazilian and international journals of production engineering, sociology of work and management.

Adriana Marques is a Lecturer at the Department of Economics, State University of Campinas and wrote her PhD about the transformation of the white goods sector in Brazil. She has published in Brazilian journals about different aspects of the white goods industry including changes in economic performance, ownership and the labour process.

China

Tongqing Feng is Professor and Vice President, China Institute of Labour Relations, Beijing, China. He has written widely on labour relations and related issues in China. He is the author of several books on labour relations in China and the position of Chinese workers and their future.

Wei Zhao was Associate Professor at the China Institute of Labour Relations, Beijing and is currently a post graduate researcher at the School of Social Sciences, Cardiff University. She has written books, in Chinese, on changes in workers' conditions in the private sector and the changing structure of white- and blue-collar employment.

South Africa

Andries Bezuidenhout is a researcher at the Sociology of Work Unit, University of Witwatersrand, South Africa. He recently completed his PhD on the white goods industry in Southern Africa and is continuing to research in this area and to work more widely in the political economy of the region.

South Korea

Soon-Ok Chun is Director of SPARK (Social Programme for Action and Research in Korea), Seoul, South Korea. A former Lecturer at Sungkonghoe University, she has now committed herself to SPARK, a social welfare organisation that she has founded to help poor Korean garment workers. She is author of *They Are Not Machines: Korean Women Workers and their Fight for Democratic Trade Unionism in the 1970s* (2003).

Taiwan

Wen-chi Grace Chou is Associate Professor, Department of Labor Relations and Institute of Labour Studies, National Chung-Cheng University, Chi-Yi, Taiwan. She has conducted research in Taiwan on a range of industries, including white goods, electronics, textiles and cars.

Turkey

Nadir Sugur is Professor of Sociology, Faculty of Communication Sciences, Anadolu University, Eskisehir, Turkey and was formerly Research Fellow, School of Social Sciences, Cardiff University. He is co-author, with Theo Nichols, of *Global Management and Local Labour: Turkish Workers and Modern Industry* (2004) and co-editor, with Erol Kahveci and Theo Nichols of *Work and Occupation in Modern Turkey* (1996).

1

The World of White Goods – Markets, Industry Structure and Dynamics

Theo Nichols and Surhan Cam

For some time it has been a common criticism of the widespread discussion of globalisation and the vast literature that fosters this that it lacks specificity and evidence. This is so both with respect to national variables and sector variation (ILO 1996; Hirst and Thompson 1996; Smith and Meiksins 1995). Such deficiencies are to be regretted because globalisation and related ideas about the emergence of a new international division of labour raise questions about the form and meaning of work. Such ideas should stimulate us to think about the range and scope of management strategies and forms of work organisation, the patterns of change and development occurring in different countries and the emergent character of paid work. Above all, they should drive us beyond the practice of what might be termed 'research in one country' but, for a variety of reasons, this is rarely the case. This book is intended as a contribution to overcoming some of these limitations by means of a single sector study. It focuses on the production, in different countries, of products that are increasingly familiar in both advanced and emergent economies – so called 'white goods'. In this first chapter the emphasis is on providing a broad overview of the structure and dynamics of the industry and its market world-wide. The implications for labour feature more prominently in the country-specific chapters and in chapter 8.

The term 'white goods' is a trade term that covers a wide range of domestic appliances which are chiefly for kitchen or laundry use. Usually a distinction is made within the general category of domestic appliances between large kitchen appliances – including refrigeration appliances, dishwashers, large cooking appliances and microwaves; and small electrical appliances – these comprising food preparation appliances; small cooking appliances; other small kitchen appliances; vacuum cleaners; heating/cooling appliances; irons; and an assortment of hair care appliances, body shavers, oral hygiene appliances; and other personal care appliances. (White goods are generally distinguished from so-called 'brown goods'. These are consumer electronic products such as TVs, video recorders, hi-fi systems, telephones, computers and cameras.)

Large kitchen appliances have been critical to the development of new patterns of food consumption and domestic activity. They have important implications for what and when we eat and for where and when we shop for food. Hardyment 1988 has provided an historical account of the mechanisation of housework 'from mangle to microwave'; Cockburn and Ormrod 1993 have contributed an original gender-related study of microwave oven development and technology; and Silva (2001) has written of household technology and time use. Yet in recent years despite the increased concern of social scientists with consumption – and the increased familiarity with the use of such white goods by people in all the continents of the world – few writers have directed their attention to how and where such commodities are produced and what this entails for those who produce them. Exceptions include Lambert, Gillan and Fitzgerald (2005) in Australia, Wells 2001 in North America, Paba 1986 in Italy and among only a few others Baden-Fuller and Stopford 1991 and Segal-Horn, Asch and Suneja 1998 in the UK and Europe.

The description of these goods as 'white' is no longer entirely accurate but as we have seen the main 'large' white goods can be identified readily enough as refrigeration appliances (for instance refrigerators and fridge-freezers), cooking appliances and laundry appliances (washing machines). This book is mainly concerned with the first two which are the two largest components of the large white goods category – refrigeration and cooking appliances – and most especially with refrigeration appliances. These are common to many urban areas of the world (though ovens, as opposed to hobs, are relatively less common in Asia because of different traditions of cooking). They are also, despite a profusion of different brands, relatively similar products which are relatively simple to produce. There are product innovations such as sensors on cooker hobs that turn off the burners if no pan is present or fast thaw and cooling systems for refrigerator appliances but new models tend to incorporate relatively minor improvements together with changes in external restyling.

There are some differences between products in different national markets. Industrialists have been long wont to explain that, even within Europe, ovens add up to a complex picture, because of the variety of national cooking methods; and that 'UK housewives do more baking and want even browning. The French want a different heat balance' and so on (Batchelor 1992). Managers who work for international corporations can also recite at will how refrigeration appliances can vary in the number of doors (Germany and the UK two, China three, Japan five) and in terms of whether the fridge part of the fridge-freezer typically goes on top (the UK), which adds to cost because of technical considerations, or underneath (Turkey). But such variation is of limited importance and although manufacturers have to take into account national differences in the size of apartments, electricity voltage and environmental regulations, white goods remain essentially comparable products in different countries and remain recognisable despite different colours, which include black, with stainless steel, aluminium and titanium finishes now also available. Relevant here is that Whirlpool was able to launch a 'world cooker' in 1998, which used common product technology, despite having different doors, shelf layouts and controls (Marsh and Tait 1998) and as other authors have observed, the proliferation of product features occurred at the same time as standard-isation of product design and most especially of standardisation of the manufacturing process, and not as an alternative to this (Segal-Horn et al 1998: 107). Indeed, the point of 'platform thinking' is to make use of stan-dard engineering frameworks to which parts can be added or subtracted. Fewer platforms mean the ability to design global products with, for example, regional features and with further gains through reductions in procurement costs (Brown-Humes 2002; Marsh 2002b; Appliance Magazine 2003).

Testimony to the essential simplicity of many of the products on offer, sometimes despite their apparent differences, is the double-oven which has recently gained popularity in the UK and the US. This is essentially two single ovens put together. Manufacturers, who are well able to produce single ovens, have been more than pleased to put two of them together and charge a premium price for their little additional effort. Expensive fridge-freezers have attracted criticism along just these lines – as for example in the suggestion made by a less than enthusiastic Amazon-type reviewer of a £8,000 unit, who suggested to potential buyers 'OK why not buy a fridge without the gadgets, £2,000, and a laptop, £1,500. Glue the laptop to the front of the fridge and save yourself a small fortune!' (Firebox 2004). Whatever the merit of this particular claim, it is the essential similarity of these products which informs the logic behind this book – namely to look at the production of large white goods, and what this entails for labour, in several different areas of the world; in fact in Brazil, China, Taiwan, Turkey, South Africa and South Korea.

The book brings together research in each of these countries, each chapter drawing upon the specific features of each particular social forma-tion and in addition making use of the results of research into at least one specific white goods factory in each country.

The plants will be introduced later in the chapters devoted to individual regions and countries and, as will be evident already, most chapters relate to what are commonly referred to as emerging market economies. The concern throughout is to examine aspects of the production of these rel-atively simple commodities in just such countries, prefaced by a discussion of the state of the industry in the UK (considered in the next chapter). To begin with, though, it is necessary to outline the extent, problems and dynamics of an industry which – judged by its presence in so many regions of the world – may now be considered to be a global one.

At the turn of the century the industry (as represented essentially by refrigeration appliances, large cooking appliances and home laundry appliances) had sales of around $100 billion worldwide (Euromonitor 2002, Table 4.5). Such is the industry's size that by 2002 over 100 million cooking appliances (a category that includes hobs) were sold world-wide; as were over 80 million refrigeration appliances to a value of US$32 billion. Big though the industry is however – and in part as a consequence of its own success in producing so much – it faces problems.

One problem that the industry faces that arises out of the sheer volume of production takes the form of increased concern for the environment and regulation that has been introduced to prevent the depletion of the ozone layer by chlorofluorocarbons (CFCs) and hydrochlorofluorocarbons (HCFCs). It is estimated that in the UK alone up to three million domestic refrigeration appliances are disposed of each year. In recent years, in some countries the existence of 'fridge mountains' has become a topic of everyday conversation. What is less well remarked – which is also in a way a consequence of the industry's success – is that in the most advanced industrial countries the market is saturated. This is particularly so in the case of refrigeration appliances but largely so for large cooking appliances also. Indeed, household penetration rates for both refrigeration and cooking appliances stand at around 99 per cent for Australia, Canada, Germany, Italy, Japan, the UK and the US (Euromonitor 2001: Table 3.3).

The white goods industry is highly cyclical – so much so that it is sometimes used by economists and policy makers as a short term cyclical indicator. In any given country it can also be affected by a range of demographic and other factors – by changing patterns of marriage (and indeed by variation in the proportion of separate households, including those of single persons) and by rises and falls in house-building, the availability or otherwise of credit and interest rates, all of which can make for different levels of demand. But the advanced industrial countries listed above, together with many others, have in common that they lack the optimum conditions for rapid growth – in particular a young and growing population, which is becoming urbanised, is setting up new households and which, ideally, has newly found disposable income.

There are three main regions in the refrigeration appliance market – Western Europe, the Asian Pacific and North America. In 2002 these regions accounted for about 70 per cent of units sold world-wide (Table 1.1 and Figure 1.1). The three of them have fared differently. Western Europe has fared worst, units sold increasing by less than four per cent 1992–2002. By contrast, in North America units sold increased by 28 per cent and in Asia Pacific by 36 per cent.

In the case of cooking appliances these same three regions account for nearly 80 per cent the units sold world-wide (Table 1.2 and Figure 1.2). The differences in their patterns of development are even more pronounced. For these same years Western Europe registered a gain of about nine per cent, North America of 17 per cent in units sold and Asia Pacific of 79 per cent.

For both sets of commodities Asia Pacific is clearly becoming a leading market, with smaller but increasing shares being taken by Eastern Europe, Africa and the Middle East (Latin America does not show well for the period reviewed because of political and economic instability). Generally, though, saturated markets are a problem. As will be seen in later chapters, even in China there is now a high level of household penetration in the urban areas and both in China, and as we shall also see, in South Africa, the promise of expanding into markets in the rural areas is frustrated by lack of electrification or adequate gas supply and, not least, lack of disposable income.

So far, though, white goods have only been considered as physical commodities – in terms of the number of fridges or the number of cookers and so on – and not in terms of price. Increased competition, partly a consequence of saturated markets, partly as a consequence of trade liberalisation and of reductions in the cost of components have meant that the growth already reported in the number of both refrigeration and cooking appliances sold has not been matched by an equivalent increase in the value of sales.

In the case of refrigeration, a 20 per cent increase in the number of units sold worldwide 1992–2002 amounted to an increase in sales value of only about six per cent (cf. Tables 1.1 and 1.3 and related Figures). The performance in value terms in Western Europe was even worse than this. Over the last decade (1992–2002) the value of refrigeration appliance sales in North America increased about 20 per cent. It increased nearly 30 per cent in the Asia Pacific region. In Western Europe total sales value fell 7 per cent (Table 1.3).

In the case of cooking appliances the 40 per cent rise in units sold world-wide over the same period amounted to a rise in sales by value of only 8 per cent (cf. Table 1.2 and Table 1.4 and related Figures). Cooking appliance sales increased over 20 per cent by value in North America and by nearly 75 per cent in the Asia Pacific region. In Western Europe they fell by 10 per cent (Table 1.4).

There are, then, important differences between regions, with the situation generally worse in Western Europe. The failure of sales values to keep up with number of units sold is, however, a feature of all three major regions and applies to both major sets of commodities. In nearly all cases, unit values lacked any impressive or sustained rise and fell toward the end of the period in line with global trends in the industry (Figure 1.5). (Only Eastern Europe failed to fit this pattern. The increased availability of better quality products in the region contributed to a

Table 1.1   Global Sales of Refrigeration Appliances by Regions, 1992–2002, Units (thousands)

	Asia Pacific	Western Europe	North America	Latin America	Eastern Europe	Africa and Middle East	World Total
1992	17288.0	18716.5	11825.9	8709.7	4814.1	5211.6	66566.1
1993	18345.8	18902.2	11806.4	8369.6	3849.0	5809.3	67082.7
1994	17288.0	18716.5	11825.9	8709.7	4814.1	5211.6	66566.1
1995	18345.8	18902.2	11806.4	8369.6	3849.0	5809.3	67082.7
1996	20086.8	18668.6	12150.8	10139.1	4333.8	6472.7	71851.9
1997	23023.9	18768.7	12210.3	9823.0	5175.7	6217.5	75219.4
1998	21368.6	18720.0	12464.5	8493.7	4204.1	6472.7	71723.6
1999	23689.8	19463.0	13470.5	8275.6	4454.4	6376.4	75729.7
2000	24290.5	20070.0	13569.0	8465.3	4963.1	7589.2	78947.1
2001	23900.9	19425.0	14003.9	9216.2	5202.7	7905.9	79654.6
2002	23511.4	19372.0	15105.5	8554.6	5829.7	8333.7	80706.9

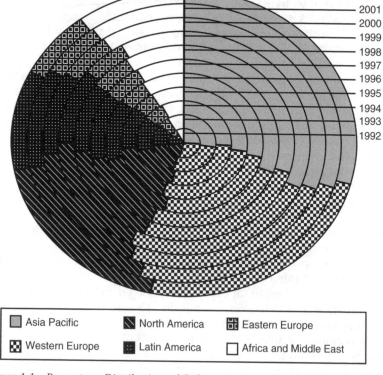

Figure 1.1 Percentage Distribution of Refrigeration Appliance Unit Sales in the World, 1992–2002
Source: Data for 1992 to1996 from Euromonitor 1999, Table 2 and Table 4; for 1997 to 2002 reworked from Euromonitor 2003a. Based on US$. Re-chained to 2002 Series.

Table 1.2　Global Sales of Cooking Appliances by Regions, 1992–2002, Units (thousands)

	Asia Pacific	Western Europe	North America	Latin America	Eastern Europe	Africa and Middle East	World Total
1992	27121.5	22295.7	10770.8	6928.7	4351.4	4694.9	76163.2
1993	30970.8	22725.3	10488.2	7904.7	3797.8	4909.1	80796.0
1994	27121.5	22295.7	10770.8	6928.7	4351.4	4694.9	76163.2
1995	30970.8	22725.3	10488.2	7904.7	3797.8	4909.1	80796.0
1996	32531.6	22450.8	10714.3	8965.1	4331.2	4884.3	83877.5
1997	33766.6	22568.6	10907.1	8737.9	5178.1	4604.3	85762.9
1998	32168.5	22795.1	11158.3	7703.4	4208.0	5559.8	83593.1
1999	35769.8	23823.4	11838.1	7988.2	4514.4	5577.3	89511.2
2000	40914.7	24830.2	11929.8	8179.3	4958.3	6723.0	97535.3
2001	44677.4	24336.1	11916.9	8149.8	5487.8	7071.9	101639.9
2002	48630.1	24230.0	12603.5	7785.7	6231.4	7477.8	106958.5

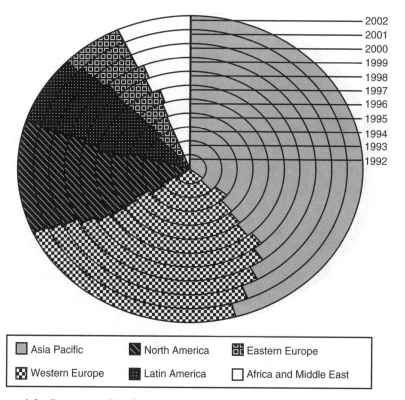

Figure 1.2　Percentage Distribution of Large Cooking Appliance Unit Sales in the World, 1992–2002
Source: Data for 1992 to 1996 from Euromonitor 1998 Tables 7.1, 7.2 and 7.5; for 1997 to 2002 reworked from Euromonitor 2003a.

Table 1.3 Global Sales of Refrigeration Appliances by Regions, 1992–2002, Value ($US million, 2002 Prices)

	Asia Pacific	Western Europe	North America	Latin America	Eastern Europe	Africa and Middle East	World Total
1992	7280.7	8821.4	5762.6	5368.6	1188.4	1862.7	30284.6
1993	7600.6	9066.7	5859.1	5523.4	1126.4	2110.3	31286.8
1994	7280.7	8821.4	5762.6	5368.6	1188.4	1862.7	30284.6
1995	7600.6	9066.7	5859.1	5523.4	1126.4	2110.3	31286.8
1996	8159.0	8978.3	6276.4	6951.7	1279.5	2411.8	34057.0
1997	9788.8	9065.6	6407.6	6773.6	1550.4	2347.2	35933.6
1998	8983.0	9092.2	6604.0	5483.5	1308.7	2433.4	33904.8
1999	10103.3	9094.6	6886.6	4312.1	1344.3	2514.0	34254.9
2000	10190.6	8216.1	6651.6	4125.8	1365.0	2436.3	32985.4
2001	9594.5	7731.5	6774.3	3816.0	1457.3	2335.5	31709.1
2002	9410.2	8160.6	7027.8	3270.5	1709.0	2411.2	31989.3

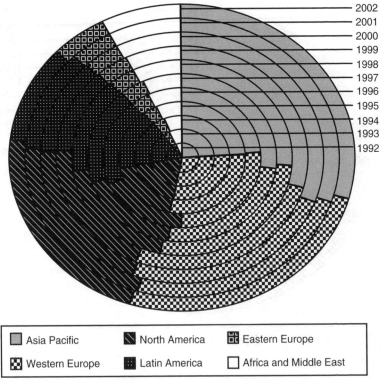

Figure 1.3 Percentage Distribution of Refrigeration Appliance Sales in the World, 1992–2002

Source: Data for 1992 and 1996 is from Euromonitor 1999 Tables 2 and 4; data for 1997 to 2002 reworked from Euromonitor 2003a.

Table 1.4 Global Sales of Cooking Appliances by Regions, 1992–2002, Value ($US million, 2002)

	Asia Pacific	Western Europe	North America	Latin America	Eastern Europe	Africa and Middle East	World Total
1992	2436.9	10571.8	4250.9	2913.2	792.5	807.3	21772.7
1993	2848.6	10769.4	4259.3	3532.0	729.2	850.1	22988.8
1994	2436.9	10571.8	4250.9	2913.2	792.5	807.3	21772.7
1995	2848.6	10769.4	4259.3	3532.0	729.2	850.1	22988.8
1996	2995.4	10721.8	4478.5	4171.1	917.8	850.1	24134.9
1997	3158.1	10547.4	4638.3	4057.8	1140.6	801.2	24343.6
1998	2880.0	10675.5	4843.5	3046.8	978.6	978.6	23403.0
1999	3388.6	10710.8	5146.7	2397.8	1010.1	1010.1	23664.1
2000	3759.3	9647.8	5103.4	2281.8	1074.0	1074.0	22940.3
2001	3838.0	9084.0	5029.6	1878.9	1245.9	1245.9	22322.3
2002	4232.7	9507.1	5222.9	1569.9	1477.3	1477.3	23487.2

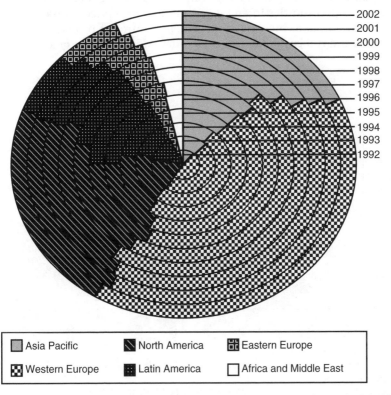

Legend:
☐ Asia Pacific   ◪ North America   ▦ Eastern Europe
▨ Western Europe   ▦ Latin America   ☐ Africa and Middle East

Figure 1.4 Percentage Distribution of Large Cooking Appliance Sales in the World, 1992–2002
Source: Data for 1992 and 1996 from Euromonitor 1998 Tables 7.3, 7.4 and 7.8; data for 1997 to 2002 reworked from Euromonitor 2003a.

30 per cent increase in unit prices in the ten years up to 2002; those for cooking appliances increased by 18 per cent.) Reviewing the wider situation in 2001 Electrolux Chief Executive Michael Treschow reflected that it was 'a very competitive environment in which customers are paying less and less for the products' (George 2001). In short, this is the overall problem. Good news as it is for customers, the industry has been subject to continual price erosion.

The industry has adopted a number of strategies to fix or at least to seek to ameliorate the effects of saturated markets and declining or flat unit prices. One such strategy, which is in evidence world-wide, has been to re-vamp production – to cut the labour force; to outsource; to strip production down to an assembly operation; and to bring to bear a number of systematic modern management techniques. Prominent examples of the latter are the introduction of Six Sigma (sigma being the term for the degree of variation that is the standard deviation and the six sigma level indicating that there are no more than 3.4 defects per million opportunities in any given product or service transaction) and other attempts to increase management control of production, reduce defects and run customer-driven factories. Most common of all, from the

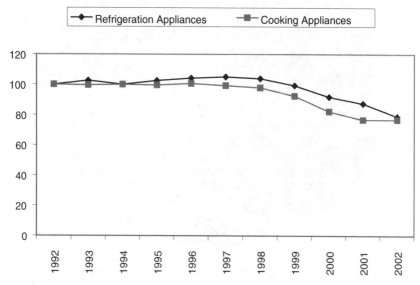

Figure 1.5   Global Sales of Refrigeration and Cooking Appliances, 1992–2002, Unit Prices (US$ Index, 1992 = 100)
Source: Data for large cooking appliances for the period 1992 and 1996 from Euromonitor 1998 Tables 7.4, 7.5 and 7.8; for refrigeration appliances for the same period Euromonitor 1999 Tables 1, 2, 3 and 4. Data for large cooking and refrigeration appliances for 1997 to 2002 are reworked from Euromonitor 2003a.

1990s onward, is TQM (Total Quality Management). These methods figure in later country-specific chapters of this book and again to some extent in chapter 8. But there are several other strategies – or attempted fixes – that have been attempted that merit mention here. One of these entails Marketing/Design; another entails Concentration; another Relocation of Production. These are not mutually exclusive.

Marketing/design

Attempts have been made to shift products up the value chain in order to attract a premium and lift unit price. Moves have also been made to bundle products into entire kitchen suites and/or to selling what might be best described as kitchen furniture to form part of the kitchen-as-display area.

A whole constellation of ovens, refrigeration appliances, steam ovens, microwaves, coffee machines and other aesthetically integrated designer objects may be found advertised in upmarket magazines, often slipped between advertisements for other expensive items like Rolex or Chophard watches. At the very top of the market, the display of what money can buy really counts. As the author of an article on kitchens advised readers of *How to Spend It*, the appropriately if odiously entitled *Financial Times* magazine, 'a big, fancy-brand kitchen ... has serious cachet'. As she further advised: 'Beautiful cabinetry will probably eat up half the £50,000 budget and appliances – now huge and ultra high-tech – will finish the job'. Items listed included

> free-standing dual-fuel range cookers – the kind with at least six gas burners and one or two electric ovens, by manufacturers such as Smeg, Britannia or Viking [which] can cost anywhere between £3,000 and £10,000...Domino hobs (rectangular elements each comprising a pair of burners or, say, a griddle) [that] can be configured to offer every kind of cooking possibility: to barbecue, deep-fry, steam, wok, to use gas or electricity...Vast American-style fridges with pukka ice-dispensers and stainless-steel or glass doors are almost a given in the top-end kitchen (and cost from £3,000). The Gaggenau IK300 fridge freezer is big, beautiful and filters mains water to make crystal-clear ice (£9,000 if free-standing, £7,500 built in). Newer, for the crowd who have to have the latest, is the internet fridge (made by LG Electronics and available here from the American Appliance Centre, from around £6,000). The screen on the door allows you to check your shopping list on-line, order something you've run out of, catch up on emails and even call up a recipe (van der Post 2003).

Such products and such white goods displays of conspicuous consumption are not only aimed at the top end of the market in North America and

Western Europe. In China and India a burgeoning middle class, keen to display its new found wealth, provides an important target market for such products as the internet fridge, with its door mounted 15″ LCD, built-in 56k modem, TV tuner, FM radio and digital still camera, MP3 player and rest of it. In similar vein, Electrolux is targeting 'consumers with strong purchasing power' in Korea with a high-priced robot vacuum cleaner (Korea Times 2004a). It has plans to sell this into China too. In 2002 the same company introduced the 'Washy-Talky' washing machine in India that talks to its users (Brown-Humes 2002). The machine is reported to speak in a soft, Indian middle class female accent and to use 90 different phrases in Hindi and English, gently giving instructions like 'drop the detergent, close the lid and relax'.

Looking to the future, manufacturers toy with the idea of entirely re-constituting the kitchen, so that, among other things, their appliances become central features rather than be confined to the walls. This is the idea behind Whirlpool's prototype 'Theatre kitchen', unfurled in 2004. Cooking takes place in a U-shaped table projecting from a central appliance block whose refrigerator, oven and wine cooler are accessed from either side. Under-table sensors generate induction heating when they detect a pan on the aluminium cook-top while the table's maple outer surface doubles as a bar. The meal is served 'backstage', behind the appliance block. The project designer declares excitedly 'Theatre is both stage and stalls – a double-faceted environment where the cook and guests perform as actor and audience. It allows the play to become interactive and the roles to intertwine' (Swengley 2004). As is implicit in some of the other examples referred to above, other 'post-kitchen' prototypes put the empha-sis on multi-functionality – 'culinary zones' (no longer kitchens as we have known them) providing sites in which to socialise, download music, send emails and surf the net, as well as to store and prepare food.

Relatively long replacement cycles, usually of ten years or longer, are a feature of white goods in most societies and are themselves an incentive for manufacturers to incite customers, including those on lower incomes, to buy new models with additional functions. The move to adding higher value functions can be expected to continue and so can innovations in design, whether of a futuristic or retro kind, whatever sells. Some pro-ducers admit that products are given additional features to entice cus-tomers but without much or any practical benefit. Thus most washing machines have 12 to 20 programmes whereas most buyers will use only two to four (Bonnema 2004: 7)

Manufacturers are twisting every which way. In the year 2000 alone Electrolux ran a networking experiment in Sweden which offered pay-per-use as an alternative to purchasing its dishwashers; in America, Whirlpool revealed plans for an Internet-enabled combination refrigera-tor/oven that allowed the user to prepare food ahead of time, keep it safely cooled, then initiate cooking remotely so that the meal was ready upon arriving home; and Merloni Elettrodomestici in Fabriano, Italy, launched a washing machine in France and the UK that could be remotely controlled and monitored by either Internet or fixed or mobile phone. Earlier in the year Merloni had demonstrated a prototype kitchen monitor and home controller that let users download cooking programmes from the Internet into Merloni Ariston cooking appliances; the same year Matsushita of Japan signed a multimillion dollar licensing agreement with emWare of Salt Lake City to use a networking software device to embed remote access, management and diagnostic capabilities in its products (Babyak 2000).

Notwithstanding the hi-tech, or the appearance of this, white goods production is mainly production for a mass market. Mostly the objective is to sell essentially similar products in large numbers, 'to pile them high and wide'. Lack of sustained growth during the 1990s meant cost-cutting and rationalisation especially in Western Europe and the pressure to cut costs continues.

Concentration

Much growth in the industry has been by acquisition and merger, Electrolux alone swallowed up 450 companies in 30 years, with considerable duplication of facilities (and brands, of which it had 25 in Europe alone as late as 2002). In fact, the top companies have owned a considerable number of brands, a far from exhaustive list including Kitchenaid, Roper, Estate, Bauknecht, SMC and Brastemp from Whirlpool; Zanussi, AEG, Elektro-Helios, Tricity Bendix, Frigidaire, Kelvinator, as well as Electrolux, from Electrolux; Monogram, Profile, and GE from General Electric; Bosch, Siemens, Pitsos, Balay, Profilo, Gaggenau, Neff and Continental from Bosch-Siemens Hausgeräte; and Ariston, Hotpoint, Creda and Indesit from Merloni (which changed its name to its best known brand, Indesit, in late 2004).

Sometimes these brands have migrated from one of the top companies to another (for example in the USA Hoover is owned by Maytag but in the UK it is owned by the Italian firm Candy who bought it from Maytag in 1995). Often they reflect the take-over or merger of smaller companies in particular local markets. It is sometimes claimed that brands mean that new unfamiliar companies can find it difficult to break into markets and it is noteworthy that most of the major players in all regions – the Asia Pacific being a clear exception – have long established ones. Whatever the case about this, there is no doubt that the industry is highly concentrated – much more so than the number of its brands would suggest.

In 2002 the top five manufacturers of the large kitchen appliances that constitute large white goods accounted for 30 per cent of global volume sales. The top ten manufacturers accounted for 44 per cent of global sales (Table 1.5). For refrigeration appliances, the top five manufacturers accounted for 39 per cent of sales and the top ten for 53 per cent (Table 1.6).

The most concentrated refrigeration appliance market is Australasia, where in 2002 the top five companies accounted for 87 per cent of the region's volume sales. Electrolux accounted for over 33 per cent and Fisher and Paykel of New Zealand accounted for another 22 per cent. However, this is a small market, which accounts for less than one per cent of world unit sales. Of the three main regions considered here, concentration has progressed furthest in North America where the top five manufacturers account for nearly 64 per cent of the region's refrigeration appliance sales. Three companies, General Electric, Whirlpool and Maytag – all US corporations – each had around 15 per cent of sales in 2002; followed by Electrolux

Table 1.5   Large Kitchen Appliances: Top Ten Global Manufacturer Shares, 2002 (volume)

Per cent volume		
Whirlpool	US	7.9
Electrolux AB	Sweden	7.1
Bosch-Siemens Hausgeräte	Germany	5.7
General Electric Co (GE)	US	5.4
Haier Group	China	3.8
Matsushita Electrical Industrial Co Ltd	Japan	3.2
Maytag Corporation	US	3.1
LG Group	Korea	2.6
Sharp Electronics Corp	Japan	2.6
Merloni Elettrodomestici SpA	Italy	2.5

Source: Adapted from Euromonitor 2003a Table 29.

Table 1.6   Refrigeration Appliances: Top Ten Global Manufacturer Shares, 2002 (volume)

Per cent volume		
Electrolux AB	Sweden	12.0
Whirlpool Corp	US	10.8
Bosch-Siemens Hausgeräte	Germany	5.6
Haier Group	China	5.6
General Electric Co (GE)	US	4.6
Maytag Corp	US	3.0
Guangdong Kelon Electrical Appliance Co	China	2.9
Merloni Elettrodomestici SpA	Italy	2.8
Matsushita Electrical Industrial Co Ltd	Japan	2.7
LG Group	Korea	2.5

Source: Adapted from Euromonitor 2003a Table 38.

from Sweden, followed by Haier from China. In Western Europe, where the top five manufacturers had 52 per cent of refrigerator volume, two major European companies head the list, Electrolux from Sweden and Germany's BSH, with Italy's Merloni in fourth place and Whirlpool and General Electric in third and fifth place respectively. The tendency for regions to be dominated by 'local' companies – General Electric and Whirlpool in North America; Electrolux and BSH (with Merloni now probably increasing its share) in Western Europe – is also evident in the Asia Pacific where the top five manufacturers' share amounts to 46 per cent, the top three places going to Haier and Guangdong Kelon Electrical Appliance (both China) and Matusushita (Japan), Electrolux holding fourth place and fifth place being occupied by Henan Xinfei Electrical Appliance, another Chinese company (Euromonitor 2003a Table 48).

Concentration offers economies of scale and greater leverage over supply chains. Further advantages have been sought by concentration of function and reducing non-core activities (over the last few years for example Electrolux has sold off its commercial refrigeration and leisure appliance lines); and by moves to develop global manufacturing bases, as attempted by both Electrolux and Whirlpool.

Above all, concentration has meant job losses. Electrolux provides a leading example of this. During Michael Treschow's five year reign as CEO, April 1997–April 2002, the company closed 33 factories, 50 warehouses and cut 21,000 jobs – more than 20 per cent of the work force (McLannahan 2003). By December 2002 it was planning to lose another 5,000 jobs (Watkins 2003).

Relocation

The challenge posed by mature markets in the advanced industrial coun-tries has meant a scrabble to get into newly developing ones. China has figured prominently as a host in attempts to shift from North to South into less developed and newly emerging markets. In 2002 about a third of world demand for major appliances came from the Asia Pacific region, with almost half of this from China. Indeed, white goods have become such big business in China that in 2002 Zhang Ruimin, the capitalist entrepreneur who heads Haier, the giant Chinese white goods company, was made an alternate member of the Communist Party's Central Committee. China's proportionately small but numerically vast urban population is itself now experiencing high levels of saturation for refrigerators and washing machines but the market remains vast, labour is cheap and in recent years foreign companies have increased their market share, in some cases considerably. For example, the foreign share of the washing machine market increased from about 15 per cent in 2000 to more than 25 per cent in the first six months of 2003, and for automatic machines it rose from

15 per cent in 1999 to 42 per cent (McGregor 2003). This has meant that several indigenous companies have been driven out of business and the process of concentration amongst Chinese owned companies, already well advanced in the mature markets of the world, is expected to strengthen in future.

It is widely expected that the 40 to 50 large indigenous players which existed in China in the mid-1990s will soon reduce to a much smaller number, the big fish eating the little ones, just as has happened in the long established capitalist markets in Europe and North America. In Europe for example the 350 producers of major household appliances that existed in 1982 had reduced to 15 by 1998 (Segal-Horn et al 1998: 105) and have reduced yet further since then.

A similar process of concentration is likely in India where there is considerable overcapacity and Haier is now attempting to make inroads in the Indian market. The Korean companies Samsung and LG are already a significant presence (Business Standard 2003; Mishra and Mukherjee 2004) and in 2004 Korea's LG announced plans to make India its second largest global production base after China in order to penetrate the Asian, Middle eastern and African markets (Song 2004). (Relocation is not necessarily a one-stop process. For example, GE, helped by the market liberalisation made possible by the North American Free Trade Agreement (NAFTA), contracted its production of refrigerators, stoves and ranges to Grupo Mabe SA in Mexico. In turn, Mabe now produces ranges and washing machines in Columbia and refrigerators in Venezuela (Millman 2000)).

The other ex-socialist block, Eastern Europe, has also attracted inward investment in white goods (as, at another point on the EU periphery, has Turkey). In fact, there has been a general tendency for manufacturing to relocate to low wage areas. Whereas this has sometimes taken the form of moves to the periphery of a region (to Mexico from the US for example), it has also taken the form of movement into different regions. Eastern Europe is not only becoming a new and important market for foreign companies but, at the same time, a new manufacturing base. An industry insider predicts 'intense competition between US, European and Korean manufacturers in Eastern Europe – more than in any other market' (Esgin 2003).

In Eastern Europe, as in China, indigenous white goods firms have also found themselves facing a difficult challenge as modern, competitive products have become more widely available. Only a few of them have been able to stay competitive and survive independently, many having become part of international groups.

Looked at from the standpoint of corporate strategy, BSH provides an indication of what has been happening world-wide. In 1990 the company had only factories in Germany, Spain and Greece. Since then, through acquisition and new developments, the number of plants has almost trebled and BSH has added production sites in eleven other areas, including Eastern Europe, Turkey, South America and China (Marsh 2002a). The company already produces refrigerators and other products in China and holds more than 50 per cent of the high-end washing machine market. In 2004 it plans to begin producing cookers there (China Daily 2004). Other big companies in white goods have moved in much the same direction – or more precisely directions.

In 2002, Whirlpool took over one hundred percent of the cooking appliance, refrigeration and laundry operations formerly operated with Vitromatic SA de CV in Mexico and purchased Polar in Poland, and it cut jobs at its Amien plant in France with a view to transferring production to its plant at Poprad in Slovakia.

In 2003, Merloni, having sunk £80 million into its Lodz cooker plant, which exports 80 per cent of it production, was actively reviewing the purchase of shares of its rival Amica Wronki and announced plans to spend EU100 million over the next three years to increase its manufacturing operations in Russia (it had built a plant at Fryasino in 2000) and Poland, mainly to take advantage of the expanding demand for domestic appliances in eastern Europe (Polish News Bulletin 2003; Marsh 2003). In the same year, Electrolux indicated that it was planning to move more and more of its production to low-cost countries to cope with relentless price pressures (George 2003) and it has announced projects totalling over $350 million to shift production to lower cost countries – Mexico, Russia, Thailand, Poland and Hungary (Bauer 2004).

In 2004, Vittirio Merloni, Merloni's chairman, confirmed that it would continue to develop its international business, including expansion to other continents (La Stampa 2004). Also in 2004, Whirlpool, having played the Slovakian and Polish governments off against each other, reputedly extracted promises of 44 million in cash, tax breaks and exemptions to set up oven production at Wroclaw, Poland (Polish News Bulletin 2004). Meanwhile, Maytag closed a fridge factory in Illinois with the loss of over 1,500 jobs to switch production to a new plant being built in Mexico.

Within the Asia Pacific region, the industry in Japan has come under intense pressure. The domestic market reached its peak in the early 1990s, and production has been shifting overseas. Japanese companies, like Matsushita, reckon the cost of manufacturing in China is roughly one sixth of that in Japan. And according to Sharp's President, Katshiko Machida, although there might be some potential for Japanese companies to develop revolutionary technology in some sectors, without this they will be pushed out entirely in 10 years, it being 'difficult to compete with China in the white goods sector' (Nakamoto 2004). In 2004, Matsushita began construction of a massive global production base for home electrical appliances in Zhejiang, China; and Toshiba, which is already in Thailand, agreed to set up production and marketing joint ventures in China with TCL International Holdings of China with plans to produce refrigerators and washing machines, first for the Chinese market and then Southeast Asian markets and in the longer term also for export to Japan (Japan Today 2004a, 2004b). Competitive pressures have already paved the way to international tie-ups of various kinds between, among others, Hitachi and Bosch-Siemens, Toshiba and Electrolux and Sanyo Electric and Maytag (Euromonitor 2003b).

The obvious question is: do all roads lead South? In particular: must production shift to China? In considering such questions it is first important to bear in mind that it is a long way from China or Korea to the US or Europe. Shipping freight costs are based on cubic capacity, not weight, and large white goods, which are often described in the industry as 'empty boxes of air', are therefore relatively expensive to transport over great distances by sea (consider the value per cubic metre of a fridge compared to even a small car).

For some time producers in the established markets such as the US were protected from long distance imports by this high value/volume ratio but eventually a combination of cheap wages and low production costs (often facilitated by the import of western technology and by a high level of knowledge of competitors' plants) has meant that companies like China's Haier and South Korea's LG have successfully moved on from selling small to large appliances. As a consequence of such processes, by 2001 China was exporting refrigerators to the USA to the value of about $150 million, dominating US imports of refrigerators followed by Mexico and then, some way behind, South Korea (*World Appliance Companies* 2002, Table 3.4.3.3 and Chart 3.1.1.3)

It is now no longer a question of white goods produced inside China being sold to the US however – whether by a wholly owned foreign company; by a joint venture; by a local original equipment manufacturer (OEM) to be sold under another company's brand label; or by an indigenous company under its own brand name. Haier already produces inside the US. The same is true for the relation between South Korea and the US. South Korea's LG Electronics (then 'Goldstar') established its first off shore manufacturing facility in Alabama in 1981 (Korea Times 2004b). Again, if the relation between Turkey and other countries in Europe is considered, it is apparent that Turkey not only now sells them white goods. In 2002, for example, Arcelik of Turkey took on a significantly more international profile. It purchased the 'Leisure' and 'Flavel' cooking brands from Aga Foodservices in the UK; it acquired the Elektra Bregenz Produktionsgesellschaft ovens business in Austria from the French company Elco Holdings; and it took 51 per cent in the Artic refrigeration business in Romania.

There are considerations of a strategic kind that can lead white goods producers in the South to both enter markets in the North (when foreign producers are squeezing the domestic market in China for example) and sometimes to actually set up production there (adjacency to markets can reduce transport costs for producers from North and South alike). There are also, however, strategic considerations that mean there is no one way that the established producers in the North have responded to pressures arising from the cheap labour advantages of the South and here some important additional qualifications must be entered to the view that everything must go to China.

A case in point is what has happened at the US corporation Maytag. Faced with increased imports from China, it did not respond on the 'if you can't beat them, join them' principle and shift production there. This was partly because it wanted to stay close to its end market and it was partly because with some products there was thought to be a greater chance of proprietary technology being stolen. Instead of adopting an all or nothing response, Maytag developed a variety of mixed strategies. For example the company now buys motors for dishwashers in China – from a plant owned by GE – because the design is standardised and stable and China offers the lowest price. On the other hand, it makes wire harnesses for dishwashers in Mexico because those harnesses tend to be different in each dishwasher model, so sudden shifts in demand could make it difficult to supply from farther away. In fact, as far as dishwashers are concerned, Maytag uses Chinese motors, Mexican wiring and does the main assembly in America. As Aeppel (2003) comments, it tries to stay ahead of imports by using a 'triad strategy'. Sometimes, though, Maytag has simply decided to stop making products itself. Refrigerators with the freezer on top are a case in point. Competition from cheap imports made for such thin profit margins on these that the corporation decided to get them made by Daewoo in Korea and then sell them under the Maytag label.

Electrolux provides another example. This corporation has also developed a range of responses to the emergence of low wage producers. In 2004, in the context of moving the production of 1.6 million refrigerators from Greenville in the US to the Texas-Mexico border, Hans Straberg, Electrolux President and CEO outlined the company's own mixed strategy. Part of this was to expand manufacturing in Asia, both for the Asian market and beyond. 'In time' he said, 'we expect to ship from low cost Asian plants to markets around the world'. But another prong in the strategy was to shift some plants to lower cost countries adjacent to markets. As Straberg pointed out 'for the US market, a Mexican plant is fully competitive with an Asian plant' (because higher shipping costs from China offset cheaper labour there). The same policy was followed in Europe, where production is shifting to Eastern European countries that are close to Western Europe. Yet another prong of the company's policy entailed outsourcing components from low cost countries. The aim here is that existing plants should double the proportion of components that they outsource from 20 to 40 per cent. In addition, moves are being made to increase the pooling of resources at the Group level by simplifying, standardising and consolidating products. If this was done, Straberg reasoned, 'Some plants can stay right where they are and they can remain competitive for now' (quoted in Bauer 2004). Just how long 'for now' will be remains to be seen of course and the best bet must be that more production will move South. But, as the above suggests, relocation of all production is unlikely. A mixture of strategies is likely to persist.

It is possible that in the USA the outsourcing of components from China and Mexico has been more common than the re labelling of entire products and that the same may be true for Western European products in relation to China and also Turkey and Eastern Europe. What is clear is that the decisions taken in individual cases are driven by a mix of pragmatic considerations – proximity to end market, transport costs, consideration of the alternative production sites on offer and the financial inducements sometimes associated with them and so forth; and that the part of the industry that has been traditionally located in the highly industrialised countries has been persistently pressured to make decisions on just such matters. One way or another, this spells the emergence of some developing economies as production sites for white goods as well as increasingly important markets for their consumption.

As we said at the outset, however, much talk about globalisation lacks specificity. Looking now within the world of white goods, the rest of the book therefore considers the industry in different countries. Most of these are in the South – China, Taiwan, South Korea, Turkey, Brazil, South Africa – but the next chapter provides a more detailed view from within the North, from the UK, to examine in more detail how the industry and its workers have fared over the last quarter century.

References

Aeppel, T. (2003) 'Three Countries, One Dishwasher', *The Wall Street Journal*, 6 October.

Appliance Magazine (2003) 'Whirlpool Corporate Overview', Whirlpool Special Section *Appliance Magazine*, April.

Babyak, R. (2000) 'Getting Connected: Network News', *Appliance Manufacturer*, September.

Baden-Fuller, C. W. and Stopford, J. M. (1991) 'Globalisation Frustrated: The Case of White Goods', *Strategic Management Journal*, 12 (7).

Batchelor, C. (1992) 'Burning Ambition to Succeed: A Look At a Company That Has Adopted Advanced Manufacturing Methods To Take on the World', *Financial Times*, 10 November.

Bauer, J. (2004) 'Electrolux Remains in Pursuit of Low Cost Factories', *The Grand Rapids Press*, 13 February.

Bonnema, L. (2004) 'European Appliance Industry: Surviving in a New Europe', *Appliance Magazine*, July.

Brown-Humes, C. (2002) 'Electrolux: A Careful Clean-up to Consolidate the Company', *Financial Times*, 6 June.

Business Standard (2003) 'Electrolux Looking at Contract Jobs', *Business Standard*, 12 September.

China Daily (2004) 'BSH Plans Expansion in China', *China Daily*, 21 June.

Cockburn, C. and Ormrod, S. (1993) *Gender and Technology in the Making*, London: Sage.

Esgin, N. (2003) 'Manufacturing for Eastern Europe', *Appliance Magazine – European Edition*, November.

Euromonitor (1998) *Global Market Information Database*, London: Euromonitor Ltd.

Euromonitor (1999) *International Market Review: World Market for Refrigeration Appliances*, London: Euromonitor Ltd.

Euromonitor (2001) *Global Market Information Database: Market Background*, London: Euromonitor Ltd.

Euromonitor (2002) *Large Kitchen Appliances: Market Survey*, London: Euromonitor Ltd.

Euromonitor (2003a) *Global Sales of Refrigeration and Large Cooking Appliances*, http://euromonitor.com/gmid/default.asp.

Euromonitor (2003b) *Domestic Electrical Appliances in Japan*, London: Euromonitor Ltd.

Firebox (2004) www.firebox.com (reviewer's comment originally made August 2003).

George, N. (2001) 'Electrolux to Cut a Further 2,800 Jobs', *Financial Times*, 15 December.

George, N. (2003) 'Electrolux Considers Closing US Plant', *FT.com site*, 21 October.

Hardyment, C. (1988) From Mangle to Microwave, Cambridge: Polity Press in association with Basil Blackwell.

Hirst, P. and Thompson, G. (1996) *Globalisation in Question. The International Economy and the Possibilities of Governance*, Oxford: Blackwell.

ILO (1996) *World Employment 1996/7: National Policies in a Global Context*, Geneva: ILO.

Japan Today (2004a) 'Matsushita Begins Construction of Giant Industrial Complex in China', *Japan Today*, 18 October.

Japan Today (2004b) 'Toshiba, TCL to launch Appliance Venture in China', *Japan Today*, 4 November.

Korea Times (2004a) 'Electrolux Aims to Boost Volume Here', *Korea Times*, 2 February.

Korea Times (2004b) 'LG Electronics on Global Map from Moscow to LA', *Korea Times*, 14 November.

La Stampa (2004) 'Merloni: Ci Svilupperemo in Altri Continenti' [Merloni Aims to Expand Beyond Europe], *La Stampa*, 6 July.

Lambert, R., Gillan, M. and Fitzgerald, S. (2005) 'Electrolux in Australia: Deregulation, 'Industry Restructuring and the Dynamics of Bargaining', *Industrial Relations Journal* 47 (3).

Marsh, P. (2002a) 'Top of the Range to the Rest of the World', *Financial Times*, 3 April.

Marsh, P. (2002b) 'The World's Wash Day: How Platform Development Works', *Financial Times*, 29 April.

Marsh, P. (2003) 'Merloni to Expand in Eastern Europe', *Financial Times*, 30 October.

Marsh, P. and Tait, N. (1998) 'Whirlpool's Platform for Growth', *Financial Times*, 26 March.

McGregor, R. (2003) 'China Tumbles in White Goods', *Financial Times*, 11 September.

McLannahan, B. (2003) 'Black Days for White Goods', *CFOEurope.com*, 16 December.

Millman, J. (2000) 'The World's New Tiger on the Export Scene Isn't Asian; It's Mexico', *The Wall Street Journal*, 5 May.

Mishra, R. and Mukherjee, G. (2004) 'Haier Buys Out Entire Stake in Indian Unit', *The Hindu Business Line*, (Internet Edition) 4 March.

Nakamoto, M. (2004) 'Matsushita Shake-Up To Cut Costs', *Financial Times*, 9 January.

Polish News Bulletin (2003) 'Producer of Household Appliances Plans More Investments in Poland', *Polish News Bulletin*, 25 July.

Polish News Bulletin (2004) 'Giving to the Rich', *Polish News Bulletin*, 6 April.

Segal-Horn, S., Asch, D. and Suneja, V. (1998) 'The Globalization of the European White Goods Industry', *European Management Journal*, 16 (1) January.

Silva, E. B. (2001) 'Time and Emotion in Studies of Household Technologies', *Work, Employment and Society*, 16 (2).

Smith, C. and Meiksins, P. (1995) 'System and Dominance Effects in Cross-National Organisational Analysis', *Work, Employment and Society*, 9 (2) June.

Song, J. (2004) 'LG Aims for $10bn Sales in India by 2010', *Financial Times*, 6 October.

Swengley, N. (2004) 'The Kitchen Has Landed', *How to Spend It*, 6 November.

van der Post, L. (2003) 'A New Kitchen or a Merc?', *How to Spend It*, 7 October.

Watkins, M. (2003) 'Electrolux Sees Flat Demand as Losses Widen', *Financial Times*, 12 February.

Wells, D. (2001) 'Labour Markets, Flexible Specialisation and the New Microcorporatism', *Relations Industrielles / Industrial Relations*, Fall, 56 (2).

World Appliance Companies (2002), *World Appliance Companies*, Third Edition. Report published by Appliance magazine and Industry Statistics Ltd, Oak Brook: Dana Chase.

2
The View from the UK – Mature Markets, High Imports and Other Problems

Theo Nichols and Surhan Cam

This chapter examines the changing position of the UK domestic appliances industry with respect to a number of dimensions – consumption, production, ownership, trade relations and employment. It does so in the context of what might be called the 'regional idea'. This is the idea that, in the modern political economy, 'trade flows are dominated by exchanges within and between the three major regions of the global economy (the so-called triad): Europe, North America, and East Asia' (Hoekman and Kostecki 2001: 9); and that over the last two decades or more there has been a regionalisation of trade and foreign direct investment flows (Kozul-Wright 1995; Ohmae, 1995).

Following an outline of the history of cooking and cooling products in the UK, the chapter focuses on the industry over the last quarter of a century. To anticipate: it points to the industry as one that has been in secular decline as far as employment is concerned. The now mature domestic market is seen to be subject to continued domination by foreign ownership and high levels of market concentration. With respect to the regional idea set out above, both imports and exports are seen to have taken a largely (European) regional form, although recent evidence also suggests that the source of imports has been shifting from the EU to the EU periphery and may now be beginning to move outside the region. In this respect, the picture to emerge is compatible with the wider notion that the UK is undergoing a reconfiguration of its economic relationships to two specific parts of the world: Eastern Europe and East Asia (GPN 2001). However, our main purpose is to examine the situation of the UK white goods industry (in particular large cooking and cooling appliances). In doing so, we hope that the situation in the other countries reviewed in later chapters may be better viewed in comparative perspective.

The origins of domestic appliance production in the UK

But a few years ago a Refrigerator was regarded purely as a luxury and only within the purchasing power of the well-to-do. Today, however, there is a definite trend toward universal adoption and it is only a matter of time and of the recognition [of] the essential need of a refrigerator when this appliance will be as commonly used as a domestic cooker....

This refrigerator is British-made at Electrolux works, Luton, Bedfordshire. Precise manufacturing detail, the finest workmanship and material, and careful selling and distribution planning, allied to the exclusively simple principle of operation, have made the Electrolux successful, and the testimony of householders, builders, tenants, and architects confirm the acceptance of this most modern and improved automatic refrigerator, as the refrigerator of today (Electrolux 1933: 2, 3).

The production of electric domestic appliances in the UK goes back to the late nineteenth century. As a new industry, it was in part an adaptation of more established ones, such as the general engineering industry, foundries and related product industries. One sequence of development was for existing engineering companies to move into domestic appliances, presumably in response to a perceived potential demand. To illustrate, Davis Gas Stove Company bought into T. and J. Jackson Ltd (electric lighting specialists) in 1912 and went on to produce the Jackson electric cooker (Corley 1966: 30–31). For the first part of the twentieth century, the British market was dominated by foreign companies, via imports or by operations run through British subsidiaries. The industry has its social roots in the beginnings of a broader based consumer market for such products, first among the middle classes and then slowly extended to the working classes in the first part of the twentieth century.

Cookers

The forerunner of the domestic appliances industry came in the form of cookers, first gas cookers and then electric. Sometime in the 1820s, following the supply of gas to houses, the first gas cooker was developed and used in the UK (Houghton 1972). These early models were adaptations of the coal range. They were cast iron boxes, insulated with straw and heated by piped gas. There was little development and refinement of these units for most of the century. However, by the First World War they had acquired a position as a prestige domestic unit. Even by the 1930s the author of a prodigiously titled work (*Domestic Scientific Appliances: Being a Treatise for the Guidance of Users and Manufacturers of Domestic Appliances, Architects and Teachers of Domestic Science, with Special Regard to Efficiency Economy and Correct Method of Use*) felt able to declare, thus conveying a sense of wonder:

In no branch of domestic science has greater progress been made in recent years than in that relating to the cooking of food, and with the appliances now procurable it is possible to conduct this part of the home routine with less labour and at a lower cost than hitherto.

The author went on to note, referring to gas cookers:

> [The] inherent defect of all cooking apparatus in which solid fuel is used is that a single, small operation cannot be conducted without consuming a considerable quantity of fuel unless a range is already in use for other purposes. By using gas, however, this difficulty is overcome.

And about 'electric cooking appliances':

> electrical contrivances are clean and convenient in use, and for these reasons, electric cooking has replaced the coal-fire method to a large extent in localities in which a cheap supply of electricity is provided (Darling 1932: 98, 107,111).

The author of a handbook on domestic electrical appliances from about the same period also emphasised the advantages of cleanliness:

> Cooking by electricity is first and foremost absolutely clean, there are no fumes, smoke or smell, and the pots and pans never blacken.
> The heat is under perfect control and can be regulated to a nicety, the stoves themselves do not require black-leading, are easy to keep clean (Hobbs 1930: 62).

The development of the electric cooker was dependent on the extension of electricity supply to households. In 1895, it was reported that the Gloucester Road School of Cookery, London was using a 'miraculous' method of cooking with 'trained lightning'; namely electricity. In a public demonstration of these 'new' products, the demonstrator, a Miss Fairclough, claimed that it was possible to cook food 'without any apparent signs of heat' and she went on: 'no other means of cooking is so eminently satisfactory and free from all disagreeable accompaniments' (Conacher 1971: 1). This effectively was the beginning of electric cooking. Before this, cooking was largely carried out in iron stoves, using wood and other combustible material, having developed over the centuries, from the open fire through to the enclosed fire and then to the bakers' oven.

The first electric stoves were unrefined: the forerunner of the modern oven was a square metal box with a door. This so-called Dutch oven stood on high feet or on a hob in front of the fire and contained a clockwork mechanism from which a joint hung and rotated while cooking (Conacher 1971: 1). As with the gas cooker, these units were slow to develop. Initially they were adaptations of the gas cookers that were available, simply involving the replacement of gas heating with electricity. By the turn of the century the electric cooker had begun to develop a distinctive form and appearance.

Cookers gradually evolved with the attributes and features that are taken for granted today. The Belling company, an early domestic appliances producer, developed the boiler grill (heat above and below) for the electric cooker in 1915. Originally switch controls had only three settings, High, Medium and Low, and it was not until 1946 that the 'Simmerstat' was developed, which gave a choice of six different settings for boiler rings (Conacher 1971: 4)

As with many of the innovations on gas and electric cookers, wartime developments were important. Research development for war purposes in the First World War and particularly the Second World War resulted in initiatives that were later utilised in the domestic appliance area. The now popular microwave technology has its origins in defence development, which was subsequently transferred to domestic household use.

Refrigeration

The development of refrigeration units occurred at a later stage and outside the UK. It began in the USA with the development of cooling systems, in the first instance these were insulated ice-boxes (sold for example by Sears Roebuck), and it then proceeded via kerosene powered units to the modern refrigerator. The modern refrigerator was created with the development in the 1920s of compressors and evaporative technology. The first residential electric refrigerator was developed in the 1920s by General Electric. By 1928 the company estimated there were over one million refrigerators in US homes. By 1937 it is estimated there were nearly 3 million. At first these 'luxury items' were for the few who could afford them but by 1950, 90 per cent of Americans living in towns and 80 per cent living in rural areas owned domestic refrigerators (Russo 2002; Weightman 2003: 189–90).

By 1927, the United States provided the bulk of refrigerator imports into Britain (Corley 1966: 107). In the same year, Electrolux began producing the first small gas refrigerator in Britain. This development foreshadowed the later move in Britain towards 'waist high' or small refrigeration units (Hardyment 1988: 141–142). The compressor, an essential unit for electric refrigerators, was only introduced into Britain in 1933. But demand for refrigerators was also delayed in part because the American penchant for ice in the home (initially stimulated and supplied by the frozen ice trade) had no counterpart in the UK or in Europe generally (Weightman 2003: 144). Compressor production did not assume any major importance in the British market until after the Second World War, when a franchise was granted to L. Sterne of Glasgow by the American Tecumseh Co. to make its sealed units, which were small enough to be incorporated into the refrigerator (Corley 1966: 107–108). By the mid-1960s Sterne supplied compressors to most refrigerator manufacturers in the UK, apart from Hotpoint, Frigidaire, Kelvinator and Lec, which all produced their own compressors.

Design and users

Initially, these appliances were very utilitarian, with little emphasis on style. Until the 1940s, the design of domestic appliances was largely dominated by engineering considerations about the layout of the appliance's chassis, or inside mechanism (Corley 1966: 105). The result was an approach to product development in which relatively little attention was given to users. In fact, it is claimed that the view amongst appliance manufacturers was 'that since appliances were finely engineered products, the housewife ought to value their qualities even if the specification did not exactly suit her needs' (Corley 1966: 51). It was only in 1956/7 that Hotpoint (principal products – cookers, refrigerators, vacuum cleaners and washing machines) carried out market research with 'housewives' to see what they wanted in relation to their electrical domestic appliances, this being the first time that this had happened in the electric domestic appliance industry (Corley 1966: 51). Until relatively recently, these products were designed and developed by men for largely 'imagined' women (Cockburn and Furst-Dilic 1994).

The beginning of a mass market: 1950s–1970s

Initially, the acquisition of domestic appliances was confined to the middle classes, and it was to them that the early advertising was directed. It emphasised that the new products were clean and scientific (an idea later traded on by Zanussi, which advertised its products under the rubric of 'The Appliance of Science'). It also made a definite play on the idea that they were 'fashionable' and 'modern' (an example is provided by the 1930s Electrolux advertisement reproduced in Figure 2.1).

It was during the 1950s that the more affluent working class began to purchase such items. As reported by Goldthorpe et al (1969: 22), real earnings increased sharply during this decade, and this was reflected in the acquisition of consumer goods:

> ... it was estimated that the average real earnings of industrial workers had risen by more than 20 per cent between 1951 and 1958; and that by the spring of 1959 the average working-class household income was about £850 per year (gross), with nearly half of all employed working-class families having an annual income of over £1,000. It was revealed further, as a result of national surveys, that by 1959 among this more prosperous half of the working class 85 per cent of all household had a television set, 44 per cent a washing machine, 44 per cent a lawnmower, 32 per cent a car and 16 per cent a refrigerator. In addition 35 per cent of the families in question owned, or were buying, their own house.

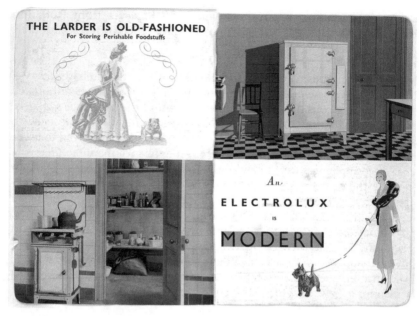

Figure 2.1   White Goods, Fashion and Modernity in the 1930s

Lockwood had noted in an earlier article that these developments were part of a desire to acquire the material goods necessary for a relatively comfortable life. Rather than these working class families seeing such consumer durables as 'status symbols' (a matter about which there was much popular discussion at the time), he argued that they recognised that: 'A washing machine is a washing machine is a washing machine' (1960: 253).

Gradually, consumer durables became an increasing feature of working class as well as middle class family life in Britain. Nonetheless, during the 1950s and into the 1960s, the production of domestic appliances in Britain had remained largely focused on middle class families, with little attention paid to the potential of a broader consumer base (Corley 1966: 54). It was an industry which, in Paba's words, consisted essentially of 'unspecialised, over-fragmented, undynamic' firms (Paba 1986: 306). These firms had limited product lines. Many firms manufactured under licence, particularly for the large US firms that led the industry. It was an industry that had been led either by subsidiaries of US multinationals (Frigidaire, Hoover, General Electric and Kelvinator) or divisions of other large diversified firms (AEI-Hotpoint, English Electric, Thorn, Simplex (Tube Investments) and Electrolux). By the 1960s, in the context of competitive pressures around quality, development and innovation, the smaller entrepreneurial units began to withdraw from the British domestic appliance market (Paba 1986: 306–07).

Thus, the British industry was largely nationally based – in the sense that production took place in Britain largely for a British market – although shaped by the presence of multinational firms. The British market expanded as the acquisition and use of the basic domestic appliances increased throughout the early to mid-twentieth century, such products being popularised as labour-saving goods for the modern household (Slater 2000: 179–180). This expansion is reflected in the focus of advertising on the consuming households, predicated on an expanding 'affluent working class'.

> The emerging affluent working class in western societies from 1950 onwards was seen as a new relatively undifferentiated 'mass' market by producers, department stores, advertisers and distributors of all types of what were termed 'consumer durables', such as televisions, washing machines, cars, transistor radios and record players. (Bocock 1992: 133)

The white goods industry had been relatively closed to imports for a number of decades. One reason for this was that after 1946 imports were tightly controlled by the Board of Trade, against a pre-war background of an increasingly restrictive import policy for the electrical domestic appliance industry, so as to protect Britain's electrical industry. In 1932 an Import Duties Act had placed tariffs on many goods based on preferential principles, with a first level of protection for British manufacturers, a second level for Commonwealth manufacturers and no protection for others. After the Second World War, imports from the dollar area were restricted until 1959. However these policies had the effect of encouraging foreign firms to produce inside the UK domestic appliance market.

Government concern about the balance of payments led to policies to promote exports. In 1951, at the time of the Korean War, refrigerator manufacturers were required to increase their exports. The result was that aggregate appliance exports increased to about 42 per cent of total production. Following this short term measure however exports declined to 35 per cent in 1954 and were down to 19 per cent by 1964 (Corley 1966: 122–23).

As far as imports are concerned, it is argued by Paba that the principal barrier to import penetration in the UK industry during this period was 'high product differentiation' (1986: 307). In brief, he argues that domestic appliances is an industry in which it is very difficult to judge the quality of the product before purchase and consumers were drawn towards known and familiar brands. Such a situation gave established brands a considerable advantage, making it difficult for new entrants to persuade consumers to try them out. The fact that both Whirlpool and MDA (Merloni) later told a Monopolies and Merger Commission into domestic electrical goods that they had experienced difficulty because 'brand awareness and brand loyalty were important features of the market' and that the Commission reported 'both these suppliers told us that they had experienced difficulty in over-coming consumer (and also retail) loyalty to established names when launching their brands in the UK market', adds some credibility to this view (Monopolies and Merger Commission 1997 Vol. 2, para 7.17). Coupled with this resistance, as Paba (1986: 307–08) points out, it may also be the case that consumers had negative views about products from partic-ular countries. During the 1950s and 1960s this may have constituted an additional barrier to import penetration.

During the 1960s and 1970s, the patterns of production and marketing of domestic appliances in Europe began to change, with major conse-quences for the UK in the 1980s and 1990s. One feature of this period was the growth of a few European based firms, principally, through merger and acquisition. In fact, it is argued by Paba that in Europe the domestic appliances industry was marked by growth of firms through merger and acquisition rather than by increasing production or entering new markets (1991: 22–24). But another particular feature, critical for the UK, was the development of the Italian domestic appliance industry.

The modern Italian domestic appliance industry (refrigerators, washing machines, freezers, and dishwashers) dates from the 1950s, when the industry was transformed by the entry of new generation specialised firms, such as Zanussi, Ignis, Zoppas, Castor, Candy and Indesit. During the 1950s and 1960s these few firms came to dominate the industry, with Ignis, Zanussi, Indesit and Zoppas accounting for 77.8 per cent of the total refri-gerator production in Italy in 1964. This level of concentration in domestic appliance production was quite unlike any other European country at the time (Paba 1986: 308–9).

Significantly, these firms, unlike their larger European competitors, focused on the emerging mass market, developing products that were reasonably priced and produced at low cost. To achieve these goals, these firms built up their productive capacity, and capitalised on the relatively low cost of Italian labour. Thus this was an industry that was highly con-centrated, aimed at the mass market, with products that were relatively cheaply priced. This made the UK market, which had not been oriented to the bottom end of the market, highly vulnerable.

In targeting the low income segments of the market the Italian firms pursued a two pronged strategy. First, UK companies were provided with non-branded goods, which they then sold under their own name. General Electric, Hotpoint, English Electric, Frigidaire and Imperial all participated in such brand-naming. The appeal of this strategy to the British-based com-panies was that it helped them to widen the model range in a particular product. Sometimes companies also used this method to open up new product markets. For example, Hoover, with 30 per cent of the domestic British market for washing machines pursued this approach in the mid-1960s to enter the refrigerator market.

Second, the Italian firms sought agreements with retailers and commercial houses to market the Italian goods under the firms' own labels, thereby seeking to assure potential purchasers of the quality of these goods. This second approach was an important way of building brand recognition over time. Of the main Italian firms, only Indesit always sold under the 'Indesit' label, attributed by Paba to the fact that the firm was closely linked to Fiat and influenced by this multinational company (1986: 312, fn 2).

The Italian firms were successful in pursuing the 'own label' strategy in the UK and across Europe. Paba notes that during the 1960s, Italy became the second largest producer of domestic appliances in the world, and the largest exporter of domestic appliances. In 1963, Italy became the largest European producer of washing machines and in 1966 of refrigerators (Paba 1986: 308). The Italians had rapidly developed an innovative, expansionist industry based on big plants with low-cost labour and more efficient mass production techniques.

During the 1970s, changes took place with implications for the pattern of production and consumer demand in Britain, as well as the other main European countries. On the one hand, the Italian industry began to lose its way. The European market began to show signs of saturation, replacement demand coming to the fore towards the end of the 1960s. In this situation, increased emphasis was placed on product differentiation and after-sales service rather than production skills, as had been the case earlier (Paba 1986: 312–13). On the other hand, after 1969 the Italian firms could no longer maintain their low cost advantage that had characterised the earlier period.

There then followed a period where key Italian firms, such as Ignis and Zanussi, which were both actively involved in 'own label' exports, were either absorbed as a managerial division of a multinational (Phillips in the case of Ignis) or entered into part ownership (AEG-Telefunken in the case of Zanussi from 1973 to 1979) or were subsequent taken over (Electrolux taking over Zanussi in 1984). Some firms, such as Smeg, began to specialise in high quality products, which were still sold abroad through non-branded channels (Paba 1986: 314–15). However, overall there was increased emphasis on branded goods.

Problems of a mature market: from the 1980s onward

Value of the UK market

Class-related patterns of consumption have remained in evidence to some extent as the range of domestic appliances has extended, and products such as microwave ovens have come onto the market (Table 2.1). Generally, the professionals, employers and managers have been the first to buy new products (as no doubt is the case the world over). However, by the 1980s, the UK market for cooling appliances, washing machines and cookers was mass-based, with the emphasis moving from first-time purchase to replacement.

Table 2.1   **UK Households with Selected Domestic Appliances, 1988**
(Percentages)

Households with:	Deep-freezers (incl. fridge-freezers)	Washing machines	Tumble drier	Microwave oven	Dishwasher
Professional	88	93	60	51	32
Employers and Managers	91	95	62	60	27
Other non-manual	84	89	45	50	19
Skilled and semi-skilled manual	85	91	50	48	6
Unskilled manual	75	83	36	32	1
Economically inactive	61	72	25	21	4
All	77	84	42	39	10

Source: Social Trends 1991, 109, Table 4.6.

The market has become a mature one with high levels of penetration for most products, so that, in 2000, 99 per cent of households had refrigeration and cooking appliances (ONS 2002 Table 9.3). Moreover, the UK market for domestic appliances has lacked overall growth in value terms. Domestic appliance markets are sensitive to changes in consumer demand and in the UK cyclical fluctuations made for falls in the overall market in the early 1980s and early 1990s, followed by upswings in each decade.[1] But the market was still worth less in 2000 than it had been in 1979. At the start of this period, the market had stood at £3,891 million at 1995 prices. It reached a highpoint of over £4,000 million in 1989 but was still only £3,500 million in 2000 (Figure 2.2).

When the overall market is disaggregated into cooking appliances on the one hand and cooling appliances on the other[2] it can be seen that these two product groups have followed a similar pattern of movement to that of the overall domestic appliances market (cf. Figures 2.2 and 2.3). As with the overall domestic appliances market, the declines at the beginning of each decade were followed by increases in later years. The most notable difference is in the performance of the cooking appliance market in the 1990s. Although cooking and cooling products did see a small amount of growth in contrast to the fall in the domestic appliance market as a whole, such growth was very limited. Over the entire period between 1979 and 2000 the cooking appliances market increased by only 23 per cent from £447 million in 1979 to £548 million in 2000. Cooling appliances

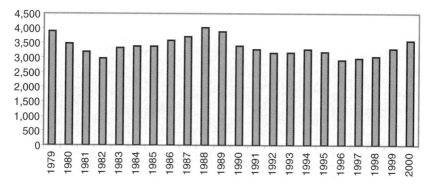

Figure 2.2 UK Market for Domestic Appliances (£ Million, 1995 Prices)
Source: ONS 2004.

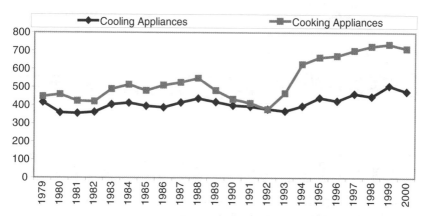

Figure 2.3 UK Market for Cooking and Cooling Appliances (£ Million, 1995 Prices)
Source: AMDEA 1985, 1992 and 2001.

increased by only 14 per cent from £415 million in 1979 to £475 million in 2000. These changes amounted to annual average rates of growth of only one per cent and two thirds of one per cent respectively.

Turnover, value-added and unit price

Just as the value of the UK market failed to grow, so did the turnover of UK based manufacturers. In 1979 total turnover of UK-based domestic appliances stood at £3,120 million. In 2000, it was down to £2,433 million. Only the second half of the 1980s saw year on year increases. This trend was not maintained in the 1990s, which were characterised by gradual decline (Figure 2.4).

The unimpressive performance for turnover was matched by an equally unimpressive performance for share of value added in turnover. The share

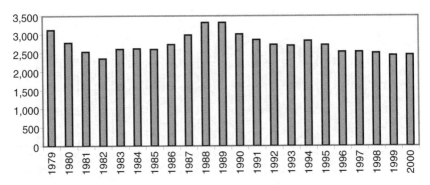

Figure 2.4   Turnover in UK Domestic Appliances Manufacturing (£ Million)
Source: ONS 2003a.

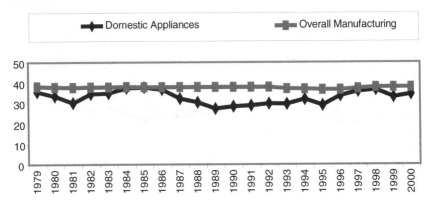

Figure 2.5   The Share of Value Added in Overall Turnover in UK Domestic Appliances and Overall Manufacturing (Percentages)
Source: ONS 2003b.

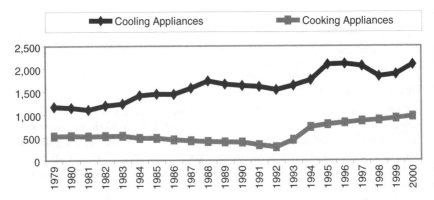

Figure 2.6   UK Production of Cooking and Cooling Appliances (Thousands of Units)
Source: AMDEA, 1985, 1992 and 2001.

of value added in domestic appliances turnover fell below that in manufacturing as a whole for the entire period (Figure 2.5). In UK manufacturing as a whole the share of value added remained stable with an average of 38 per cent 1979–2000. In domestic appliances, it averaged only 33 per cent for the entire period, the high points of 1984–86 and 1997–98 which approached the level for manufacturing as a whole proving transitory.

The lack of a sustained upward movement in both turnover and the share of value added has to be seen in the context of increased UK based production. In short, over the period 1979–2000, more units have been produced but without significant benefit to the total value of production or the share of value added.

Both the number of cooking and cooling appliance units produced in the UK between 1979 and 2000 increased (Figure 2.6). In the case of cooking appliances, the growth occurred in the 1990s and overall the number of cooking appliances almost doubled to one million. In the case of cooling appliances, the rise was steadier, but units produced again almost doubled rising from 1.2 million in 1979 to 2.2 million in 2000. In the context of a lack of growth in the turnover of UK based manufacturers the increase in the number of units produced meant a more or less continuous decline in the price of UK manufactured units over the past two decades.

UK-based production has of course undergone some changes in product mix over the past two decades. In the case of cooking appliances, for example, the 1990s saw some rise in gas cookers at the expense of electric ones and there have been changes in the share contributed by hoods. In the case of cooling appliances, the share taken by refrigerators has tended to fall and those of freezers and fridge-freezers have grown. However, all major categories underwent a decline in unit price (Figures 2.7 below and 2.8).

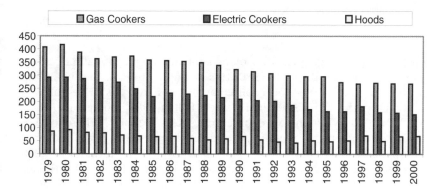

Figure 2.7   UK Wholesale Unit Prices of Different Cooking Appliances, 1995 prices, (£s)
Source: AMDEA 1985, 1992 and 2001.

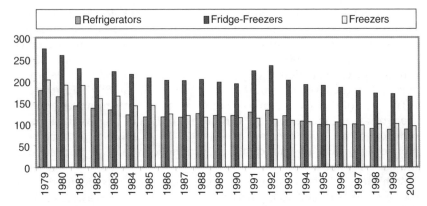

Figure 2.8   UK Wholesale Unit Prices of Different Cooling Appliances, 1995 prices, (£s)
Source: AMDEA 1985, 1992 and 2001.

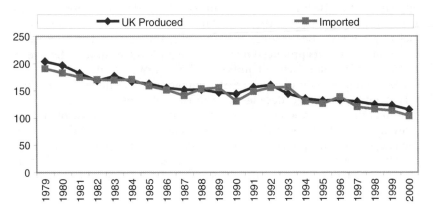

Figure 2.9   UK Cooling Appliances, Wholesale Unit Prices
Source: AMDEA 1985, 1992 and 2001.

In 1979, the average price for cooking appliances was £219 (all prices here are wholesale). By the early 1980s this had fallen to £167 and by 2000 it was more like £100. For cooling appliances average price followed a similar path – from £203 in 1979 to £171 in 1983 and again to about £100 in 2000. While there are sometimes substantial price differences between the different sub-products, the general trend is born out in the major cases. Gas cookers have declined from £407 in 1979 to £268 in 2000. Electric cookers have declined from £292 in 1979 to £151 in 2000 (hoods, in any case a low price item, have held up better). Amongst cooling appliances, fridge-freezers fell from £274 in 1979 to £163 in 2000. The pricing of refrigerators and freezers underwent falls that are even more pronounced.

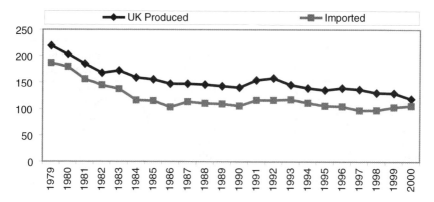

Figure 2.10   UK Cooking Appliances, Wholesale Unit Prices
Source: AMDEA 1985, 1992 and 2001.

The problem of falling unit prices relates to a further problem that besets domestic appliance production in the UK and is significantly driven by it. Prices in the UK have been depressed by cheaper and/or cheapening imports (the extent of imports is discussed later). In cooling appliances the prices of UK produced and imported products have been closely matched, but in both cooking (where imports have typically been cheaper) and in cooling appliances there has been a long-term downward trend in unit price, shown in Figures 2.9 and 2.10. Lower unit prices have exacted their cost on labour.

Employment and labour costs

Lower unit prices have meant job cuts. Over the past two decades, the number of employees in UK domestic appliance manufacturing dropped from 70,000 in 1979 to 30,000 by 2000. In electrical domestic appliances 30 per cent of jobs went, in the smaller non-electrical part of the industry fewer jobs went but this still amounted to more than a quarter of the 1979 labour force (Table 2.2).

Other things being equal, from capital's point of view, more units produced by fewer workers might suggest a significant improvement in economic outcome. However, we have already seen that unit prices were falling and in addition to this, despite a fall of nearly 60 per cent in domestic appliances employment between 1979 and 2000, which represents a loss of over 40,000 jobs, employee compensation fell only 22 per cent (ONS, 1984 Table 1; ONS, 2001 Table 2).

The share of employee compensation in gross value added in the domestic appliances industry underwent a sharp rise 1979–1981, reaching 95 per cent in 1981. This was at a time when the first Thatcher government's policies hit British manufacturing badly. In the domestic appliances industry about

Table 2.2   UK Employment in Domestic Appliances Manufacturing, 1979–2000 (000s)

	Electric Appliances	Non-Electric Appliances	Total Employment in Domestic Appliances
1979	54.7	15.8	70.50
1980	50.8	14.4	65.20
1981	45.1	10.6	55.70
1982	38.3	10.4	48.70
1983	36.9	11.2	48.10
1984	37.9	10.1	47.98
1985	37.5	10.7	48.20
1986	38.1	10.6	48.70
1987	38.1	10.4	48.50
1988	42.1	10.1	52.20
1989	39.6	10.3	49.90
1990	36.9	9.4	46.30
1991	31.2	7.7	38.85
1992	29.2	7.4	36.51
1993	28.2	7.3	35.47
1994	28.6	7.2	35.77
1995	30.2	7.2	37.39
1996	31.0	7.4	38.30
1997	27.8	7.4	35.13
1998	26.0	7.3	33.25
1999	23.5	7.3	30.78
2000	22.3	7.3	29.59

Source: ABI 2000, ONS 2000.

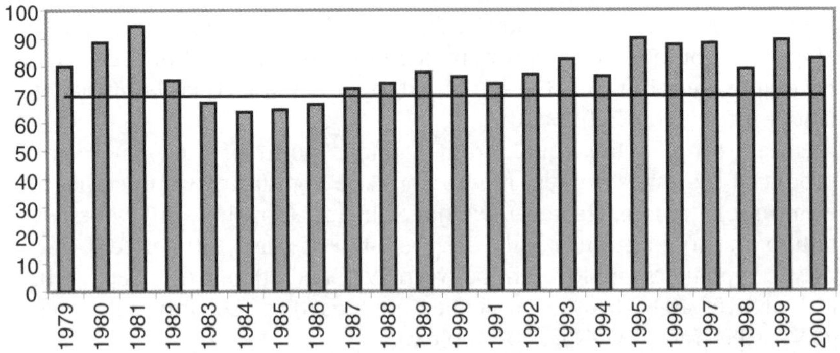

Figure 2.11   Labour's Share of Gross Value Added in UK Domestic Appliances (Percentage)
Source: Value added from ONS 2003b; Labour's Share (Employees' total compensation) from ONS 1984 Table 1; 1992 Table 2; 1999 Table 1; 2001 Table 2.

15,000 employees lost their jobs (employee compensation includes redundancy payments). Employee compensation then fell, bottoming out in the mid-1980s and thereafter it has undergone a steady rise. By 1990 it was 76 per cent of gross value added and in 2000 it was 83 per cent.

Labour's share of gross value added (Figure 2.11) is a measure of the trouble facing the UK-based domestic appliance industry. A financially successful firm or industry has been said to require a labour share in value added which is steadily 'at or below 70 per cent' (Williams et al 1994: 174). Whatever the precise validity of this claim may be, for much of the last two decades labour's share in value added has been at a higher level than this.

International trade (exports and imports)

In domestic appliances as a whole there has been some rise in exports over the last quarter of a century but the rise in imports, up to 80 per cent by 2000, amply underlines that UK-based producers have been unable to hold on to the home market (Figure 2.12 below). High levels of imports characterise several sub sectors. Amongst cooking appliances, 38 per cent of cooker hoods were imported in 2002, 39 per cent of free-standing electric cookers, 63 per cent of electric build in ovens and 86 per cent of build in electric hobs. Among refrigeration appliances, imports have penetrated yet further and amount to 83 per cent of fridge freezers, 91 per cent of refrigerators and 92 per cent of upright freezers (AMDEA 2003). To the problem of a lack of growth in value in the UK market there therefore has to be added the problem of a growing percentage of imports.

Trade relations in the industry have typically centred on Europe. A closer examination of two particular products, freestanding electric

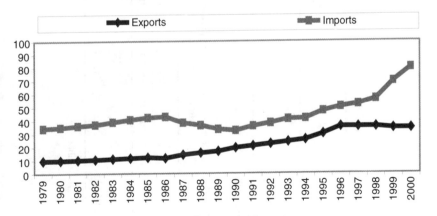

Figure 2.12   UK Domestic Appliance Exports and Imports
Source: ONS 2003c.
Notes: Exports as percentage of output of UK-based domestic appliance manufacturing. Imports as percentage of domestic appliances sales in the UK.

Table 2.3 UK Direction of Trade for Electric Cookers: 1985, 1990, 1995, 1999 (As Percentage of Total Value)

	1985		1990		1995		1999	
	Imports	Exports	Imports	Exports	Imports	Exports	Imports	Exports
EU	82.5	86.5	91.1	77.1	87.5	85.3	78.1	83.6
North America	1.1	0.9	1.1	0.3	1.0	1.4	0.7	1.0
Rest of the World	16.4	12.4	8.8	19.9	12.5	13.3	21.2	15.4

Source: AMDEA 1988, 1992 and 2001.

Table 2.4 UK Direction of Trade for Refrigerators: 1985, 1990, 1995, 1999 (As Percentage of Total Value)

	1985		1990		1995		1999	
	Imports	Exports	Imports	Exports	Imports	Exports	Imports	Exports
EU	86	71.5	72.3	54.9	57.5	60.9	57.1	68.5
North America	1.7	2.4	2.8	8.8	4.4	7.9	4.7	8.9
Rest of the World	12.3	26.1	24.9	36.3	38.1	31.2	38.2	22.6

Source: As for previous table.

cookers (Table 2.3) and refrigerators (Table 2.4) makes clear that in both cases the majority of trade took place within Europe as late as 1999 (a geographical breakdown is not possible for the year 2000 for technical reasons).

In 1999, 78 per cent of imported electric cookers came from EU countries. Italy was the largest provider with 52 per cent and Germany contributed 10 per cent. In the case of imported refrigerators, 57 per cent came from the EU countries. More than half of them (29 per cent) came from Italy, followed by Germany with 19 per cent. As far as exports are concerned, the lion's share of cookers goes to Ireland, described by one British white goods manager as part of the 'home market', as do a significant proportion of refrigerators (data on particular countries is given in Table 2.5).

Even so, British trade with the EU countries has undergone considerable changes: the share of EU countries in imports of electric cookers and refrigerators has declined. Whereas EU countries still contributed 78 per cent of freestanding electric cooker imports into the UK in 1999 this was below the levels in 1995, 1990 and 1985. Moreover, whereas EU countries still contributed 57 per cent of refrigerator imports in 1999, they had contributed over 70 per cent in 1990 and 86 per cent in 1985. In particular, Italy's share fell from 68 per cent to 52 per cent of cooker imports between 1990 and 1999 and its share of refrigerator imports fell from 41 per cent to 28 per cent.

There has been little change in the share of North American imports to UK. In the case of electric cookers imports to the UK, the share of North America averaged about one per cent throughout the 1980s and 1990s (1.1 per cent in 1985 and 0.7 per cent in 2000). The share of North America in refrigerator imports to the UK increased from 1.7 per cent of in 1985 to 4.7 per cent in 2000.

The share of imports from 'Rest of the World' – essentially low wage-countries has increased. The change has been relatively modest in the case of electric cookers. There was an increase from 16 to 21 per cent between 1985 and 1999, and this with some fall in the middle years. The increased contribution of Turkey is however plain to see, with a rise from one to 17 per cent over the decade until the end of the century. In the case of refrigerators, it is a different story.

Refrigeration imports from 'Rest of the World' countries have undergone a marked change. The UK is now the world's leading importer of refrigerators (World Appliance Companies 2002: 8, Table 1.2) and the countries so classified increased their share from 12 per cent to 38 per cent between 1985 and 1999. The major growth until recently has again come from Turkey, its share rose from 9 per cent in 1985 to over 17 per cent in 1999. Since Slovenia and Hungary also made a contribution it might well be said that the trade pattern remained essentially regional but with some move to the

Table 2.5 UK Direction of Trade by Selected Countries: 1990, 1999 (Percentage Contributions by Value)

| | Electric Cookers | | | | Refrigerators | | | |
| | 1990 | | 1999 | | 1990 | | 1999 | |
	Imports	Exports	Imports	Exports	Imports	Exports	Imports	Exports
Total EU	**94.0**	**77.1**	**78.1**	**83.6**	**68.1**	**54.9**	**57.1**	**68.5**
France	5.1	0.2	3.2		3.5	9.0	4.4	6.5
Belgium/Luxembourg					0.4	2.6	0.1	0.0
Netherlands				0.1	0.3	1.9	0.1	4.1
Germany	13.9		7.0		19.3	13.4	18.9	18.7
Italy	68.7	0.5	52.2		40.5	10.8	28.2	1.4
Irish Republic	2.5	75.9	2.5	83.4	0.1	12.0	0.1	31.4
Denmark						1.9	2.0	3.2
Portugal	0.3		11			0.4	2.2	0.4
Spain	0.5	0.1				2.9	0.3	0.3
Sweden							0.5	0.3
Austria	2.1		2				0.4	1.0
Finland							0.0	0.3
Greece		0.3				0.2	0.0	0.3
Total Non-EU Developed Countries	**1.4**	**0.3**	**1.0**	**9.2**	**3.3**	**17.2**	**5.6**	**3.7**
Norway	0.3					1.4	0.0	0.3
Switzerland			0.3		0.3	1.9	0.9	2.1
USA	0.7	0.3	0.7	1.0	3.0	8.8	4.7	1.2
Canada	0.4							
Japan						5.1	0.4	0.1
Australia				7.0				
New Zealand				1.2				

Table 2.5 UK Direction of Trade by Selected Countries: 1990, 1999 (Percentage Contributions by Value) – *continued*

	Electric Cookers				Refrigerators			
	1990		1999		1990		1999	
	Imports	Exports	Imports	Exports	Imports	Exports	Imports	Exports
Rest of the World*	**4.6**	**22.6**	**20.9**	**7.2**	**28.6**	**27.9**	**38.2**	**27.8**
Turkey	1.0		17.7		9.1		17.4	0.9
Hungary			0.5		2.6		6.1	0.0
Poland	3.7		0.6					
Czech Republic	0.1		0.3				0.0	0.8
Slovenia					5.6	1.9	2.7	0.0
Romania					2.5	0.8	0.0	0.5
Russia					1.1			
Bulgaria					1.1			
South Korea					2.8		7.1	0.0
China							1.8	0.0
Nigeria						7.1	0.0	0.0
Ghana						1.6	0.0	3.5
Kenya		15.1		0.8			0.0	1.2
Qatar		1.4						
Mauritius		4.2						

Source: AMDEA 1992 and 2001.

inclusion of the European periphery (a term now complicated by politics catching up with economics in the 2004 EU enlargement). But in 1999 South Korea also achieved an increase in its share of refrigerator imports, up from nearly three per cent in 1990 to seven per cent. This gives some pause for thought about the regional idea and that this is in order is underlined by the latest import data in relation to another East Asian country – China.

The latest data for imports show that by 2003 China accounted for 38 per cent of refrigerator imports by volume and 12 per cent by value (AMDEA 2004). Refrigerators are in fact a relatively low cost cooling appliance and the discrepancy between the Chinese share on the volume and value measures indicates that, even within refrigerators, the Chinese appliances are at the bottom of the price range. When Turkish goods entered the market, they were first aimed at the bottom end and often took the form of OEM products that were sold by independent retailers who presented them as their own brands. They now commonly appear under their own brand names (Beko from Arcelik for example) and have begun to climb the market. The strategies pursued by firms in China would appear to be much the same. Haier launched in the UK in 1997, following its entry into Germany and the US; and it also produces some OEM products for the UK market (Ward 1999). The growth in refrigerator imports from China is however already remarkable, especially in terms of unit sales. In round terms, these have risen from about 150,000 in 2000 to 250,000 in 2001 to 350,000 in 2002 to a million in 2003 (AMDEA various years). Some special factors apply. Haier is now the world's leading producer of refrigerators and refrigerators are only one sub-sector of large cooling appliances, let alone of all white goods. Furthermore, as noted already, refrigerators are relatively low value items. These things said, it is difficult to believe that the range and penetration of white goods products from Rest of the World countries will not increase.

Concentration of ownership (and the hidden face of oligopoly)

To a significant extent, competition between firms in the UK is not competition between British companies or even between British firms and non-British ones. For the most part, the British white goods industry is owned and operated by non-British companies, with the UK the site of competition between global players. However, this development is not necessarily evident to the consumer. Brand names can make it difficult to tell which firm's products they are buying. Such is the situation with respect to cooking appliances that in 2000 UK buyers were offered, among others, Cannon, Creda and Hotpoint machines (all from GDA, the last two at that time accounting for 12 and 9 per cent of the market respectively); they were also offered machines which were apparently made by firms called Zanussi, AEG, Electrolux, Tricity Bendix and Parkinson Cowan (all of which came from Electrolux, the first three accounting for 9, 8 and

3 per cent of the market respectively); and they could also choose Indesit machines, actually from Merloni (accounting for another 3 per cent of the market). In effect, in 2000, despite the several brand names, five firms controlled over half the UK cooking appliance market (Table 2.6). In cooling appliances the market is even more concentrated than in cooking (Table 2.7). In 2000 the top five companies accounted for 68 per cent of the refrigeration appliances market.

The recent history of UK white goods, certainly as far as cooking and cooling appliances are concerned, is epitomised by the Hotpoint brand. This is widely regarded as reliable, good quality – and British. The company was established in 1909. It became wholly owned by GEC in 1983, which also acquired Creda, established in 1932, from Tube Investments in 1987. In 1989, Hotpoint became part of General Domestic Appliances Limited (GDA), a company equally owned on a 50/50 basis by GEC and GE of the US. In 2002, the British half of this joint operation (now called Marconi) experienced mounting difficulties in its other operations and sold its share in GDA to the Italian firm Merloni. At this point, any British ownership was voided from the top five, the Marconi share of GDA now belonging to Merloni. But Merloni then proceeded to take effective ownership of GDA entirely, undertaking to buy shares from GE, which had owned the other half of GDA. This made for further concentration. Merloni's acquisition of GDA has now given it 30 per cent of the UK white goods market (Marsh 2002), simultaneously making Hotpoint, Creda and Cannon Italian brands.

Amongst other recent developments, in 2002 the Turkish firm Arcelik bought out the brand names, 'Leisure' and 'Flavel' from the British oven producer Leisure Consumer Products. The ultimate owner of these products, Glynwed International, changed its name to Aga Foodservice in 2000, its decline having rightly been said to signal 'the further decline of the once-mighty Midlands metal-bashing industry' (Guthrie 2001). The turn of the century also saw Glen Dimplex, a private Republic of Ireland firm, take over Stoves, which had manufactured cooking products on Merseyside under various brands and ownership since 1920, and which had bought the loss making Valor Cookers from Yale and Valor ten years earlier, and more recently New World. Stoves thereby joined Belling, another well-known brand name, and a producer of cooling and cooking appliances and other white goods brands, which Glen Dimplex had taken over in 1992.

It is tempting to conclude that we have here an example of a British industry being taken over by foreign capital. It is as well to remember therefore that although there have been British firms that have supplied white goods for many years, so too have there been foreign white goods firms in the UK. Electrolux for example has manufactured in the UK for three quarters of a century. Even so, it is now clearly better to refer to the 'White Goods Industry in the UK' – not to the 'UK White Goods Industry'. How, then, does the white goods industry in the UK cope?

Table 2.6 Ownership and Brand Shares of Retail Volume in the UK: Cooking Appliances, 2000

Ownership	Country of Brand Owner	Brand names	Brand share in retail volume (per cent)	Company share in retail volume (per cent)
General Domestic Appliances Ltd	USA / UK	Creda Hotpoint	12.1 9.3	21.4
Electrolux UK Ltd	Sweden	Zanussi AEG Electrolux	9.2 8.4 3.5	21.1
Whirlpool UK Ltd	USA	Whirlpool	4.1	4.1
Merloni Domestic Appliances Ltd	Italy	Indesit	3.5	3.5
Bosch Home Appliances Ltd	Germany	Bosch Siemens	3.0	3.0
Share of Top Five Companies				53.1
Private Label*			3.4	3.4
Others			43.5	43.5
Total			100	100

*Exclusive to certain retailers
Source: Euromonitor 2001, Part II, Table 16 and 17.

Table 2.7 Ownership and Brand Shares of Retail Volume in the UK: Refrigeration Appliances, 2000

Ownership	Country of Brand Owner	Brand name	Brand share in retail volume (per cent)	Company share in retail volume (percentage)
General Domestic Appliances Ltd	USA / UK	Hotpoint	22.0	22.0
Lec	Malaysia	Lec	12.5	12.5
Electrolux	Sweden	Zanussi	11.5	21.5
		Electrolux	10.0	
Merloni	Italy	Indesit	7.2	7.2
Bosch	Germany	Bosch	5.0	5.0
Share of Top Five Companies				68.2
Private Label			6.9	6.9
Others			24.9	24.9
Total			100	100

Source: Euromonitor 2001, Part II, Table 10 and 11.

The future of the domestic appliance industry in the UK

In many ways, the industry has performed worse than British manufacturing as a whole. The bare bones of this adverse comparison are signalled by the fact that whereas in the 1990s turnover remained more or less flat in manufacturing as a whole, even showing a slight increase, it actually fell in domestic appliances (Figure 2.13).

As we have seen, the share of value added in turnover in domestic appliances also trended below that in manufacturing for the whole of the period and whereas in the case of manufacturing as a whole imports increased from 15 per cent in 1979 to 46 per cent in 1999, in domestic appliances the same years saw a rise from 34 per cent to 80 per cent.

It is difficult to attribute the industry's comparatively worse UK performance to any special characteristics of the work force. According to LFS data although in 2002 trade union density was slightly higher in domestic appliances (34 per cent) than in manufacturing as a whole (26 per cent), the industry's employment profile was rather similar. Temporary workers of all kinds – contracted workers, agency workers, casual workers and others – amounted to three per cent of the workforce in domestic appliances and four per cent in all manufacturing. Part-time workers amounted to eight per cent of the work force compared to nine per cent. The industry was not even a bastion of white male workers – not to a greater extent than manufacturing as a whole anyway. In domestic appliances 30 per cent of the labour force were women, compared to 27 per cent for all manufacturing; similarly six per cent were non-white compared to five per cent for all manufacturing. Indeed, the key difference with respect to the workforce, is that factories in the industry are generally located in low wage areas and that wages in domestic

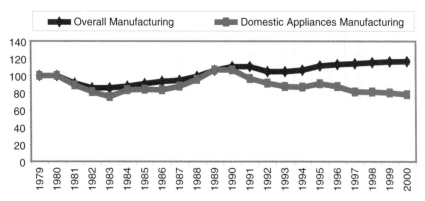

Figure 2.13   Turnover in UK Domestic Appliances Manufacturing and in Overall Manufacturing (1995 prices, 1979 = 100)
Source: ONS 2003a.

appliances are lower than in British manufacturing generally. In Autumn 2002 average gross weekly earnings for domestic appliance workers stood at £355 compared to £410 in manufacturing as a whole and they were 10 to 20 per cent lower than for manufacturing as a whole for the whole of the decade (LFS 2002). The problem is that although wages in domestic appliances are lower than for UK manufacturing as a whole, they are not low when compared to some of the international competition.

In the post-war period, Italian producers invaded the UK. Later, it was exposed to increased imports from Turkey and other countries on the periphery of the EU. Now it is exposed to increased competition from East Asia. Whatever else these countries have offered – and Italy contributed design just as today South Korea contributes electronics – the common element has been cheap labour. This is notably so for China.

In the 1990s, redundancy pay swelled labour costs and squeezed value added. If redundancies ceased this would make for some reduction in labour costs. Even then, compared to Turkey, East Europe and East Asia wages would still be 'too high'. It is most unlikely that they will be driven low enough to compete with foreign imports – or indeed that redundancies will cease.

The industry appears to be a prime example of some of the causes of British manufacturing's more general decline. Take GDA. The company, with its Hotpoint brand, might well be regarded as the flagship of the British white goods industry and most certainly of those parts of it under review here. In 1997 a Monopolies and Merger Commission Report into domestic electrical goods noted with some incredulity that only 9.7 per cent of GDA's 1994/95 turnover arose from exports (Monopolies and Merger Commission 1997: para 8.9). In 2002 over 90 per cent of its revenues still came from the UK (Marsh 2002). This seems to fit the idea of a domestically focused company, which lived off the home market, and when push came to shove, was unable to compete with imports and to defend the home market against external aggressors. The story is not quite that simple. First of all, Hotpoint was an exporter in the mid-1970s but, faced with declining profitability, it sold its European distributive network to concentrate resources on the UK market, after which it became profitable in the 1980s (Baden-Fuller and Stopford 1991: 505). Second, as we have seen, Hotpoint was merged with GE's European appliance business in 1989 in recognition of the limited defensibility of a national position (Stopford and Baden-Fuller 1990: 411). Some industry insiders attribute its export performance in the 1990s to the negative effects of this merger, as a consequence of which, in the words of one of these, 'Europe was left to GE'. Other industry insiders claim less specifically that the merger never worked and that the two sides could not get on. Shorn of these particularities, however, the image of a long established company, focused on the home and Empire market, remains a plausible one.

We saw in Chapter 1 that most of the world's regions are dominated by a few multinationals. These corporations are likely to implement their own production systems wherever in the globe they settle and this means that low wage overseas producers are therefore unlikely to be left behind in terms of technical and organisational innovation. In these circumstances, white goods companies in the UK have adopted a number of strategies in an attempt to safeguard the home market.

The pressure has been on to develop common platforms and to gain from other economies of scale by further rationalisation and the purchase across sites of materials and components (not least of course components cheaply produced abroad). In the UK, Stoves, a long established producer of cooking appliances, was badly affected by imports from East Europe in 1999 and when faced with falling profits because of this, it began to eagerly search for alliances with other white goods firms across Europe to get better prices for steel and components (Gracie 1999). Glen Dimplex, an Irish based company that also owns British production facilities (now including Stoves, which it took over in 2001) exemplifies a different tactic. It buys in $100 million of electrical components every year from China (Brown 2002).

Production operations, which are often situated in old factories, have been stripped down. As an industry trade union official put it:

> Oven factories used to have their own foundries, paint shops and machine shops. Today, they're like big Meccano shops.

Attempts have been made to increase productivity in other ways and to revamp management practice. In the mid to late 1970s, Hotpoint introduced a number of changes: single status dining areas, sick-pay for hourly paid workers, shop floor rest areas, a suggestion scheme and profit sharing. In the 1980s, faced by increasingly aggressive and sophisticated competitors, it changed its work methods. A Total Quality programme began in 1989 and, after an initial failure, this was pushed further. Management was de-layered. Company plans were cascaded down into departmental and individual plans. Shop floor training audits were instituted. An appraisal system and teamwork were introduced. As a result substantial cost savings were claimed at the Peterborough factory, which was recognised as an Investor in People. Company managers claimed response times for customer order to delivery fell for 19 weeks to 8 days, with Peterborough Hotpoint claiming to achieve results equal to those at General Electric's Louisville plant. A former work study engineer reports that the changes at Hotpoint were vigorously introduced. He attributes the 'Japanese' turn taken by the company in the 1990s to the strong influence of GE managers. Most of the initiatives introduced at Hotpoint had already been introduced by GE in its North American operations – reductions in work in progress;

training operators to analyse their own jobs to improve efficiency by eliminating wasted actions; a stress on quality and continuous improvement
(Jones 1997: 19). Such changes did not escape the attention of the wider
business community. In 2001, a writer in an Institute of Quality Assurance
journal singled out GDA as an example of the 'success of Six Sigma within
the UK' (Caves 2001).

In the 1990s, the oven producer, Stoves, adopted another strategy. It
introduced a flexible manufacturing system which by a remarkable applica-
tion of engineering offered customers 2000 or so variants. Stoves was cele-
brated for this in the business press (Gracie 1999). Yet highly flexible as the
production system was, it did not last. Within months of Glen Dimplex
taking over Stoves, it had cut the number of variants to less than half.

Especially in cooking appliances, there are niche markets. Established
companies and, more often, small new ones, sometimes try to open these
up. Promar, a small company based in Anglesey, Wales, makes specially
designed cookers for Whirlpool. Other small companies make ceramic hobs
(Marsh 1998). There are also small companies that make cast iron cookers.
But to flourish in volume production is much more difficult. Prominent
strategies that have been attempted already are to specialise in fridges/
fridge freezers/chest freezers or to specialise in built-in or free-standing
cookers in order to combine the advantages of speciality and longer production runs; or to add some bells and whistles or do both. Generally, the
pressure is on toward making higher value goods.

Such is the level of competition that producers place a great deal of
emphasis on after-sales service agreements, through which they seek to
tie-in customers. In any case, according to some company managers,
these are a more profitable use of time than the business of actually
producing domestic appliances. (GDA made about 20 per cent of sales
from servicing products in people's houses: Marsh 2002.) There have also
been moves to get into the market for fitted kitchens, which are stocked
with a range of a particular producer's white goods – the oven, washing
machine, fridge-freezer, even small appliances such as kettles. But here
too there is competition.

It is not only that UK producers are in a market that lacks significant
expansion for refrigeration appliances and to a lesser extent for cooking
appliances or that they cannot compete on production costs with some
other countries. Compared to Germany or Italy, they face the additional
problem that the retail market is highly concentrated. Two firms, Comet,
owned by Kingfisher and Currys, owned by the Dixon group, dominate
the retail market and account for about 40 per cent of retail volume. The
buying power of these specialist multiples allows them to exert considerable leverage. Specialist independents and department stores account
for about a further 15 per cent of the market each (Euromonitor 2003:
Tables 124, 126). New entrants, like Haier today, have generally sought

to escape the hold of the big specialist multiples by selling through independent retailers.

Thus far, the supermarket food chains have made little incursion into this sector. One of them, Sainsbury's, is however planning to sell white goods from catalogues at its sales points in 50 stores, not stocking these products on its premises and thus making considerable economies. Internet sales may also increase – though the specialist multiples are there already. At February 2003 for example Comet's website was offering 310 different cooling appliances, priced from £150 to £1,300 and around 360 different cooking appliance items priced from £500 to £1,900.

A strategy that remains to be tried to any great extent in cooking and cooling appliances is the one recently pursued by Dyson, the vacuum cleaner producer. In 2002, in the pursuit of cheap labour, the company switched production of its bag-less cleaner from the semi-rural location of Malmesbury, Wiltshire to Malaysia with the loss of 800 local jobs (Gibbs 2002). Practically speaking, both the complete relocation of manufacturing and the long distance importation of components could prove imperfect solutions on logistical grounds in as far as the objective is to sell in the UK market. Even if such strategies are not pursued further, however, continued foreign dominance of the UK market and further contraction of employment look likely. Whether concentration will increase will depend in part on whether and to what extent imports increase, particularly those from Turkey, South Korea and China. Whatever the case, it bears consideration that in recent years the industry has actually been lucky in one respect. A boom in house prices has seen many householders re-mortgage their property and use the money to upgrade their homes. This will not go on forever.

Where, though, does this leave the 'regional idea' with which we began? It is helpful here to go back to a review of white goods in Europe in the 1980s (Baden-Fuller and Stopford 1991). These authors distinguished three categories of white goods makers – 'global players'; 'exporters'; and 'national players'.

Global players manufactured and sold their product in more than one country. Included here were Electrolux and Whirlpool.

Exporters produced in a local market but exported more than 30 per cent of their output. Examples here included Bosch-Siemens, AEG, Merloni, Candy, Hoover and Indesit.

National players included Hotpoint, Thorn and Lec, who manufactured at home and sold more than 90 per cent of their output locally. These firms, it was claimed, enjoyed a superior profit performance to the others, with the implication that globalisation strategies were therefore inferior to localisation ones in white goods.

What is interesting about the above list is what has happened since. Briefly, it is this:

- The global players Electrolux and Whirlpool remain
- Among the exporters, AEG is now owned by Electrolux, Indesit by Merloni, Hoover in the UK, having been owned by Maytag, was sold to Candy in 1995
- Among the national players, Thorn was taken over by Electrolux; Creda was taken over by GDA, which in turn was taken over by Merloni; and Lec, although based at Bognor Regis since 1942, and although vaunting the slogan – 'Lec Products the Best of British' – was taken over by the Malaysian company Sime Darby in 1994.

What is to be made of this? First, of course, the big fish have been eating the little fish – and the not so little fish too. In Europe, Electrolux had bought Zanussi in 1984. Whirlpool had bought the Dutch consumer electronics firm Philips in 1988. GEC (later Marconi) had formed GDA with GE in 1989. Other mergers and acquisitions had followed.

Second, though, it is equally evident that the meaning of 'national' player is by no means unproblematic. It is still the case, for example, that 95 per cent of Lec's domestic products are sold in the UK (Way 2002) but, in view of its ownership, the idea that the company is a 'national' player requires some qualification.

Third, these developments add some credibility to the claim made by Segal-Horn et al 1998 who, reviewing the situation at the end of the 1990s write – with respect to the strategies of particular companies – of 'the globalisation of the European white goods industry'.

In advancing this claim, Segal-Horn et al are careful to point out that firms may pursue more than one strategy. They may pursue both global strategies (where a firm serves multiple national markets with internationally branded goods produced in a single location) and local ones (that is national ones, whereby a firm aims to serve each country from a series of national centres) and no doubt, other company strategies are possible. Wider discussion of the globalisation or otherwise of the UK white goods industry is, however, bedevilled by the need to specify in respect to what it is that terms such as 'local' and 'global' – and also 'regional' – are used; and by the need to clearly specify the subject at issue – for example, ownership of factories in the UK? Destination of goods produced in the UK? Origin of goods sold in the UK?

In conclusion, *UK ownership of white goods factories in the UK*, most especially of refrigerators, is minimal. The last significant British ownership went when Merloni took over Marconi's share in GDA (Hotpoint).

Amongst cooking manufacturers, several products that serve niche markets remain. An example is the Aga cooker produced by Aga Foodservices. A long established product, favoured by the British upper class and country dwellers, this has been manufactured in the UK since 1932. Aga now sells over 10,000 units a year. But it is very much a niche product, both because of its symbolic value and not least its price (up to £25,000). Such, indeed, is the current degree of market differentiation within the UK that the company sells pink and lavender Agas in the greenbelt and cheaper and smaller Rangemasters to city customers with country aspirations – the so-called 'Fulham farmers'. Consistent with our earlier comment that it is misleading to think in terms of a once British industry ceasing to exist, however, even this seemingly perfect 'British' example is not all it seems. The castings for Agas are made at the Coalbrookadale Foundry, Shropshire, on the site on which Abraham Darby smelt iron using coke instead of charcoal in 1709 but the Aga cooker was originally a Swedish invention and first imported from there in 1929.

As for *the destination of goods produced in UK factories*, we have seen that most of these go to Europe, in which respect we may clearly talk of an important European regional dimension.

As for *the countries of origin of imports*, for some time these, too, have had a European regional dimension. As we have seen, the European companies Merloni/Indesit and Electrolux account for over 50 per cent of UK refrigeration appliance sales; these two companies also account for 45 per cent of cooking appliance sales. The situation with respect to imports is not static in either economic or political terms, however. There has been a shift from Italy to cheap wage countries on the so-called 'EU periphery' – such as Turkey and some Eastern European countries. (In this context, Merloni's entry into production in the UK via its purchase of GDA looks like an attempt to make up its threatened decline in market share.)

Recently, of course, Turkey and the Eastern European countries have undergone a change in status. In Turkey's case, the country joined the Customs Union in 1996. Hungary and other 'EU 15' countries actually joined the EU in 2004. This change of status has not been lost on Electrolux, or Whirlpool or Merloni. They are developing production there (a move that is reminiscent of the influx of US companies to Mexico following NAFTA, the 1994 North American Free Trade Agreement). This may mean, in future, that more white goods may come into the UK from the European periphery rather than, say, in the case of Merloni, from Italy. On any reasonable definition, such relations remain regional in nature, and to this extent, the 'regional idea' with which we began would remain in tact. As we have seen, though, imports from East Asia have begun to gain ground. This development – from outside the European region – may mark the beginning of a real departure.

References

ABI (2000) *Annual Business Enquiry*, http://www.statistics.gov.uk/CCI/article.asp?ID=74&Pos=2&ColRank=1Rank=224.

AMDEA (various years) *The AMDEA Yearbook*, London: Association of Manufacturers of Domestic Appliances.

Baden-Fuller, C. W. and Stopford, J. M. (1991) 'Globalisation Frustrated: The Case of White Goods', *Strategic Management Journal*, 12 (7).

Bocock, M. (1992) 'Consumption and Lifestyles', in R. Bocock and K. Thompson (eds) *Social and Cultural Forms of Modernity*, Cambridge: Polity Press in association with the Open University.

Brown, J. M. (2002) 'Glen Dimplex Has Hot Idea for Cold China', *Financial Times*, 6 June.

Caves, A. (2001) 'Does the UK Need a Six Sigma-Style Makeover?', *Quality World*, January.

Cockburn, C. and Furst-Dilic, R. (1994) *Bringing Technology Home: Gender and Technology in a Changing Europe*, Buckingham: Open University Press.

Conacher, G. (1971) *Electric Cookers*, London: Forbes Publication Limited.

Corley, T. (1966) *Domestic Electrical Appliances*, London: Jonathan Cape.

Darling, C. R. (1932) *Modern Domestic Scientific Appliances: Being a Treatise for the Guidance of Users and Manufacturers of Domestic Appliances, Architects and Teachers of Domestic Science, with Special Regard to Efficiency, Economy and Correct Method of Use*, London: E & F. N. Spon.

Electrolux (1933) *All the Facts about Electrolux Refrigerators*, London: Electrolux Ltd.

Euromonitor (2001) *Global Market Information Data Base, Large Kitchen Appliances*, London: Euromonitor.

Euromonitor (2003) *Domestic Electrical Appliances in the United Kingdom (August 2002)* http://www.euromonitor.co/gmid/default.asp

Gibbs, G. (2002) 'Beating a Retreat from Britain', *Guardian*, 4 October.

GPN (2001) *Global Production Networks and the Analysis of Economic Development*, GPN Working Paper 1, University of Manchester, School of Environment and Planning.

Goldthorpe, J., Lockwood, D., Bechhofer, F. and Platt J. (1969) *The Affluent Worker in the Class Structure*, Cambridge: Cambridge University Press.

Gracie, S. (1999) 'Coping with the Over-heated Pound', *The Sunday Times*, 11 July.

Guthrie, J. (2001) 'Latest Chapter of the Aga Saga Reaches a Close: The Break-up of Glynwed Marks Another Stage in the Decline of Midlands Engineering', *Financial Times*, 23 January.

Hardyment, C. (1988) *From Mangle to Microwave*, Cambridge: Polity Press in association with Basil Blackwell.

Hobbs, E. W. (1930) *Domestic Appliances*, London: Cassel & Co Ltd.

Hoekman, B. and Kostecki, M. (2001) *The Political Economy of the World Trading System: The WTO and Beyond*, Second Edition; Oxford: Oxford University Press.

Houghton, J. (1972) *Gas Cookers*, London: Forbes Publications Limited.

Jones, O. (1997) 'Changing the Balance? Taylorism, TQM and Work Organisation', *New Technology, Work and Employment*, 12 (1).

Kozul-Wright, R. (1995) 'Transnational Corporations and the Nation State', in J. Michie and J. Grieve-Smith (eds) *Managing the Global Economy*, Oxford: Oxford University Press.

LFS (2002) Labour Force Survey, http://www.dataarchive.ac.uk/lfsAbstract.asp

Lockwood, D. (1960) 'The "New Working Class"', *European Journal of Sociology*, 1 (2): 248–259.

Marsh, P. (1998) 'When the Thoughts of Tumble Dryer Makers Turn to Summer', *Financial Times*, 27 March.

Marsh, P. (2002) 'Italian Group in Hotpoint Deal', *Financial Times*, 27 June.

Monopolies and Merger Commission (1997) *Domestic Electrical Goods*, Vol 2, London: HMSO. Cm 3676–II.

ONS (1984) Data Provided Directly by Office for National Statistics from Annual Employment Survey: Employee Analysis.

ONS (1992) Data Provided Directly by Office for National Statistics from Annual Employment Survey: Employee Analysis.

ONS (1999) Data Provided Directly by Office for National Statistics from Annual Employment Survey: Employee Analysis.

ONS (2000) Office for National Statistics, http://www.statistics.gov.uk/statbase/tsdtimezone.asp.vink=ims

ONS (2001) Data Provided Directly by Office for National Statistics from Annual Employment Survey: Employee Analysis.

ONS (2002) Office for National Statistics, Family Spending 2000–2001.

ONS (2003a) Office for National Statistics, http://www.statistics.gov.uk/statbase/TSDtimezone.asp Updated on 24/ 1/2003.

ONS (2003b) Office for National Statistics, http://www.statistics.gov.uk/statbase/TSDtimezone.asp?vink=pgdp Updated on 24/ 1/2003.

ONS (2003c) Office for National Statistics, http://www.statistics.gov.uk/statbase/tsdtimezone.asp: MQ10: 1 and MQ10: 2, Updated on 4/ 3/2003.

ONS (2004) Office for National Statistics, http://www.statistics.gov.uk/STATBASE/Product.asp?vlnk=242

Ohmae, K. (1995) *The End of the Nation State: The Rise of Regional Economies*, London: Harper Collins.

Paba, S. (1986) '"Brand-naming" as an entry strategy in the European white goods industry', *Cambridge Journal of Economics*, 10: 305–318.

Paba, S. (1991) 'Brand reputation, efficiency and the concentration process: a case study', *Cambridge Journal of Economics*, 15: 21–43.

Russo, L. (2002) 'What's Cooking in Kitchen Collectables', *The Collector Newsmagazine*, www.drspublishing.com/thecollector/feature.htm

Segal-Horn, S., Asch, D. and Suneja, V. (1998) 'The Globalization of the European White Goods Industry', *European Management Journal*, 16 (1) January.

Slater, D. (2000) 'Looking Backwards', in M. Lee (ed.) *The Consumer Society – Reader*, Oxford: Blackwell, pp. 177–191.

Social Trends (1991) *Social Trends*, No. 21; London: HMSO.

Stopford, J. M. and Baden-Fuller, C. W. (1990) 'Corporate Rejuvenation', *Journal of Management Studies*, 27 (4).

Ward, C. (1999) 'Chinese Takeover', *ERT Weekly*, 5 August.

Way, R. (2002) 'No Hassle with Lec', *ERT Weekly*, 12 November 21.

Williams, K., Haslam, C., Johal, S. and Williams, J. (1994) *Cars: Analysis, History, Cases*, Oxford: Berghahn Books.

Weightman, G. (2003) *The Frozen Water Trade: How Ice from New England Lakes Kept the World Cool*, London: HarperCollins.

World Appliance Companies (2002) *World Appliance Companies*, Third edition. Report published by Appliance Magazine and Industry Statistics Ltd, Oak Brook: Dana Chase.

3
South Africa, Swaziland and Zimbabwe – White Goods in Post-Colonial Societies: Markets, the State and Production

Andries Bezuidenhout

White goods in Southern Africa

Finding explanations for the inability of numerous postcolonial African states to transcend many of the legacies of colonialism has led to a position that is best described as Afro-pessimism.[1] In the context of 'global informational capitalism', argues Manuel Castells (1998) for example, the African continent can be considered to be part of the 'Fourth World' – a space that has become irrelevant to the global economy. Yet, renewed interest in some of the concerns of now unpopular theories of underdevelopment, in the form of what has become known as commodity chain analysis, shows that Africa does indeed link into the global economy, but mostly at the lower ends of commodity chains (Gereffi 1999; Kaplinsky 2000; Gibbon 2001). In the last decade, there has been a mining boom in many parts of Africa, often driven by South African mining firms, but sometimes linked into wars for control of mines in the context of 'collapsed states'.[2]

But relative to many other African states, South Africa has succeeded in building up a significant manufacturing industry. In this, argue some, lies the difference between South Africa and the rest of Africa. The country dominates not only the economy of Southern Africa, but also sub-Saharan Africa. Its economy accounts for approximately 44 per cent of the total gross domestic product (GDP) and 52 per cent of the industrial output of sub-Saharan Africa (Saul and Leys 1999: 23). In 2003, manufacturing accounted for 62 per cent of South Africa's exports, mining for 33 per cent and agriculture for just under five per cent (DTI 2004a). However, when one disaggregates manufacturing, what is termed 'raw products' and 'semi-manufactured goods' still account for two thirds of exports. Beneficiated metal products, such as steel, account for a major part of this (DTI 2004b). The country also has a negative manufacturing trade balance of 49 per cent, which is offset by a positive mining trade balance of 57 per cent (DTI

2004a). The automobile industry is the only major real segment of the manufacturing sector that has succeeded in moving to a global economy of scale and an export orientation (Masondo 2004).

In the Southern African context, white goods are manufactured in South Africa, Swaziland and Zimbabwe. South Africa manufactures all the major kinds of white goods products. Only two major manufacturers located in Southern Africa are left in the game: Defy and Whirlpool. Defy is owned by its directors and a major South African banking group. It manufactures refrigerators, freezers, stoves, washing machines and tumble dryers locally. The company also imports some of its branded products – its gas cookers are imported from Brazil, and some of its washing machines are imported from Korea. Its refrigerator and freezer manufacturing operations are located in Ezakheni (near Ladysmith) and East London. Its major plant in Jacobs, an industrial area in the south of Durban, manufactures the rest. The US multinational, Whirlpool manufactures only refrigerators and freezers locally – at its Isithebe plant near Mandini in northern KwaZulu-Natal. The rest of its products are imported. It set up its manufacturing facilities by buying out a locally owned loss-making firm in 1996.

During the 1990s and the early 2000s, several factories closed down, including the Kelvinator[3] and Univa[4] factories in Alrode, an industrial area near Johannesburg, as well as a fridge factory in Bronkhostspruit (owned by Masterfridge). In Swaziland, white goods were manufactured from 1990 onwards, originally by Swaziland Refrigeration, which later became known as Masterfridge. This firm captured a significant share of the refrigeration market in South Africa, but was liquidated towards the end of 1999. However, the former director of Masterfridge came out of retirement to set up a new company, Palfridge. He did this by buying some of the equipment from the liquidators and setting up shop in one of the factory complexes left empty by the previous manufacturer. By 2003, this firm was in the process of introducing a number of brands to the South African market under licence, including the Kelvinator brand that had previously been manufactured by one of the liquidated South African firms.

In Zimbabwe, three factories manufacture white goods. In Harare, Imperial and Innscor manufacture refrigerators, and in Bulawayo, a company called Tregers manufactures stoves. All three firms are owned by Zimbabwean corporations, with Innscor's holding firm listed on the country's stock exchange. These companies principally manufacture for the local market. They also do not operate at full capacity in the context of the political and economic turmoil in the country.

Most of these companies – with the exception of Whirlpool – are not major players in the global white goods manufacturing industry. Indeed, in contrast to other regions of the world, the industry is characterised by its relative isolation. None of the firms are major exporters. Only one South African firm features when one breaks down sales by regions of the world.

Defy only has a significant presence in Africa, with a market share of 7 per cent in 2001. Thus, the white goods manufacturing industry in Southern Africa remains isolated. In contrast to cases in developing countries where new managerial techniques such as Six Sigma are implemented to reduce manufacturing defects and waste (Nichols, Sugur and Demir 2002; Nichols and Sugur 2004: Part 2), the seven factories surveyed in Southern Africa seemed somewhat backward. Indeed, only in the Whirlpool factory were processes in place to implement this technique. In other cases, concepts such as 'multi-skilling', 'total quality management' and 'lean manufacturing' were familiar, but in practice, very little had changed over the past decade.

While imports are increasing steadily, Southern African manufacturers have not been able to penetrate export markets. Compared to emerging mega-factories, such as an LG factory in Korea that produces 2.5 million fridges annually, the annual output of 350,000 fridges of the three remaining South African factories seems almost immaterial. Indeed, an overview of the world appliance industry in 2002 did not even bother to provide a summary of any of the markets or producers of white goods in Africa (World Appliance Companies 2002).

Whilst Castells (1998) considered Africa's fate as part of the 'Fourth World' almost as a fact of life, he allowed for the possibility of South Africa 'connecting' to the 'information superhighway' in ways that other African countries could not. Thus, in the African context, South Africa could be considered as an exception. This view is also reflected in an argument put forward by Gay Seidman. 'South Africa... holds out unusual promise', she argued, 'both to its citizens and to the rest of the developing world... especially given the general good will and support accorded the new government, South African experiments may illustrate new strategies for addressing problems of growth or persistent inequalities in a globalized world'. With regard to the workplace, Seidman framed the challenge as follows: 'Given the persistence of racial divisions at work, can labor and management work together to replace the authoritarian labor practices of the past with the kind of cooperative arrangements often considered essential for higher productivity and industrial flexibility?' Thus, according to Seidman, South Africa may be different from other post-colonies. Instead of being a 'mirror', if South Africa is able to manage its transition towards a democratic society, it may actually be a 'beacon' for the 'rest of the post-colonial world' (1999: 433).

If one wants to understand why the white goods industry in Southern Africa has not significantly linked into the global economy, one has to see South Africa not as an exception to the African rule, but rather, following Mahmood Mamdani (1996: 8), understand that 'apartheid, usually considered unique to South Africa, is actually a generic form of the colonial state in Africa'. He argues that 'neither institutional segregation nor apartheid was a South African invention ... both idealised a form of rule that the British Colonial Office dubbed "indirect rule" and the French "association".' (1996: 7).

Hence, colonial states in Africa were 'bifurcated'. In urban areas, colonial powers *ruled directly* through settler populations. The urban order was a racialised one, based on settler capitalism and its associated institutions. In rural areas, however, *indirect rule* implied the manipulation of 'tribal' chiefs and customs in order to assert dominance – it 'signified a mediated – decentralised – despotism' (1996: 17). According to Mamdani, '[u]rban power spoke the language of civil society and civil rights, rural power of community and culture'. Thus the colonial state was Janus-faced: 'Its one side, the state that governed a racially defined citizenry, was bounded by the rule of law and an associated regime of rights. Its other side, the state that ruled over subjects, was a regime of extra-economic coercion and administratively driven justice'. Also, whereas civil society was 'racialised' by the colonial order, rural areas were 'tribalised' (1996: 18–19).

Post-colonial African states were constructed on this bifurcation between urban and rural and were unable to move beyond this situation. Whilst the struggle against settler colonialism often creates a vibrant civil society, post-colonial transitions in Africa succeed in deracialising the state, but not civil society. Indeed, anti-colonial social movements, such as trade unions and nationalist groupings are often incorporated into the state after in-dependence and become demobilised. Hence, those in urban areas achieve some levels of 'citizenship', whilst tribal authority is often maintained in rural areas – where people remain 'subjects' (Mamdani 1996).

By presenting South Africa as an exception to the rule – as a special African case with a more substantial urban population and higher levels of industrialisation – we fail to understand the constraints to post-colonial reconstruction imposed by the legacy of colonialism. In the case of the white goods industry in South Africa, bifurcation between urban and rural areas plays out in the realms of the state, markets and production. This chapter concentrates on some of the most significant developments and factories in South Africa and also considers some of the dynamics in Swaziland and Zimbabwe in order to understand South Africa comparatively. In this vein, an attempt is made to show how, in the context of social transition – of discontinuity, certain key structural elements of the past can be reasserted in new ways. The argument is that one can identify continuity in discontinuity itself.

In the first part of this chapter, the bifurcated nature of the market for white goods in South Africa is analysed. It is shown how the economy's marginality is reinforced by relatively small consumer markets that are still constrained by inequality shaped by 'race' and space. In the second part of the chapter, the concept 'apartheid workplace regime' is explained and its development is located in the bifurcated nature of the state in South Africa,

Swaziland and Zimbabwe. In the third part of the chapter, our attention again turns to the present. It is argued that racial tension remains a salient feature of the post-colonial workplace regimes found in South Africa and also in Swaziland and Zimbabwe. Tensions revolve around the grading of jobs, as well as the perceived lack of authority of African supervisors and managers. The concepts 'informal wage colour bar' and 'upward floating colour bar' are used to describe these dynamics. In addition, a key feature of the apartheid manufacturing regime – its location in a bifurcated industrial geography – is replicated in the context of Southern African regional integration. In the case of the white goods industry, Swaziland provides for a space where authoritarian labour practices can be continued.

The perspective presented here is mainly based on documentary research and fieldwork, the latter drawing on an analysis of 78 semi-structured in-depth interviews that were conducted with workers and trade union officials at seven factories in the three countries (see Table 3.1 below).

Table 3.1   Companies in South Africa, Swaziland and Zimbabwe where Interviews were Conducted

Company	Factory	Products	Number of employees
Defy Appliances	Jacobs, Durban in KwaZulu-Natal, South Africa	Cookers and laundry equipment	1,300
	Ezakheni, near Ladysmith in KwaZulu-Natal, South Africa	Refrigerators, freezers and chest freezers	470
	East London in the Eastern Cape, South Africa	Refrigerators and freezers	600
Whirlpool	Isithebe, part of Mandeni in KwaZulu-Natal, South Africa	Refrigerators and freezers	900
Palfridge	Matsapha Industrial Area in Manzini, Swaziland	Refrigerators, freezers and commercial refrigerators	436
Imperial	Willowvale Industrial Area, Harare in Zimbabwe	Refrigerators, freezers and commercial refrigerators	170
Innscor	Graniteside Industrial Area, Harare, Zimbabwe	Refrigerators, chest freezers, commercial freezers	250

The interviews were conducted between 2001 and 2003. In South Africa, interviews were set up by the National Union of Metalworkers of South Africa (NUMSA) as part of their preparations for a summit between government, the union and industry representatives to consider industrial policy options for the engineering sector. During these interviews, many of the union members raised issues related to 'apartheid' and 'discrimination' when discussing approaches to production, supervision and industrial relations. In Swaziland and Zimbabwe, some interviews were set up by management, but a number of interviews with workers were also conducted outside working time. In Zimbabwe, the National Engineering Workers Union (NEWU) kindly assisted in this process, and in Swaziland the Swaziland Manufacturing and Allied Workers Union (SMAWU) provided valuable information. Workers provided their perspectives on the basis of anonymity. Since linking their perspectives to certain factories might compromise their anonymity in some cases, the interview data is presented in a way that takes these sensitivities into account. The analysis of interview data is supplemented by impressions gained from factory visits, as well as an analysis of secondary data and reports in the print media.

The market for white goods in South Africa: bifurcation between urban and rural

South Africa's home grown white goods company, Defy, still dominates the market, with a market share of 39.9 per cent in 2001, aided by the liquidation of Masterfridge in Swaziland. Several other competitors are registered as companies in South Africa, but do not manufacture their products locally. LG, for instance, imports all its products, and Whirlpool only manufactures refrigerators and freezers locally. Hence, Defy is followed by Whirlpool, with a market share of 19.8 per cent. LG accounts for a further 14 per cent, followed by Bosch, with 6.7 per cent and Samsung, with 4.8 per cent. Often brands are licensed to manufacturers – such as the Kelvinator brand to Masterfridge after the liquidation of Kelvinator SA, and before the subsequent liquidation of Masterfridge itself. The firm that was set up at the Masterfridge premises in Swaziland, Palfridge, reintroduced the Kelvinator brand during 2003. But the major players remained Defy, Whirlpool and LG (Euromonitor 2003).

Although many factories were closed down during the 1990s in South Africa, the number of units produced by the industry has remained stable in the 1990s, dropping slightly from its 1990 levels, but picking up again towards the 2000s to equal those levels. Figure 3.1 expresses output in the industry as an index of 100, taking the average production levels of 1995 as baseline. In 1990, the index was at a level of 117, dropping to its lowest in 1994, at just under 97, and then picking up again to 117 in 2000. This implies that manufacturing activities have been concentrated in fewer factories with higher output.

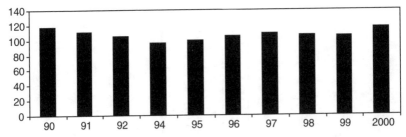

Figure 3.1 Production of Household Appliance Units in South Africa, 1990–2000
(1995 = 100)
Source: Calculated from RSA (2002).
Note: This figure includes all household appliances and not only white goods.

This process of rationalisation in South Africa follows a broader trend in the industry globally. Increasingly firms move to rationalise production facilities and to increase volume at their remaining facilities. Multinational manufacturers were able to do this because of a general reduction in import tariffs globally. Between 1990 and 1997, world trade in white goods accelerated by 13 per cent per annum, amounting to US$23,136 million in 1997 (IDC 2000: 35).

The size of the market for white goods in South Africa – and Africa generally – is negligible when compared to the major consumer markets of the North.

In 2001, the size of the whole South African white goods market was R3,345.5 million (Table 3.2) – which translates to roughly US$394.8 million[5] – compared to Italy's exports to the value of US$479.8 million, Mexico's exports of US$275.4 million, and China's exports of US$253.4 million of refrigerators alone in the same year (World Appliance Companies 2002: 8). This implies that the size of the South African white goods market is relatively small when compared to the economies of scale achieved by major exporting countries.

It is in this context that from 1994 onwards the South African government pursued a policy of rapid trade liberalisation. Thus, with the transition to a more democratic dispensation internally, came the opening up of the economy to increased competition from outside. The 'protectionist' regime that started in 1924 gave way to a new 'globalised' order. Like all other manufacturing sectors of the South African economy, import tariffs in the white goods industry have been lowered. According to the Industrial Development Corporation (IDC), the weighted import tariff for white goods was at 7 per cent in 1994. They projected this to decrease to 6 per cent in 2004 (IDC 2000: 35). Import tariffs varied from 0 per cent to 25 per cent, with refrigerators and freezers being most protected; in the year 2000 the average import tariff on refrigerators and freezers was 19.82 per cent. According to the IDC, the import penetration rate in the same year for the

Table 3.2 Volume and Value Retail Sales of White Goods in South Africa, 1997–2001

	1997	1998	1999	2000	2001
'000 units	1,457.00	1,646.00	1,700.20	1,776.00	1,872.00
R million, current rsp	1,892.80	2,257.50	2,478.70	2,748.60	3,345.50
R million, constant 1997 rsp	1,892.80	2,112.20	2,204.90	2,321.00	2,670.20
US$ million, constant 1997 rsp R1 = US$0.215	406.95	454.12	474.05	499.01	574.09

Source: Euromonitor 2003; calculations of US$ based on the average Rand US$ exchange rate of 1997.
Note: data are for refrigeration appliances, home laundry appliances, dishwashers, large cooking appliances and microwaves.

white goods industry was 27 per cent. While the price of imported products increased at an annual rate of 9.7 per cent, mainly due to the depreciation of the Rand, imports increased at a rate of 20 per cent per annum since the early 1990s (IDC 2000: 35). In 2004, the reduction of the 25 per cent import tariff on refrigerators and freezers to a zero rate for products imported from the European Union will lead to additional competitive pressure for the local industry.[6]

Further strain is put on the industry by the way in which manufacturing links upstream into the South African economy. The white goods manufacturing industry, for instance, links upstream to the steel, plastics, and electronic industries. One has to consider why, in the context of a mineral rich economy, downstream manufacturers were unable to build more viable industries on inputs from mining and beneficiated metal products. Indeed, the policy of import parity pricing by Iscor, South Africa's privatised steel monopoly, has a major impact on the competitiveness of the industry. In the beginning of 2003, in order to keep up with the cost of importing steel, Iscor increased the cost of steel provided to the industry by 30 per cent. This increase in input cost is especially harsh when one considers that steel products account for 32 per cent of inputs for household refrigerators and freezers, 29 per cent of inputs for household laundry equipment, and 19 per cent of the inputs for household cooking equipment. Between 1991 and 1998, the white goods industry consumed 105,267 tonnes of steel on average per annum. Its share of total domestic primary steel sales is three per cent (IDC 2000: 34–35).

With the lowering of import tariffs, the white goods industry was unable to reorientate itself to become a significant export industry. Instead, imports increased at a rapid pace. Traditionally, South Africa imported white goods mainly from Germany, Italy and the USA (IDC 2000: 34–35). However, recent evidence shows that imports from countries such as Korea and China have also increased dramatically. In March 1997, South Korean appliance manufacturer LG Electronics launched a rebranding programme in South Africa as part of a broader programme to change the GoldStar label to LG. Barlows Appliances had acted as local agents for GoldStar products since 1991, but in 1996, LG Electronics took direct control. An initial R18 million was invested to upgrade local personnel, information technology, and service and delivery systems. A further R5 million was spent on advertising campaigns. According to a report in the *Business Day*, 'LG electronics had no immediate plans to manufacture any of its products locally, and all products would be imported from Korea, but a manufacturing plant could be established in the near future if demand warranted it.' According to the report, the company regarded South Africa as a 'springboard to the rest of Africa.' However, sales of washing machines to markets north of the South African borders had proved to be disappointing (Cole 1997).

Also, in mid-1999, Omega Holdings, a South African electronics distribution company, indicated that it had set up a new subsidiary, Sinoma International Trading, to focus on export and import trading between China and South Africa. The company was in the process of expanding its focus on brown goods to one which included white goods as well. It secured an agreement to act as an agent for Chinese brands such as Haier, Little Swan and Shangai Hitachi in South Africa. Omega's major shareholder is the Shangi Industrial Corporation (Business Day Reporter 1999).

Imports from Korea grew rapidly during the late 1990s. Refrigerator and freezer imports from Korea increased from a value of US$4,258,955 in 1998 to US$13,027,888 in 2000.[7] The value of washing machines imported from Korea increased form US$7,130,527 in 1998 to US$14,018,142 in 2000.[8] Imports from China have also grown, although not as rapidly as those from Korea. In 1998, China exported washing machines to the value of US$1,562,181. In 2000, this increased to US$2,767,098.[9] Only 6.4 per cent of white goods manufactured in South Africa were exported in 1998. These exports were mainly destined for Zimbabwe and Mozambique (DTI 2004a, 2004b).

Hence, during the 1990s, the importation of white goods exceeded the exports by far (Figures 3.2, 3.3 and 3.4).

These trade figures, expressed in Rand values, may be influenced by fluctuation in the value of the local currency. During this period, the Rand devalued significantly against a number of major currencies. However, a devaluation of the currency would imply an increase in export earnings – which is evidently not the case for these data. Nevertheless, trade figures cannot be understood without taking into account some of the dynamics related to the consumption of products in the local market. As Baumann (1995: 5–6) points out, white goods produced locally were traditionally 'geared towards the growing market of lower- to middle-income white urban-dwellers', and 'the smaller upper-income white market was served by

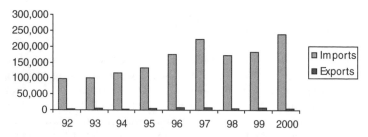

Figure 3.2   Imports and Exports for Washing Machines in South Africa, 1992–2000 (R000)
Source: Calculated from RSA (2002).
Note: Washing machines include all products listed under tariff code 84.50.

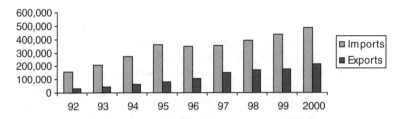

Figure 3.3 Imports and Exports for Refrigeration Appliances in South Africa, 1992–2000 (R000)
Source: Calculated from RSA (2002).
Note: Refrigeration appliances include all products listed under tariff code 84.18.

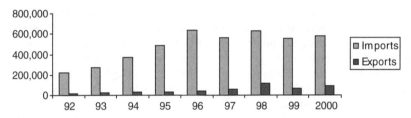

Figure 3.4 Imports and Exports for Dish Washers in South Africa, 1992–2000 (R000)
Source: Calculated from RSA (2002).
Note: Dish washers include all products listed under tariff code 84.22.

imports of sophisticated products from technology partners'. Up to the 1990s, the potential market of 'lower-income black consumers' was not 'directly served by local firms'. He argues that, apart from the invention of single-door refrigerators, very little local innovation took place in South Africa. Designs for production were taken over from US and European 'technology partners' and 'licensors'. Even until the 1990s, a substantial market for goods such as coal stoves and cast-iron pots existed in urban black townships, informal settlements and in rural areas. Indeed, the Durban Falkirk company – which later became Defy – was the last remaining firm involved in mass production geared for this market (Baumann 1995: 5–6).

Thus, one gets the impression of a relatively backward industry – one that is embedded in a colonial society increasingly isolated from the rest of the world. As one might expect, consumption patterns followed the contours of racial advantage and disadvantage. To illustrate, one should take into consideration that by 1991, whereas 62.6 per cent of white households owned a deep freeze, 2.9 per cent of African households did. Also, 97 per cent of white households had refrigerators, whereas only 20.4 per cent of African households did. 91.2 per cent of white households had electric stoves, whereas 15.5 per cent of African households did. Significantly, more African households (29.6 per cent) had stoves that were not powered by electricity than African households that did (Baumann 1995: 29). Even for African households in *urban* areas included in a survey conducted by the white goods industry in 1991, more households (32 per cent) used solid fuel stoves than electric stoves (26 per cent). However, another 20 per cent used electric hotplates. Between 1989 and 1991, only 22 per cent of the stoves sold by the white goods industry in South Africa went to African households (Baumann 1995: 30). Here one has to consider that the contours of white goods consumption were shaped by the bifurcated nature of the South African society. Migrant workers in single-sex hostels had no need for kitchen appliances, whereas their families who remained in rural areas generally did not have access to electricity. Also, the availability of cheap domestic labour done by 'maids', drawn from the impoverished black community, provided for an alternative to automation in 'white' households. Indeed, the brand name of Defy's washing machine, *Automaid*, takes on a rather ironic meaning in the context of South Africa.

An Industrial Strategy Project study of the household electrical durables sector painted a bleak picture of the early white goods manufacturing industry in South Africa:

> The finite size of the target market meant that once a situation of relative saturation had been reached, firms were unable to expand production to achieve internationally competitive economies of scale. Instead, they came to rely on continued tariff protection against import competition. Unlike firms in comparably-sized markets, manufacturing firms did not move seriously into exports in an attempt to increase throughput. This placed an upper limit on revenue and profitability and discouraged innovative investment and market strategies... Effectively, by the mid-1970s South African white goods and small appliance producers were structured into production for a small, saturated market and lacked the cost competitiveness to survive without protection (Baumann 1995: 6).

In the 1990s manufacturers of white goods in South Africa discovered a new market. In media reports and policy statements in the 1990s, the state's electrification programme seemed to give the white goods industry a new vision for expanding markets among 'black' consumers. However, despite an increase in the availability of electricity to 'black' households, the DTI pointed out that 'black households remain slow to take up some appliances for a number of reasons; ready availability of substitutes, threats of electricity supply interruption and lack of income' (RSA 1996). In contrast to the DTI's relatively pessimistic assessment of the prospects for the industry, in 1997, Ross Heron, the managing director of Defy, said that the electrification programme had brought electricity to about 2 million new homes. This had, according to him, boosted the company's financial results. The firm attributed an increase of about 20 per cent in its turnover to the electrification programme (Business Day Reporter 1997; Jenvey 1997). In the same year, Bronwyn Phillips, managing director of Masterfridge, attributed a 15 per cent growth figure to 'a combination of the electrification drive and the right product'. According to a report in *Business Day*, Phillips said that electrical fridges were the most popular product in the white goods market in South and Southern Africa. Commentators from the retail industry held the opinion that the demand for gas refrigerators had been replaced by an increasing demand for electrical refrigerators. This perceived trend was ascribed directly to the electrification programme (Parker 1997).

Some of the white goods manufacturers also looked towards Africa north of South Africa as a potential market. Phillips felt that 'the spread of TV via M-Net (a South African cable-television company) in Africa has introduced a big new market to consumerism' and that 'consumer discernment accompanies the process'. Apart from the expansion of South African television in Africa, Phillips saw the opening up of South African retail outlets, such as Shoprite Checkers (in Mozambique and Zambia) and Metro Cash (in Kenya), as creating new opportunities to penetrate African markets. She also saw the development of the Maputo Corridor[10] as an opportunity for the company to expand exports into Africa (Frazer 1997; Beresford 1997).

Indeed, Table 3.3 shows that the value of the market has grown significantly since the mid-1990s. We can see, for example, that the value of sales of refrigeration appliances has increased form R880 million in 1997 to R1.4 billion in 2001. The value of the market for microwaves has also more than doubled from 1997 to 2001. Overall, the value of the market for white goods has grown from almost R1.9 billion in 1997 to a bit more than R3.3 billion in 2001.

But the picture looks different when one considers the market in terms of volume (see Table 3.4). This shows that the market for refrigeration appliances has only grown by a 100,000 units – from 670,000 units in 1997 to 770,000 units in 2001. The number of white goods units sold has increased

Table 3.3 Value Retail Sales of White Goods in South Africa, 1997–2001

R million, current rsp	1997	1998	1999	2000	2001
Refrigeration appliances	880	1,003.80	1,136.30	1,251.20	1,452.70
Home laundry appliances	408.9	482.9	495.6	517.7	623.9
Dishwashers	52.8	65.3	78.1	89.6	105.9
Large cooking appliances	379.1	469.8	514.4	593.1	752.7
Microwaves	171.9	235.7	254.3	297	410.3
WHITE GOODS	1,892.80	2,257.50	2,478.70	2,748.60	3,345.50

Source: Euromonitor 2003.

Table 3.4   Unit Retail Sales of White Goods in South Africa, 1997–2001

'000 units	1997	1998	1999	2000	2001
Refrigeration appliances	670	700	730	750	770
Home laundry appliances	280	320	320.2	315	325
Dishwashers	22	26	30	33	35
Large cooking appliances	310	370	380	408	432
Microwaves	175	230	240	270	310
WHITE GOODS	1,457.00	1,646.00	1,700.20	1,776.00	1,872.00

Source: Euromonitor 2003.

Table 3.5   Household Penetration of White Goods in South Africa, 2001

per cent households	2001
Fridge-freezers	42
Fridges	12
Freezers	14
Automatic washing machines	17
Automatic washer dryers	0.5
Automatic tumble dryers	9
Other home laundry appliances	10
Dishwashers	4.5
Freestanding cookers	31
Ovens	17.5
Built-in hobs	17.5
Built-in cooker hoods	11
Freestanding microwaves	13

Source: Euromonitor 2003.

from almost 1.6 million units sold in 1997 to a bit less than 1.9 million units in 2001. This implies that an increase in the cost of white goods has led to the growth in the value of the market, and not necessarily a rapid increase in local output or imports.[11]

In addition, and despite all the industry's talk on the impact of electrification, there is still a major divide in South African society that limits the demand for white goods. The bifurcation between urban and rural plays out on several levels – including that of 'race'. Also, whilst the market has grown since the early 1990s, consumption patterns are still depressed (Table 3.5).

We can see that household penetration rates are still low. The product with the highest penetration rate is the combined fridge-freezer. According to market researchers, this is usually also the first product acquired by households that receive electricity. This is followed by free-standing cookers – but still only 31 per cent of households owned such products. Very few households have laundry machinery such as washing machines and tumble dryers. Some of this is explained by South Africa's climate, but one also has to consider household income and the lack of a consistent supply of water and electricity.

But these aggregated national statistics tell us very little about market segmentation by characteristics such as 'race'. The census data for the year 2001 gives us some idea of how historical patterns of advantage and disadvantage still shape consumption. When one considers household ownership of refrigerators, the product with the highest market penetration rate, striking differences emerge (Table 3.6).

In provinces where the population is mainly rural, very few households own refrigerators. Indeed, often those households do not even have access to electricity. In 2001, in the Eastern Cape, for example, 543,561 households still used wood to cook food – more than the number of households that used electricity to cook their food (419,997). A further 445,082 used paraffin. In Limpopo, another province with very low urbanisation rates, only 295,512 of the households used electricity to cook food, as opposed to a staggering 702,428 who used wood, and 131,633 who used paraffin. In a predominantly urban province, such as Gauteng, electricity and coal were used more often. There, 1,939,945 households used electricity to cook food, 567,970 used paraffin and 72,819 used coal. In Gauteng, only 18,437 households used wood (Statistics South Africa 2003b: 75).

Earlier it was pointed out that in 1991, whereas 97 per cent of white households had refrigerators, only 20.4 per cent of African households did. Table 3.7, again drawn from the census data for 2001, shows that while there has been a significant increase in the number of 'black' households with refrigerators – to almost 40 per cent – the difference still remains striking.

Table 3.6 Number and Percentages of South African Households in Each Province with Refrigerators

Province	Percentage urban population	Number	Percentage
Gauteng	97	1 646 713	62.1
Western Cape	90	862 339	73.5
Northern Cape	83	115 094	55.6
Free State	76	356 344	48.6
KwaZulu-Natal	46	978 643	46.9
North West	42	468 198	50.4
Mpumalanga	41	370 549	50.5
Eastern Cape	39	480 122	31.7
Limpopo	13.3	459 546	38.9
South Africa	*58*	*5 737 536*	*51.2*

Source: Statistics South Africa (2003a, b: 97, c).

Table 3.7   Number and Percentages of Households in South Africa with Refrigerators by Population Group of the Head of the Household

Population group	Number	Percentage
Black	3 439 129	39.9
Coloured	650 471	73.2
Indian or Asian	272 282	96.2
White	1 375 654	97.6
Total	*5 737 536*	*51.2*

Source: Statistics South Africa (2003a, b: 98).

These differences are also reflected in the consumption of energy for cooking food. Of the households with an African as their head, 3,393,372 used electricity to cook food. A further 2,337,480 used paraffin, and 2,220,884 used wood. 304,387 used coal and 108,063 used animal dung. Of the households with a 'white' head, by far the majority used electricity – adding up to 1,362,217 households. This is followed by 32,899 households who used gas. Only 2,487 used paraffin, 4,480 used wood, and 2,183 used coal (Statistics South Africa 2003b: 77).

In summary, whilst white goods are still manufactured at a number of factories in South Africa, Swaziland and Zimbabwe, the volumes produced are very small relative to the emerging global economies of scale. There has been some investment from outside the region – notably in the case of Whirlpool – but generally capital remains in the hands of Southern African entrepreneurs. Since the 1990s, several firms and factories closed down, and there has been a concentration in the industry. Whilst remaining firms have boosted production, output has remained relatively stable. The South African government has reduced import tariffs, and is committed to reducing those further. Local firms generally produce for local markets, and imports have increased at a rapid pace. The industry is further affected by currency volatility, high interest rates and the problem of import parity pricing by the South African steel monopoly. Whilst an attempt to change patterns of electricity consumption has boosted the market for white goods by about 50 per cent, consumer markets remain segmented. The bifurcation between urban and rural areas still exists in a post-apartheid South Africa. In rural areas, wood, paraffin and coal are used to cook food, and very few households have refrigerators or even electricity. In the context of a very high unemployment rate, demand for such products will most probably remain low.

Production and the legacy of bifurcated states in Southern Africa

Three of the remaining white goods plants in Southern Africa were set up by one industrialist – a man called Charlie Palmer. In the early-1960s he set up a factory in Harare (then Salisbury, in Rhodesia). This company now operates under the name Imperial Refrigeration. Because of an apparent fall out with one of the other directors at this firm, Palmer moved on to Mozambique, where he set up another factory. In 1975, at the time of Mozambique's independence, Palmer fled the country, and then moved on to set up shop in Isithebe – one of South Africa's Bantustan industrial de-centralisation zones. He stayed here for a long time, only to move to Swaziland in 1990 to set up 'Swaziland Refrigeration', which later on became 'Masterfridge', and then, after liquidation, 'Palfridge'. Hence, the Imperial plant in Harare, the Whirlpool plant in Isithebe, and the Palfridge plant in Manzini were all originally set up by Charlie Palmer.

In both Swaziland and Zimbabwe the labour movement, and responses to the imperatives of modernisation flowing from the demands of an urban working class, shaped the outcomes of post-colonial regimes. In Swaziland, the monarchy established a form of *traditionalist unitarism*. (Davies, O'Meara and Dlamini 1985; Daniel and Stephen 1986; Levin 1997). In Zimbabwe, an initial phase of *state corporatism* gave way to liberalisation coupled with violent political repression (see Raftopoulos and Phimister 1997; Raftopoulos 2001). In both instances, a support base in rural areas was mobilised as a bulwark against democratisation.

In South Africa, which we concentrate on below, the legacy of apartheid has been played out in the context of simultaneous processes of political democratisation, economic liberalisation, and the need for the deracial-isation of the state, the economy and society. The term 'apartheid work-place regime' (Von Holdt 2003) has become popular to describe how the workplace operated under apartheid. A question therefore arises: what kind of workplace regime has been constructed on the ruins of the 'apartheid workplace regime'?

In concentrating on this question, we first have to consider how the 'apartheid workplace regime' operated, and how it related to bifurcation in apartheid South Africa.

A first characteristic is the 'racial division of labour'. 'Black' workers initially occupied the positions of labourers and assistants to artisans. Later on they became 'semi-skilled operators' (see also Webster 1985). 'Whites' were artisans and managers – including 'foremen', who supervised 'black' production workers. These foremen were assisted by 'black' *indunas* or *baas-boys*.[12] In the administrative departments, a similar colour bar was maintained – no white employee could be trained by a 'black' assistant training officer, for example. Whilst 'black' workers were not allowed to be trained as artisans, on an informal level they often possessed the practical skill to do these jobs, because 'their white superiors were frequently too lazy or ignorant to perform their own work' (Von Holdt 2003: 29). But as Von Holdt points out, 'while the racial division of labour was rigid, it was not static.' Indeed, 'racial boundaries shifted over time in response to changes in production processes and changes in the labour market' (2003: 29). Following the demise of craft production and the waning of craft unionism along with that, new forms of control emerged under the subsequent rise of Taylorism and Fordism in production (Braverman 1974; Friedman 1977; Edwards 1979). In South Africa and Zimbabwe, where a significant industrial base was built up under colonialism, mass production was introduced in the context of craft unions which mainly had 'white' members. The historical irony was that the deskilling of their work paved the way for a militant industrial unionism to emerge from the ranks of the 'black' semi-skilled operators who took their place. But still racial dominance was maintained by a strict colour bar related to supervision of work, as well as in the realm beyond the workplace. Indeed, Defy's Durban-Falkirk site was South Africa's first foundry to introduce production based on the principles of machinofacturing, which created the context for a significant cadre of semi-skilled African workers to emerge. Faced by this challenge, historically 'white' craft unions attempted to maintain their dominance over key positions (Webster 1985). Hence, apart from a 'racial division of labour', as Von Holdt calls this, one might argue that this division of labour implied a strict racial hierarchy.

Thus, a second characteristic of the apartheid workplace regime is 'the racial structure of power in the workplace'. This refers to the idea of *baasskap* (meaning 'boss-hood' or 'being the master') according to which any black person is by definition a servant of any white person, no matter what their position in the formal hierarchy. Von Holdt traces this back to 'deep colonial roots', where 'blacks' were seen as 'servants of whites'. He argues:

> The relationship between managerial authority and the racial structure of power was complex. Not all whites were managers. However, any white had the 'right' to issue instructions to any black. This meant that there was no clear line of managerial authority or job demarcation – at least, as applied to black workers. White men made the rules and the cardinal rule for black workers was 'to obey that man's rules', however arbitrary or senseless. For black workers this rule spelt extreme insecurity: one white man's rule might contradict another's, and in trying to follow both a worker was bound to transgress one or other instruction (2003: 31).

As pointed out by Burawoy, *baasskap* was often violently enforced, but also supported by the ability of supervisors to arbitrarily dismiss any 'black' worker without recourse to procedure, or by withholding bonuses for offences such as 'coming late' or 'insubordination' (Von Holdt 2003: 32–33).

Interpositioned in a dubious role between the 'white' supervisors and 'black' workers was the *baas-boy*, or the *induna*. Often 'white' supervisors were unable to speak an African language, and 'black' workers could often not speak English of Afrikaans. Thus an old colonial practice – what Mahmood Mamdani (1996) calls 'decentralised despotism' – was also employed *in the workplace itself*. Von Holdt points out that the deployment of the term *induna* 'reflects white efforts to affirm, strengthen or if necessary even create, traditional and ethnic identities for blacks as a bulwark against "modernisation" and its attendant demand for modern rights such as democracy or trade unions' (2003: 35). But unlike 'traditional chiefs' in the rural parts of colonies, these *indunas* did not bridge physical space between the village and the city, but the *social space* between the worlds of supervisors and workers. The (often brutal) power of *baas-boys* was derived from the positions of the 'white' supervisors and their role in the system as a whole. Their role was seldom a hegemonic one – no wonder that they were sometimes called *impimpis* ('informers'), and not *indunas*, by workers.

A third characteristic of the apartheid workplace regime is what Mamdani (1996: 30) would call 'the rural in the urban'. The workforce at the steel mill in Witbank studied by Von Holdt (2003: 40–46) was divided – or segmented – into workers who had lived in the local township for some time, and migrant workers who were housed in a hostel administrated by the local municipality. These two categories of workers did not only live in two distinct social spheres, but they were consciously allocated to different positions inside the workplace by management. According to Von Holdt, 'migrants were preferred for jobs in hot, dangerous places such as the iron plant tap floors or the steel plant furnaces, and for hard labour... Locals were recruited for "softer" jobs – such as artisan assistants' (2003: 40). He explains:

> This differentiated recruiting strategy was related to control, discipline and cost in the workplace. For migrant workers, pressed upon by the large reserve army of labour penned up in bantustans, and desperate for work, dismissal or non-renewal of a contract would be disaster. This imposed on them the discipline to accept the toughest and most gruelling work, at the lowest pay, and under harsh treatment... (2003: 42).

Indeed, Durban Falkirk was one of the few companies in Durban that housed migrant workers in a hostel on its premises (see Webster 1985).

A fourth characteristic of the apartheid regime was that, up to 1983, government formally legislated a racial segregation of facilities. However, as Von Holdt (2003: 29–30) points out, when this legislation was repealed in 1983, many firms continued with the practice of providing separate canteens, change houses and toilets. He makes an important point in this regard:

> Labour legislation reform – an alteration in the national regime of labour regulation – did not necessarily translate into change in the

workplace regime. Racial identity was constructed by white political, managerial, trade union and social power, rather than by the law alone, and it was the basis of that power. Power in the workplace was *racially constituted* (2003: 30).[13]

A fifth important element of the apartheid workplace regime was the way factories were inserted into the *industrial geography of colonialism*. Mamdani (1996) refers to the bifurcated state, and the different logics of colonial rule in urban centres and rural areas. In the South African context, 'indirect rule' took the form of the Bantustans created by the migrant labour system and formalised by the apartheid government. Whilst Von Holdt (2003) identifies the importance of the migrant labour system, he fails to recognise the significance of the apartheid industrial geography itself.

Until the changes to labour laws in 1979, all African workers were excluded from the legal definition of 'employee'. By using strategic court cases combined with a programme of mobilisation, the independent trade unions that emerged after the 1973 strike waves were able to slowly chip away some of the legal pillars of racial despotism. But accounts of South African labour history often fail to consider that a significant number of workers were located in areas that were not included in South African labour law. These workers were often in what became known as 'industrial decentralisation zones' in the so called 'homelands' (Bell 1973; Friedman 1987: 475; Hart 2002).

The idea of this kind of 'spatial fix' to urban worker militancy (Silver 2003) predates formal apartheid. Indeed, it was raised for the first time in the 1940s, and a limited process of state support was initiated. In the 1960s, the government stepped up its support for 'border industries', but factories were not located within the borders of Bantustans. Only from the late-1960s to the early 1970s were factory owners encouraged to set up shop within the Bantustans themselves. This had the added advantage of the location of employment relations outside the scope of the reforming South African labour regime. Thus, if one alters Mamdani's language somewhat, whereas workers in urban centres were making progress in achieving some form of *industrial citizenship*, workers in rural areas were very much the *subjects* of the neo-traditional rulers of Bantustans. In the South African context, the way in which the 'bifurcated state' shaped the industrial geography of apartheid is often ignored by a 'metro-centric' approach (Hart 2002).

To summarise, the 'apartheid workplace regime' was constituted on a racial division of labour, a racial structure of power supplemented by attempts to incorporate a colonial construction of 'ethnicity' in supervision, a system of migrant labour, the racial segregation of facilities, and a location of workplaces in a bifurcated industrial geography.

A central 'pillar' of colonial despotism, as argued here, is thus the *arbitrary nature of power* in the workplace. It is precisely this arbitrary power over the lives of workers that trade unions challenged – in the case of Zambia this started to happen in the 1930s to the 1940s, as pointed out by Burawoy (1985: 230–231). In the South African context, effectively this happened much later – from the 1970s onwards (Webster 1985; Von Holdt 2003). Any form of despotism leads to a building up of resentment, and sometimes to individualised resistance in the form of industrial sabotage, for instance, but often social movements result from such contexts – as was the case in South Africa (Webster 1985; Seidman 1994). We now turn to an analysis of what kind of workplace has been constructed on the ruins of the 'apartheid workplace regime in the white goods industry.

Continuity and discontinuity in white goods

In what follows, we examine continuities and discontinuities in the post-colonial state with respect to three issues – job grading and informal wage colour bars, the upward floating colour bar, and the reconfiguration of apartheid geography.

Job grading and 'Informal Wage Colour Bars'

In the four South African factories, workers generally held the view that important elements persisted of what is still referred to as 'apartheid', and that attempts to undo that legacy were often frustrated. These struggles were often expressed as linked to job grading – specifically what is referred to as 'grade anomalies'. During the 1990s, the National Union of Metal-workers of South Africa (NUMSA), the majority union in the sector, attempted to apply principles of 'broad banding' in union initiated restruc-turing exercises. The idea was to move away from grading systems, such as the Paterson system, where the grading principles were linked to the actual job – essentially based on the level of *responsibility* attached to a certain job. Trade unions wanted to see the grading of jobs as an exercise to contribute to the development of higher levels of accredited skills among workers; hence the term 'competency-based grading'. Working from the assumption that during the apartheid era 'black' workers had acquired certain skills that were not formally recognised by a bureaucratic system that was biased against them (Adler 1993), the argument was that first, existing 'tacit skills' had to be recognised, and second, incentives had to be built into the grading system for workers to acquire new skills.

Collapsing elaborate 'job-based' grading systems into broad banded 'com-petency-based' grading systems would, in theory, facilitate a closure of the wage gap between management and workers, but would also provide for clear 'career paths' for 'black' workers who were denied the same oppor-tunities of formal education as their 'white' counterparts (Adler 1993). At a national level, these initiatives were supported by a new bureaucracy within the framework of the National Qualifications Framework (NQF), supported by bodies such as the South African Qualifications Authority (SAQA) and several newly established Sectoral Education and Training Authorities (SETA's).

Indeed, the grading of jobs, and the linking of payment to those jobs, were very explosive issues when the interviews were conducted at the factories in South Africa. During 2002, workers at three of the factories in the sector downed tools to protest what was known as 'grade anomalies'.

Considerable tension was caused by the fact that one of the companies involved had moved from the Paterson system they were using to the one prescribed by the Bargaining Council for the industry. A worker explained: 'Before they were using the Paterson system, which was grade one to ten. Then, suddenly last year, the company [decided] to use the NIC system [National Industrial Council],[14] which has thirteen grades...' Apart from the complaint that the trade union was not consulted about this change, there were problems with 'balancing these grades as they transform them from the Paterson system...' One interviewee described the move from Paterson to the NIC system as 'a fuck-up', and another explained: 'On the Paterson system I was grade five and the other worker was grade six, but when we are transformed to [the] NIC [system], we are classified on the same grade, which is Grade G. Sometimes then we all become Grade G, but we are earning different rates.' Another said: 'The grading-system is totally corrupt, because we've got thirteen grades here and everybody here is not paid the same. Like the one artisan assistant, he's getting paid R18.57 the other one is getting paid R12.00, you understand?' There was also a feeling that the exercise was used to cut wages, since the wage levels on the new system were lower than the old one, which was based on agreements reached at the level of the factory. The result of this was the mentioned 'grade anomalies'.

Thus far the situation might seem like teething problems following the introduction of a new grading system. But an important dimension was not brought out in the media reports on the strikes that ensued in 2002. 'Grade anomalies' and allegations of 'favouritism' have an important racial sub-text:

> The grading system is buggered because, if I can put it to you that way, it is still the old apartheid regime... You take the F-grade here, [in the one department], where only coloureds work. [Then] you take F-grade in dispatch [where blacks work]. In dispatch they will be getting only R11.27 [an hour]... in [the department where mostly coloureds work] they will get R12.80, but they're both F-grade... These coloured people in F-grade are getting more money than the black people in dispatch. But the white people who [used] to work in material handling... they are also F-grade but they are getting thirty, forty rand.

At yet another factory, an interviewee had the following perspective:

> [R]acism will always be everywhere in a way... But it's not [always] that obvious [here]. But there was a big issue on grades and race, you know? It's like the Indians were getting better grades, you see? But sometimes it does happen, because when I came here it was something like fifty blacks and thirty Indians... I don't know how they rated [the whole thing]. But mostly those Indians got better grades. It's either because they applied for those positions that came up, or they just somehow got the jobs. But the thing is not every position gets advertised. So you just see someone working on higher grade and you don't even know how the hell did he get there!

Workers saw a more standardised system, with clear procedures as a way to fight discrimination based on arbitrary decisions by management. When the training of workers is linked to career paths, workers could advance in the workplace. One interviewee commented: 'This is what we have been arguing about, just because they have trained some employees here. When there are some vacancies they don't put them there, they just [take people] from outside...'.

In Zimbabwe the grading system used by factories is prescribed by the National Employment Council (NEC), a body where employers consult trade unions on matters such as wage increases. These councils are a legacy of the state corporatist industrial relations system introduced by the post-liberation regime. The grading system resembles the Paterson model to a large extent. Grades are linked to the jobs that employees perform, and not to an employee's levels of competency.

At the factory in Swaziland, most interviewees were unaware of the nature of their grading system. Someone in the Human Resources department was able to confirm that the Paterson system was used. Most factory workers fell within the 'A-band', which is the lowest in the system. One black employee, who was interviewed off the factory premises, claimed that white and African employees in similar grades, as in South Africa, were paid different wages. According to him, white employees were paid up to eleven times the salaries of African employees in similar grades. This allegation could not be verified independently.

Hence, discontinuity can be found in the removal of formal legislation that imposed racial hierarchies and the introduction of new legislation that attempts to redress the racial legacies. However, in the perspective presented in these interviews, there seems to be a competing logic – a more informal one – that still operates in the workplace. It seems as though this logic still holds that it is justified that different 'races' should receive different wages, even when, on a formal level, they perform the jobs that are graded equally. In what one might call the 'informal wage colour bar' resides continuities with the past.

The 'Upward Floating Colour Bar'

At all the South African factories, 'black' employees have steadily been promoted to the level of 'supervisor'. However, the level of 'superintendent' still remains the domain of mostly 'white' employees. 'There is an improvement, because since I came here,' said one worker, 'I think there were one or two African supervisors, but now... maybe we've got about five or six.' In the past, he said, 'supervisory vacancies were... for coloureds and Indians only, and jobs like tool-setter, which are highly skilled jobs, or quality controllers, were reserved for Indians and coloureds only. But now there are Africans.' Another said:

> In the press-shop there used to be coloured supervisors in the past. Now there are... two [Africans] on this shift, and there's one on the other shift – [so] there [are] three African supervisors in the press shop. There's an African superintendent in the press-shop, he is nightshift... I mean when it comes for there downwards, that's where they actually balance the issue of the employment equity, but at the top they don't.

Another felt that the supervisory level was still dominated by 'coloureds' and 'Indians': 'Now there are more Indian supervisors, or I should bind them together and say coloureds and Indians. The African supervisors I can count them and tell you it is so and so, so and so. When it comes to Indian and coloureds I [cannot] count [them] – they are more.'

However, whilst African workers have steadily been promoted to the supervisory level, workers felt that they did not have real authority to conduct their work. Others felt that they were under-qualified for their jobs, and that was why management was able to 'undermine' their positions. One explained: 'I can take you to [our] department, you can see the top level management disregarding the supervisor and the superintendent and [going] straight to the workforce, and say: "Work! Do your job! What's wrong?" [This] is unacceptable.' He also felt that this did not happen in the past, when supervisors were mostly coloured and Indian. At a number of factories, interviewees echoed this view: '[Y]ou find that the manager comes from top to you, instead of maybe go to the supervisor, and the supervisor must tell you [what to do].'

Another said: 'We want black people to be supervisors, then fine, they will be supervisors. [But] in some areas they are not recognised.' One interviewee went so far as to use the term 'glorified supervisors'. Ironically the union was in the process of taking up this matter with one of the companies. A union official explained: 'They [supervisors] are not empowered, although as the union we are trying to enforce that. We've got a dispute pertaining the way they're managing the factory...' The union wanted regular meetings to discuss issues related to production. However, the union was quite sceptical about the potential for such a process to make a significant impact, since it was part of ongoing attempts to address a whole range of issues, which included the issue of 'grade anomalies' and the perception from the workforce that the intensification of work had reached unacceptable levels.

At the level of management above the level of supervision, there were very few Africans at any of the factories. One interviewee said:

> We've got only one African guy who is a manager, just a stupid manager, [who] does not have power – he cannot decide [anything]... Can you imagine an IR manager taking instructions and report to the operations manager, a person who knows nothing about the Act, a person who cannot even tell you where the CCMA [dispute resolution] office is in town? But you take instructions from him!'

At another factory, workers also felt that Africans who were appointed in the Human Resources department were not taken seriously by the company. According to them, the 'black' HR managers did not get the same perks as their 'white' counterparts. At another factory, all the supervisors were 'black'. About management, however, an interviewee said: 'There's only one management here: all [are] white.' When asked about the African human resources manager, he answered: 'No [he] is not regarded as a manager... They say he's a Human Resources Manager but he's not given a power to be like that...'

But there was another African manager at this factory. As another interviewee had to point out, there was an African production manager. He did not consider him to be more approachable than the 'white' managers, and called him 'the oppressor':

> He is an oppressor, because if maybe there is a problem, even from the management, you'll find that he points [to] a worker inside... Even if maybe there is something that the company want to give us, he is the one that is a stumbling block... because [he says] now [they] spoil the people.... As a black manager, he is the one who is supposed to fight for us. [But] he's not doing that. [I'm not saying that] if you are a black manager, you [should] fight for me, even if I am wrong – if I'm wrong I'm wrong.

Workers generally felt that they were still regarded as 'second class' employees: 'The black employees in this factory are not taken into account as people who are in the company, who are making the production or making the money in the company...'

In Zimbabwe one of the factories was considered to be a 'black' and the other 'white'. At the two factories, dynamics regarding 'race' also differed. At Imperial, there were no 'white' employees. The CEO and the managing director, for example, were African. A worker who had worked at the firm for more than thirty years said that conditions at the factory had improved vastly after independence. Whilst there was a feeling that factory management was very authoritarian, the relationships between workers, supervisors and management at this factory seemed more cordial than at the South African plants. An interviewee mentioned a certain 'Mr T', a 'white' person, who had worked as a manager to implement new production equipment: 'It was not an issue. We worked on an equal footing,' he said.

At Innscor, the situation resembled some of the dynamics found in the South African factories. Up until around 1994, supervisors were 'mixed'. From then onwards, supervisors, like ordinary factory workers, became mostly Africans. The management level was also 'mixed', but the Chief Executive Officer and the Managing Director were both 'white' Zimbabweans. Workers also held the perception that 'black' and 'white' employees on similar grades were paid differential salaries.

In Swaziland, an employee who had worked in factories that manufactured similar products in Zimbabwe, South Africa, and then finally Swaziland, was asked to compare his experiences. 'In Zimbabwe, factories are often run by blacks,' he said. 'Here and there,' he said, 'whites still controlled.' Swaziland and South Africa were similar in his view. From the level of superintendent up to management, whites, coloured and Indians dominated positions. In South Africa he found it peculiar that 'the appointment of relatives in highly paid, unproductive jobs' was quite common. Another worker at this factory felt that Swaziland was less xenophobic than South Africa. According to him, rather than racism, favouritism among supervisors, team leaders and workers was more of an issue. The factory there, like the ones in Zimbabwe, did not have superintendents interpositioned between supervisors and management. Workers and supervisors were mostly Africans, whilst management were all white and Indian, except for one African. According to a worker who had previously worked in South Africa, it was 'not different from South Africa. It is the same.' One employee had a culturalist explanation for the absence of more African managers: 'It is not race, it is more like a cultural thing. Swazi's are known to be people who are polite, humble and all that jazz... But it is changing about now. Swazi's are also not confident in higher positions. We want to rely on someone else to make the decisions.'

The breakdown in the formal colour bar of the apartheid era represents a break with the past. Indeed, Africans are appointed in higher positions – specifically as supervisors, but also in some managerial positions. This slow process of deracialisation started from the early 1970s, as Nzimande (1991) showed. But many workers argue that there are still continuities with the past. They often question whether these new supervisors and managers have real authority. The process seems to show striking similarities with the 'upward floating colour bar' identified by Burawoy (1972; 1985) on the Zambian copper fields.

Reconfiguring the apartheid industrial geography

Hart points out that, even in the 1980s, the apartheid state's policies of spatial engineering had run out of fashion in the context of a dominance of neo-liberal thinking in the realm of development theory. Indeed, as she argues '[i]n development discourses more generally, places like Ladysmith and Newcastle that had featured so prominently in the apartheid era simply fell off the map'. Instead, towards the 1990s, a 'metro-centric consensus' was established, helped along by what she calls 'a group of academics associated with COSATU' who 'conjured up visions of a high-tech, high wage industrial future' (2002: 155).

But whilst the post-apartheid state does not formally support the principles of industrial decentralisation by excluding such areas from the national labour regime, they did not 'bleed away', as some policy analysts had expected (Hart 2002: 155). The KwaZulu Finance Corporation (KFC) is now called Ithala Development Finance Corporation Limited. They are still very active in former industrial decentralisation zones such as Isithebe. More than 180 companies are still 'in production' here. Their brochures inform prospective investors of different subsidies – now called supply-side measures – available to prospective investors. In addition to this, rental rates from R4-50 per m^2 are offered, sale rates from R480 per m^2, and production, electricity and water costs are advertised to be the 'lowest'. Furthermore, '[t]wo Ithala operated locomotives provide a direct link between factories and the main rail system' (Ithala Development Finance Corporation Limited n.d., Ithala Development Finance Corporation Limited 2003).

Defy's factories in Ezakheni and East London, as well as the Whirlpool factory in Isithebe, are all located within the borders of former Bantustans. In addition, Ezakheni and Isithebe were prominent industrial decentralisation zones under Apartheid. The union has been addressing the disparities in wages and conditions between these areas and factories located in urban areas. One interviewee still had concerns: 'We have two other sister-companies... So [we know] there is a disparity, the wages are not equal.'

Whereas NUMSA (and its predecessor – the Metal and Allied Workers Union) was able to organise urban factories in the 1970s, factories in these former decentralisation areas were only organised in the late 1980s. The civil war in the early 1990s, especially in KwaZulu-Natal, severely disrupted union activities. However, currently processes of 'reconciliation' in the workplace are leading to members of UWUSA, a former Zulu nationalist union, being organised into the NUMSA structures. An interviewee at a factory in a former industrial decentralisation zone pointed out: 'Even in 1988 when we joined NUMSA nothing [collective bargaining] was happening... Then in 1994, that's where they started to bargain, [later] they joined Bargaining Council and the grading system...'

As the wage levels at the different production locations in South Africa even out, workers interviewed at some of the factories were concerned about whether the company would maintain their operations in former Bantustans:

> Here we have a problem – [the company] wants to move to Durban... But we don't know when are they are going to move. We as the union asked them to give us a five or ten year guarantee that they will stay here – but they can't give us even a two year guarantee that they will stay here, you understand? Because it is still in the pipeline [whether] they are shifting.

This state of affairs is a constant source of insecurity, with workers referring to factories that are 'running away' from them. Some were aware of the fact that the discontinuation of subsidies for companies was putting pressure on the industrialisation models followed in the former industrial decentralisation zones.[15] One related the closure of companies in his area to racism:

> What makes the companies to close down? The answer is simple. It is the white men who have the money, they do not want the black government. That is why they run away with the money and hide it in another place, and sit upon it. That is the reason.

Another said 'What I mean is that business owners think that there is a problem [that they must give people jobs]. They fight the people because they want to bring back the white government'.

Whereas the industrial decentralisation zones served as a mechanism to discipline labour in the past, this dynamic is now replicated in the Southern African region. The Masterfridge factory was set up in the neighbouring Swaziland in the 1990s. Within two years it captured 40 per cent of the South African market for the product. 90 per cent of its produce was exported to South Africa. Swaziland is notorious for its labour repressive regime, and South African management and trade unions alike raised this issue publicly.

Indeed, interviewees were very much aware of some of these dynamics: 'Take a matter of Masterfridge,' said one, 'they produce goods from Swaziland... direct to South Africa... Local people, are not [benefiting] from that, they are achieving nothing from Masterfridge, because [they] don't have a plant here in South Africa, you know. That is one of the problems.' Another said: 'I think the government must try to stop taking goods from other countries and not allow so many countries to bring their goods here in South Africa – just because our factory are closing down due to that goods from outside the country.'

Whereas trade union rights in South Africa are formally recognised, unions in Swaziland often have to fight for their right to organise workers. Strike procedures are tedious and drawn out, making it almost impossible for workers to embark on legal industrial action. An interviewee at the factory in Swaziland also did not have a lot of respect for the track record of trade unions in that country: 'Unions in Swaziland are weak. They are not doing their job – they are not standing for worker's rights.' But the problem was not only a lack of effort from the trade unions. He said: 'You should remember, this is not a country, it's a kingdom...' Another said: 'The government of Swaziland is not giving power to unions.' Indeed, no collective bargaining over wages and conditions took place at the factory. Another employee pointed out that there had been a union 'across the road' who had tried to organise workers at the factory in the past. These attempts were unsuccessful: '[The manager] believes people's attitudes change when they join unions. He promised to look after the employees if they do not join a union...'

Another worker who was interviewed in Swaziland had previously worked in a factory in Zimbabwe. In his perspective, unions there were 'not weak or powerful.' According to him, 'there are not that many strikes [in Zimbabwe], but worker's rights are followed through the worker's committees.' Indeed, workers in this industry in Zimbabwe industry were organised by the National Engineering Workers' Union (NEWU). Wages were negotiated in the National Employment Council for the engineering industry, which basically prescribed minimum wages to the industry – very much like the Bargaining Councils in South Africa. However, unlike South Africa, collective bargaining for wages did not take place at the factory or company level. At this level, permanent workers elected representatives for Worker's Committees. These representatives consulted with management in a Works Council. The union as such was not involved in this process. Indeed, according to one managing director, less than 50 per cent of their workforce was unionised.

Innscor set its wage levels at a higher rate than the prescribed minimum wages – even for contract workers. This was usually discussed in the Works Council. Workers seldom went on strike as part of a collective bargaining process, but sometimes engaged in demonstrations and sit-ins. Once, when this happened, the company called the police. According to the production manager at the plant, unions were 'ineffective'.

Workers' fear that their factories may close down or relocate was compounded by another source of insecurity brought about by the segmentation of internal labour markets between workers with permanent contracts of employment and a cohort of workers with fixed-term contracts of employment. This was the case at all the factories in South Africa, Swaziland and Zimbabwe. At Defy's factory in Jacobs, these workers are known as 'STCs' – short for 'short-term contractors'. It is especially during times when production has to increase that these STCs are employed by the companies. When workers are recruited for permanent positions, they are usually recruited from the ranks of the STCs. Often, however, workers work permanently on a 'temporary' basis:

> It depends on the market – if the volumes are high, maybe, for a period of more than six months. If you start, it should be a short-term contract for a period of three months. If you exceed six months, you get a permanent position. But it depends on the market.... Currently they are plus-minus 500 – that's why I am saying it depends on the market. Like last year the company managed to employ more than 400 casual workers. Most of them were on short-term contacts, which expired at the end of last year.

At the factory in Swaziland, when the interviews were conducted, there were 436 employees. Of these, 193 were appointed on monthly contracts. One interviewee referred to these workers as 'seasonals'. At Imperial Refrigeration in Zimbabwe, of a factory staff component of 170, 60 per cent were appointed on a permanent basis and the rest were appointed on contracts that were renewed every six weeks. These contracts meant that the company could give workers 24 hours notice. At the Innscor factory, of a total workforce of 250 employees, only about 100 were on permanent contracts. The rest were all contract workers, whose contracts were renewed on a monthly basis. Contract workers range from 25 per cent of all employees at Defy's plant in Ezakheni to a staggering 60 per cent at the Innscor factory in Harare.

At none of the factories did trade unions actively recruit contract workers as members. At one of the factories, an interviewee even went so far as to suggest that '[t]he only difference [between] contract and permanent [workers] I think is being a member of the union – having a card and everything; that's the only difference.' According to her, '[e]verything [else] is just the same'.

Hence, discontinuity can be found in the levelling of the uneven labour market brought about by the industrial geography of apartheid. Nevertheless, continuities with the past point to the same logic now being replicated in the context of Southern Africa, and the availability of a labour regime in Swaziland that resembles the former 'homelands', enables a rearticulation of the logic of apartheid industrial geography. South Africa's internal spatial fix is externalised to include Swaziland. While a significant segment of permanent workers have retained some form of security, a third of all employees are in insecure temporary jobs. Even for permanent workers, however, their 'permanence' is under constant threat because of firm closures. They are constantly reminded by this as managers employ the language of globalisation. These continuities may be temporary phenomena that form part of a process of decolonisation. Also, the study is based on a sector of one industry only. One cannot generalise the findings – essentially based on opinions expressed during interviews – to include all of South Africa. However, the perspectives presented here do raise important questions about the ability of a particular formation of the post-colonial state to 'penetrate' the workplace.

Conclusion

It is perhaps understandable 'that perhaps the most striking feature of South African studies prior to the demise of apartheid was the paucity of engagement with the subject of race' (Posel et al 2001: i) but less so that '[t]he dynamics of race remain perhaps more unexplored in South Africa than anywhere else' (Seidman 1999: 434). Certainly these dynamics have had to take a central place in this analysis of the white goods industry. The industry in Southern Africa remains marginal in the context of globalisation. While imports are increasing, local firms are still hanging on to their market share. But they are unable to shift gear to become major exporters of white goods. Local markets remain small compared to the major loci of consumption in the North – and part of the problem is that they are still bifurcated according to 'race' and space.

Race makes it mark both on consumption and production. Discrimination on the basis of 'race' is no longer legal in South Africa. It is actively discouraged by state policies and legislation has been put in place to bring about 'employment equity'. However, in the white goods industry, instead of de-racialisation, the dynamics of 'race' take on the form of both an informal wage colour bar and an 'upward floating colour bar'. Workers hold strong opinions and continue to challenge these practices. An important element of the colonial workplace regime is the fact that decisions are made arbitrarily. These essentially pre-bureaucratic forms of work organisation are challenged by trade unions, who force companies to sign 'procedural agreements', and who challenge the absence of formal grading systems, or the anomalies inherent to such grading systems once they are implemented. In a way, one might argue that the struggle against colonial despotism is a *struggle for bureaucracy* – one that is based on a different logic – one that is seen as more 'rational' by workers.

When the new government came to power in South Africa in 1994, there were attempts to put in place a broader set of institutions to support such reconstruction of the workplace. But the establishment of these institutions were premised on false assumptions. The extent to which trade unions were able to establish such 'rational' procedures in the workplace was overestimated. Many sectors of the economy were never organised, and because of the particular nature of the apartheid industrial geography, significant spaces of the manufacturing industry were located outside the national regime.

Hence, a further aspect of the apartheid manufacturing regime is replicated in the context of regional integration in Southern Africa and the labour repressive regime offered by Swaziland. Where the Bantustans were used as labour reserves and disciplining mechanisms for trade unions, this logic is now regionalised to incorporate countries like Swaziland.

The authors of the labour laws assumed that one would be able to convince the players that the establishment of new institutions, or bureaucracies, in the workplace would be to their benefit – in the long run – even if they were not established yet. But instead of such institutions being established, the discourse of colonial management fused with the discourse of globalisation through the language of flexibility. The bureaucratic measures that were meant to transform the colonial despotism into some form of post-colonial hegemony, were seen as obstacles to productivity and employment. The result is the language of the market legitimising the continuing dominance of 'white' managers in the workplace and a reassertion of their despotism by using fixed term contracts, threats to relocate, and the language of neo-liberal globalisation.

Notes

1   The research fieldwork for this project was funded by the UK Government's Department for International Development as part of the 'Crisis States Programme' coordinated by the Development Research Centre of the London School of Economics. The perspectives in this chapter do not necessarily reflect those of the funding agency or the coordinators.

2   Examples are Sierra-Leone (diamonds), the Democratic Republic of Congo (diamonds, gold), and Sudan (oil).

3   Kelvinator SA manufactured products under license from Electrolux, the Swedish multinational that owns the Kelvinator brand. Kelvinator SA was originally part of Barlow Rand, a South African mining and manufacturing conglomerate. When this company unbundled, Kelvinator was sold to a local consortium led by its CEO Simon Koch, after which it was liquidated.

4   Univa was owned by Masterfridge, a company listed on the South African stock exchange.

5   This calculation is made on the basis of a Rand US$ exchange rate of R1 = US$0.118, the average exchange rate for 2001.

6   This results from the free trade agreement between South Africa and the European Union.

7   The actual Rand values of R29,433,000 in 1998 and R90,172,000 in 2000 are converted here to the constant Rand value (of R0.1447) to the US dollar in 2000.

8   Actual Rand values of R49,278,000 in 1998 and R96,877,000 in 2000, expressed in constant US dollar values in 2000.

9   Actual Rand values of R10,796,000 in 1998 and R19,123,000 in 2000, expressed in constant US dollar values in 2000. (Source: Department of Trade and Industry online database of imports and exports.)

10   This 'development initiative' basically implied the construction of a series of toll roads linking Johannesburg to Maputo in Mozambique.

11   In contrast to many of the other country case studies in this volume, the cost of white goods in South Africa increased from the mid-1990s to the early 2000s

mainly because of currency fluctuations. During this period, the Rand devalued against most major currencies. On 10 January 1996 the Rand traded at R3.6247 to the US Dollar. Since early 1996, the currency depreciated at a rapid rate, often fluctuating wildly. On 20 December 2001, the currency reached a low point of R13.4714 to the US Dollar. This led to an increase in the inflation rate. Since then, the currency has gained some of its value. In mid-2004, the currency traded at around R6 to the US Dollar (R6.0567 on 23 July 2004). The South African white goods manufacturing industry depends on significant imported inputs (such as compressors). Because of the monopolisation of the steel industry, local inputs (such as steel) are sold at import parity prices. Thus, the devaluation of the rand and the industry's exposure to imported inputs explain the rising cost of white goods in the local market.

12 'Baas' means 'boss', but implies an important element of white supremacy – a more accurate translation might be 'master', rather than 'boss'. The English version, 'boss-boy', is also sometimes used. According to the Chamber of Mines' English-Afrikaans-Fanakalo dictionary, 'baas' is translated as 'bas' in Fanakalo. The Fanakalo 'bas boy' is translated to 'baasjong' or 'voorjong' in Afrikaans. The Afrikaans translation for 'supervisor' would be 'voorman' – which is already a gendered translation. But Africans are not considered to be 'men' here – the word 'jong' is used instead, which literally means 'young'. This is similar to the colonial use of 'boy' in English. In the same dictionary, the different versions for what later became a 'machine operator' are 'machine boy' (English), 'boorjong' (Afrikaans) and 'mtshin boy' (Fanakalo). The translation for 'miner' (in English 'ganger' is presented as a synonym) is simply 'bas'. A 'fitter' ('passer' in Afrikaans), is translated as 'bas ka lo fitas', a 'shaft timberman' is a 'bas ka lo tshaf'. Here we can see how certain jobs implied a certain racial category. A 'miner' can only be a 'baas'. In fact, the two concepts were synonymous. See Chamber of Mines of South Africa. 1969. *Miners' Dictionary – Woordeboek vir Myners*.

13 Emphasis in the original text. The order here deviates from Von Holdt's discussion of the five characteristics of the apartheid workplace regime not to emphasise or de-emphasise any of them, but merely for the sake of the flow of the argument.

14 Before the promulgation of the Labour Relations Act of 1995, Bargaining Councils were known as Industrial Councils.

15 From the 1970s onwards, companies received a number of subsidies from the government to set up factories in the industrial decentralisation zones. These subsidies were phased out during the 1990s (see Hart 2002).

References

Adler, G. (1993) 'Skills, Control and Careers at Work: Possibilities for Worker Control in the South African Motor Industry', *South African Sociological Review*, 5 (2): 35–64.

Baumann, T. (1995) *An Industrial Strategy for the Electrical Durables Sector*, 'A Report of the Industrial Strategy Project', Cape Town: University of Cape Town Press.

Bell, T. (1973) *Industrial Decentralisation in South Africa*, Cape Town, Johannesburg & London: Oxford University Press.

Beresford, B. (1997) 'Fridge trade master not resting on her laurels', *Business Day*, 4 September.

Braverman, H. (1974) *Labour and Monopoly Capital: The Degradation of Work in the Twentieth Century*, New York: Monthly Review Press.

Burawoy, M. (1972) *The Colour of Class on the Copper Mines: From African Advancement to Zambianization*, Lusaka: Institute for African Studies.

Burawoy, M. (1985) *The Politics of Production*, London: Verso.

Business Day Reporter (1997) 'Defy Invests R15m to boost productivity', *Business Day*, 23 December.

Business Day Reporter (1999) 'Omega prepares itself to come in from the red', *Business Day*, 29 June.

Castells, M. (1998) *The End of the Millennium*, Massachusetts & Oxford: Blackwell.

Cole, M. (1997) 'LG launches rebranding of GoldStar trade name', *Business Day*, 19 March.

Daniel, J. and Stephen, M. F. (eds) (1986) *Historical Perspectives on the Political Economy of Swaziland*, Mbabane: Social Science Research Unit, University of Swaziland.

Davies, R., O'Meara, D. and Dlamini, S. (1985) *The Kingdom of Swaziland: A Profile*, London: Zed.

Department of Trade and Industry (DTI) (2004a) Online trade data, http://www.thedti.gov.za/econdb/raportt/rapstruc.html

Department of Trade and Industry (DTI) (2004b) Online trade data, http://www.thedti.gov.za/econdb/raportt/rapstrucben.html

Edwards, R. (1979) *Contested Terrain: The Transformation of the Workplace in the Twentieth Century*, New York: Basic Books.

Euromonitor (2003) *South African Market for White Goods*, Database, April 2003.

Frazer, H. (1997) 'Making the fridge Africa's hottest item', *Aftrade: World Trade and Investment*.

Friedman, A. L. (1977) *Industry and Labour: Class Struggle at Work and Monopoly Capitalism*, London: MacMillan.

Friedman, S. (1987) *Building Tomorrow Today*, Johannesburg: Ravan.

Gereffi, G. (1999) 'International trade and industrial upgrading in the apparel commodity chain', *Journal of International Economics*, 48 (1): 37–70.

Gibbon, P. (2001) 'Upgrading primary production: A global commodity chain approach', *World Development*, 29 (2): 345–363.

Hart, G. (2002) *Disabling Globalization: Places of Power in Post-Apartheid South Africa*, Pietermaritzburg: University of Natal Press.

Industrial Development Corporation (IDC) (2000) *The South African Downstream Carbon Steel Industry*, Sandton: IDC.

Ithala Development Finance Corporation Limited (n.d.) *Isithebe Industrial Estate*, Brochure published for potential investors.

Ithala Development Finance Corporation Limited (2003) *Ithala Business Opportunities: News for Decision-makers*, Newsletter, May 2003.

Jenvey, N. (1997) 'Electrification success boosts Defy turnover', *Business Day*, 17 December.

Kaplinsky, R. (2000) 'Globalisation and Unequalisation: What can be learned from value chain analysis?' *Globalisation and Trade*, 32 (2): 177–146.

Levin, R. (1997) *When the Sleeping Grass Awakens: Land and Power in Swaziland*, Johannesburg: Witwatersrand University Press.

Mamdani, M. (1996) *Citizen and Subject: Contemporary Africa and the Legacy of Late Colonialism*, Cape Town: David Philip.

Masondo, D. (2004) 'Trade Liberalisation and the Restructuring of Work: The Case of BMW', in: Webster, E. C. and Von Holdt, K. (eds), *Flexible Worlds of Work: Ten Years of Restructuring Post-apartheid Workplaces* [forthcoming].

Nichols, T., Sugur, N. and Demir, E. (2002) 'Globalised Management and Local Labour: The Case of the White Goods Industry in Turkey', *Industrial Relations Journal*, 33 (1): 68–85.

Nichols, T. and Sugur, N. (2004) *Global Management, Local Labour: Turkish Workers and Modern Industry*, Basingstoke: Palgrave Macmillan.

Nzimande, B. (1991) '"The Corporate Guerrillas" – Class Formation and the African Petty Bourgeoisie in Post-1973 South Africa', PhD thesis, University of Natal, Durban.

Parker, J. (1997) 'Effect of electrification on white goods unclear', *Business Day*, 18 March.

Posel, D., Hyslop, J. & Nieftogodien, N. (2001) 'Debating "Race" in South African Scholarship', *Transformation*, 47: i–xviii.

Raftopoulos, B. (2001) 'The Labour Movement and the Emergence of Oppositional Politics in Zimbabwe', in: Raftopoulos, B. & Sachikonye, L. (eds), *Striking Back: The Labour Movement and the Post-Colonial State in Zimbabwe 1980–2000*, Harare: Weaver Press.

Raftopoulos, B. and Phimister, I. (eds) (1997) *Keep on Knocking: A History of the Labour Movement in Zimbabwe 1900–97*, Harare: Baobab Books.

Republic of South Africa (RSA) (1996) *Department of Trade and Industry Annual Report*, Pretoria: Government Printers.

Republic of South Africa (RSA) (2002) *Monthly Abstract of Trade Statistics: Foreign trade statistics of South Africa released by the Commissioner for the South African Revenue Service*, Pretoria: Government Printers.

Saul, J. & Leys, C. (1999) 'Sub-Saharan Africa in global capitalism', *Monthly Review*, 51 (3).

Seidman, G. (1994) *Manufacturing Militance: Workers' Movements in Brazil and South Africa*, California: University of California Press.

Seidman, G. (1999) 'Is South-Africa Different – Sociological Comparisons and Theoretical Contributions from the Land of Apartheid', *Annual Review of Sociology*, 25: 419–440.

Silver, B. (2003) *Forces of Labor: Workers' Movements and Globalization since 1870*, Cambridge: Cambridge University Press.

Statistics South Africa (2003a) Census data for 2001, Pretoria, online at http://www.statssa.gov.za/census2001/Census/dialog/statfile.asp

Statistics South Africa (2003b) *Census 2001: Census in Brief*, Pretoria: Government Printers.

Statistics South Africa (2003c) *Census 2001: Investigation into Appropriate Definitions of Urban and Rural in South Africa – Discussion Document*, Pretoria: Government Printers.

Von Holdt, K. (2003) *Transition from Below: Forging Trade Unionism and Workplace Change in South Africa*, Durban: University of Natal Press.

Webster, E. (1985) *Cast in a Racial Mould: Labour Process and Trade Unionism in the Foundries*, Johannesburg: Ravan.

World Appliance Companies (2002) *World Appliance Companies*, Third edition. Report published by Appliance Magazine and Industry Statistics Ltd, Oak Brook: Dana Chase.

4

China – White Goods and the Capitalist Transformation

Wei Zhao, Theo Nichols and Surhan Cam

Introduction

China has developed at a dramatic pace since it began the transition to a market economy and the white goods sector, the products of which are to be seen in most homes in urban areas, was in the vanguard of this development. This chapter begins by outlining China's recent economic development, the shift toward a market economy, the change in the employment system and the position of trade unions. It then considers the specific development of the white goods industry within this larger context, following which a case study is presented, ChinaCo, which provides a closer consideration of the effects of recent changes on workers in a foreign owned white goods factory.

China's economic development and transition

China's average annual Gross Domestic Product (GDP) increased by 9.4 per cent per year from 1978 to 2001 and the total value of GDP increased from $44 billion in 1978 to $1159 billion in 2001. The rapid increase of the economy narrowed the gap between China and developed countries in macro-economic terms. According to IMF estimates, by 2001 Chinese gross domestic production ranked the sixth largest in the world.

Industrial value added increased 11.5 per cent per year from 1979 to 2001, when it amounted to approximately $515 billion (NBSC 2002a). The transformation in the rate of China's industrial growth is largely the result of the reform of state-owned enterprises (SOEs), the policy to permit the development of private enterprises and the policy of attracting foreign capital.

From the mid-1950s to the end of the 1980s, there was a single-sector system of public-owned enterprises under the planned economy. In 1978, 77.6 per cent of these were state owned enterprises (SOEs) and 22.4 per cent collective owned enterprises (COEs)[1] (NBSC 1979). The single sector and the planned economic system lacked competition, and the SOEs and COEs suffered from low productivity.

The reform of the SOEs has been a central issue of the economic reforms since the mid-1980s. The first step was to reform the internal problems of the SOEs and to adjust the relations between the government and the enterprises. This entailed the enhancement of managerial authority and the implementation of the contractual responsibility system in order to give some right to the managers in state enterprises. To stimulate the reform of SOEs and promote the economic market, a new reform strategy, namely 'Take a firm grip on the large, let go of the small' (*zhua da fang xiao*) was carried out in 1992. This meant that the state would only retain a major presence in 'pillar' industry (for instance, the national defense industry) and 'basic industry' (for instance, the energy and transport industry) and that it would allow middle and small sized enterprises to change their ownership through mergers and bankruptcies. Meanwhile, the new policy also allowed non-state enterprises to participate in SOE reform through purchase or merger. These policies changed the ownership structure and provided a significant space in which various types of ownership could develop.

As a result of the reform and adjustments in the industrial structure, the proportion of state-owned enterprises and state-owned holding companies in the national economy decreased. By the end of 2001, only 15.2 per cent of all industrial enterprises were state-owned and state holding enterprises (NBSC 2002b). At present, most state owned enterprises are super large-scale companies or company groups.

Increasing numbers of foreign capitals have invested in China in the last two decades. By the end 2001, foreign direct investment (FDI) accounted for 10.5 per cent of gross investment, which is concentrated in the industrial sector (Jiang 2002: 1). From the beginning of the century, FDI has become the most important type of foreign investment and China has been the largest recipient of FDI in the world since 2002. More than 400 out of the 500 world top multinational companies (MNCs) have invested in China, with US$390 billion of FDI having been utilised by China by the end of 2001. According to NBSC statistics, more than 390,000 companies with foreign investment have been authorised by Chinese government agencies (NBSC 2002c). As more and more foreign enterprises went into production, they played an active role in Chinese industrial development. In 2000, foreign investment enterprises accounted for 27 per cent of total industrial output and the same percentage of industrial sales income (Jiang 2002: 26).

After China entered the WTO in December 2001, a considerable amount of foreign investment entered China. Moreover, the government continued to actively attract foreign capital to invest in industrial sectors. The successful attraction of foreign capital and the setting up of foreign invested enterprises promoted technological development and the economic growth of Chinese industry. It also impacted on the employment system and the situation of Chinese workers. In fact, along with the development of different types of enterprise, continuous changes have taken place in enterprise level employment relations over the last two decades. There have been changes in the recruitment and payment system and also in trade union density and the place of the trade union.

Changes in the employment system

As a constituent part of the planned economy, the SOEs had a permanent employment system which was epitomised by the so-called 'iron rice-bowl'. The government assigned almost everyone in urban areas a permanent job with certain welfare benefits. But people did not have the freedom to choose their work and the managers of SOEs could not recruit or dismiss workers as required. An indication of what this meant is that, in 1979, total 'quits and fires' in SOEs amounted to only 0.03 per cent of the total workforce (Ding et al 2002: 432).

The traditional employment system rested on two key elements. First, all enterprises under the system were operated by the government instead of the market. The central government drew up the economic plan and transmitted it to the local government, which in turn passed it to the enterprises. Different government levels had the right to determine the supply of raw materials, investment and human resources. Managers of SOEs had the role of implementing the government's plan.

Second, there was a registration system (the hukou system). This enforced the separation of urban and rural areas. Under this system, people were categorised as urban and rural residents according to where they were born. It was difficult for people to change their units. In particular, it was almost impossible to change their place of residence from rural to urban because the government restricted people's movement in order to protect employment in the urban areas. Today, the hukou system remains but in a weakened form.

Following the initiation of liberal policies, the state held down employment in the public sector. Between 1978 and 2001, employment in the public sector as a whole (including the state bureaucracy) increased slightly from 75 and 76 million but the number of employees in collective ownership units declined from 20 million to 13 million in the same period (NBSC 1979; MOLSS 2001).

In the mid-1980s, the state also decided to introduce a labour contract system in the SOEs of some provinces. This meant that workers were employed on contracts of specified duration. According to the official statistics, the number of such contracted employees in public units had reached 9.9 million by the end of 1988, 7.2 per cent of the total number of workers and staff in the SOEs (Chen, S. H. 2003: 155). This initial implementation of the labour contract system was, in effect, only a first step to the universal abolition of the permanent employment system. Following publication of the Labour Law in 1994, both public sector companies and private enterprises – in which the number of employees had increased to 37 million by 2001 – started to use contract system nationwide (MOLSS 2001). In fact, this gives managements the unilateral right to dispense with workers' service at the end of the specified period, which is often of one year only. Workers have the right to request that they be granted an open-ended contract after 10 years but managers, on their side, have every right to refuse such requests. There has therefore been a very considerable overall gain in flexibility of employment to the clear advantage of employers.

Another important personnel reform was implemented with the SOEs reform in 1992. This was the so-called 'three systems reform', which involved the reform of employment, wage distribution and social insurances. This meant that the government would no longer be responsible for the employment norms in the enterprises and the managers of the enterprises gained the license to recruit and dismiss the workers. The reform of the employment system also resulted in the increase of labour mobility. With the ending of legal restrictions that went with the hukou system, a huge number of rural migrant workers came on to the labour market. New employees now entered enterprises through the labour market instead being allocated to them by the government. In addition, managers of SOEs gained the right to determine wages and bonus payments and the existing enterprise welfare system was replaced by a social insurance system for old age, medical needs and housing.

The reform of the employment system, the creation of the labour market and the reform of the SOEs led to a serious oversupply of labourers. In spite of the dramatic increase in national economic activity, the growth in the number of employees in urban areas was relatively limited, up from 98 million in 1978 to 112 million in 2001 (NBSC 1979; MOLSS 2001) and according to official data, despite the new flexibility of labour facilitated by the contract system, the rate of registered unemployment in urban areas has been lower than 4 per cent in recent years. However, this unemployment rate excludes the many laid off workers who are surviving at home with no pay and the large number of workers who are in fact out of work puts pressure on those actually at work and makes them fearful for their jobs. Generally speaking, the reform of employment, especially the implementation of the labour contract system has had a significant impact on employment relations. Let us now consider now the trade union situation.

The trade union situation

According to Trade Union Law in the PRC, all trade unions in mainland China must belong to the All China Federation of Trade Unions (ACFTU), which is accordingly the biggest trade union in the world. There are two main forms of organisation in China. Local federations of trade union are the main organisational form and industrial unions are the secondary form. At present, there are 31 provincial trade union federations and 7 national industrial unions in the ACFTU. The effects of industrial unions are comparatively limited.

Under the planned economic system, the Government, as the representative of the interests of the whole society, controlled the economy through various administrative units, and the workers were designated the 'masters' of the enterprise and the state. In accord with Leninist theory, the ACFTU was to serve as a 'transmission belt' between the Party and the workers. The basic function of the trade unions of enterprise level was to assist the enterprises' managers to organise the workers to fulfil the production assignment. Workers, for their part, regarded the trade union critically as 'an official union' or the 'accessory of the managers'. In other words, the trade unions were not, and were generally not seen to be, independent organisations.

With the deepening reform of the SOEs and the rapid increase of Chinese private owned enterprises (POEs) and foreign invested ones (FIEs). the contradiction between managers and employers on the one side and workers on the other has been growing, especially with respect to aspects of the payment, working hours and working conditions. For instance, the number of employees engaged in labour disputes has increased continuously in recent years and the number of workers involved in disputes has been rising over the last decade (Table 4.1 below).

Table 4.1   Labour Disputes in China Handled by All Levels of Mediation Offices, 1993–2001

	Labour disputes handled by all levels of mediation offices (10,000s)	Employees included (10,000s)
1993	1.2	3.5
1994	1.9	*
1995	3.3	12.3
1996	4.8	*
1997	7.2	22.1
1998	9.4	35.9
1999	12.0	47.4
2000	13.5	42.3
2001	18.4	61.0

Source: MOLSS (1993 to 2001).
*Not available

Currently, every worker is required to join the trade union after they sign the labour contract with the enterprise. By the end of June 2002, the ACFTU had more than 130 million members in approximately 1.67 million trade union organisations (ACFTU 2002: 57). Table 4.2 shows the change in union density over the last decade. In SOEs, POEs and TVEs (the town and village enterprises), union density is high, with even some increase over the 1990s. Union density has also been relatively high in FIEs although there was no substantial growth in the density during the 1990s. However, by 2001 trade union density in FIEs halved to 40 per cent, along with the rapid growth in the number of such companies. More than 70 per cent of FIEs are labour intensive manufacturing firms, with the investment coming mainly from Hong Kong, Taiwan and South Korea (Bill et al 2003: 127). Many employers from these areas refuse to allow trade unions, despite the illegality of this. In many small scale FIEs and POEs, the trade unions are weak or do not exist at all. Unionisation in such enterprises is also hampered by the fact that many of them recruit migrant workers from rural areas who know little trade unions and who are extremely vulnerable. But Chinese trade unions generally have little effect anyway. The ACFTU has tried to set up collective bargaining systems in various companies in order to safeguard the workers' interests, which has met with resistance in many FIEs and POEs, few of which will permit this. Nor do the leaders of trade unions at grassroots level have enough power to bargain with the employers (Zhao 2001: 97).

In China, the effectiveness of trade unions is also challenged by the legal framework. Workers, for example, have no legal right to strike. Under the existing political system, Chinese trade unions also have to continue to play multiple roles. The trade union is the organic extension of the Communist Party in enterprises and union leaders are the official representatives of the Party. Protecting employees' interests does not sit happily with serving the Government's liberalisation programme. Neither do local governments generally support trade union activities since they are primarily concerned with economic development – based on attracting foreign

Table 4.2   Trade Union Density in China by Type of Ownership (per cent)*

	1990	1996	1999	2001
SOEs	92.2	92.7	92.4	94.2
POEs	69.5	70.6	77.6	75.9
FIEs	78.3	80.2	79.7	40.2
TVEs	**	**	70.4	82.3

*In some trade unions, the density rate does not include temporary workers.
**Not available
Source: Bill et al (2003): 126.

and private investment (Chen, F. 2003: 1010). Even so, the changes in labour relations and the recent increase in labour disputes ('strikes' are illegal in the PRC) has required the trade unions to play a more positive role to safeguard workers' interests. Moreover, to some extent the ACFTU has had to re-evaluate its position and modify its policies in accordance with the changing situation.

The 1992 Trade Union Law defined a new form of industrial relations and new function for the trade unions. It began to take protecting workers' interests as the primary and the basic function of the trade union (Howell 1998: 160). Based on the transition, the trade unions in different levels began to change their system and style of work. In the mid-1990s, the ACFTU stressed that safeguarding the workers' economic interests is the basic function of the Chinese trade union. In 1999, the leader of the ACFTU promoted a series of new tasks for the trade unions, including assisting the government to provide basic guarantees for the living standards of laid-off workers and to help them to find new jobs; safeguarding the economic interests of the workers; speeding up trade union organisation in foreign and private enterprises and getting the largest possible number of workers organised in trade unions; and promoting collective contracts in different kinds of enterprises. The above reforms signify a shift from the union as the transmission belt of the Party in the direction of playing an important role on behalf of workers in the new form of labour relations.

The development of the white goods industry in China

So much, then, for the general background. What of the white goods industry? The white goods industry was one of the first to open to market forces and though the industry has its own unique features its history provides an important insight into industry development in China more generally and into changes in labour relations in enterprises since the reform process began.

The Chinese white goods industry has become fully fledged under the market economy, but its origins go back to the 1950s. Since the inception of reform and opening-up in the late 1970s, the industry has expanded rapidly. At present, the white goods industry is a major player in the national economy. Furthermore, China has emerged as one of the largest white goods producers in the world.

Refrigerator production in China began as early as 1957 and it was the first sector of the white goods industry in China to develop. At that time output amounted to only 1,600 units and such small-scale production continued till the late 1970s with output having risen to 50,000 units by 1980. Washing machine manufacture started later, in 1978, and the sector developed rapidly. Output had reached 250,000 units by 1980 (CLIA 2002: Table 1-2).

From the mid-1950s to the early 1980s, there was little market demand for household appliances because of the very low income of most Chinese people. Very few owned white goods products. For instance, there were only 0.2 refrigerators and 6 washing machines per 100 families in urban areas in 1981. The gross value of household appliance output was still only $103.8 million in 1980 (NBSC 1999). The bicycle, the watch and the sewing machine were called the 'Big Three' home appliances in urban families. To understand how the once modest white goods industry of China became a leading one world-wide, it is necessary to have a closer look at its historical development.

Giving the 'Go Ahead'

The white goods industry was one of the first industries that was opened to market forces and world competition. In particular, it was amongst the first industries in which foreign investment was permitted. Unlike the energy or defense industries, the state did not see it as a 'key' or 'pillar' industry and in the mid-1980s local governments began to encourage the import of assembly lines from abroad to set up household appliance factories in the hope of promoting their local economies. Some local governments even set aside money from their budgets for enterprises to purchase such imports. At state level, administrative control had been reduced and enterprises were given more freedom to develop, the first significant expansion of the white goods industry took place in line with these developments from the mid- to late 1980s. The number of refrigerators produced increased from 0.19 million units in 1983 to 6.7 million units in 1989 while the number of washing machines increased from 3.7 million to 8.3 million. Freezer manufacture began in 1986, though at this time there was still no microwave or cooker production (CLIA 2002: Table 1-2, 5).

A huge market demand was the primary driving force behind the expansion of the white goods industry in this period. As mentioned earlier, the growth rate of GDP was remarkable in the 1980s as well as afterwards. Meanwhile, the incomes of the Chinese people grew continuously. On average, the annual per capita national income rose by 4.1 per cent between 1985–9, and the consumption level was up by 3.1 per cent in real term (NBSC 1991). As a result, market demand for household appliances increased. However, small-scale production failed to meet the demand and imports were too expensive for the majority of the Chinese consumers. Refrigerators and washing machines were therefore in short supply, resulting in high profits. Household appliance factories found they could quickly make profits through the increased production that resulted in wider ownership of these appliances. By 1988, there were 28 refrigerators per 100 urban families (NBSC 1999).

At this time, almost all the manufacturers were small-scale, state-owned or collective-owned enterprises (SOEs or COEs). For example, in the early

1980s Meiling Company, which is now a major producer in China, had been a small-scale, state-owned factory that produced light industrial machines. The predecessor of the Haier Group, now the largest producer of the white goods in China and a major world producer, was a collective-owned factory with a workforce of less than 800 workers. Today it has 30,000 employees (Haier Group 2004). The managers of what had originally been relatively small factories had been given more managerial authority by the government and the white goods industry and benefited by belonging to one of the first industrial sectors to operate according to the market system.

Another feature that explains the rise of white goods is the large number of foreign technologies and production lines that were introduced to China. For instance, by the mid-1990s more than 100 white goods production lines had been imported by factories in different provinces, nine modern refrigerator production lines being introduced from Italy alone (Fan 2004). Meiling was one of those to import from Italy, commonly referred to as 'the nine brothers of Ariston'. Haier imported from Germany. On the one hand, the imported modern technology helped to promote rapid development and laid the foundation for the Chinese white goods industry that exists today. On the other hand, though, this soon led to over-production.

The first half of the 1990s witnessed the restructuring of the industry. Production of refrigerators and washing machines declined slightly from 1989 till 1991 (Table 4.3). The decrease was connected to a wider economic restructuring. At that time, the national economy was in the adjustment period, and the profit of state-owned enterprises dropped significantly. As the macro-economic situation took a turn for the better in 1992, the manufacture of white goods began to grow steadily, the industry going through a period of structural readjustment up until the mid-1990s.

Table 4.3   Production of Refrigerators and Washing Machines in China, 1989–1995

Year	Output (000 units)	
	Refrigerators	Washing machines
1989	6,710	8,250
1990	4,630	6,630
1991	4,700	6,780
1992	4,860	7,080
1993	5,970	8,880
1994	7,680	10,940
1995	9,190	9,480

Source: CLIA (2002: Table 1.2).

Especially in the refrigerator sector, large enterprises merged or acquired small enterprises, thus increasing their market shares. For instance, by 1995, there were a total of 186 refrigerator enterprises in 19 provinces, most of them small. In that year, the top five companies among them contributed 50 per cent of the total output and 61 enterprises made loses (NBSC 1995; Chen, S. H. 2003: 240). In terms of the market share, several large domestic companies controlled the market and some famous brands such as Haier, Kelon, Meiling and Little Swan became well-known among the Chinese consumers.

In general, from the late 1980s to the mid-1990s, the output of Chinese household appliances went up and a balance was basically struck between production and the market. Through mergers and acquisitions, several large companies have developed swiftly and their brands have become very popular among the Chinese consumers. Domestic companies were dominant in the Chinese market. Furthermore, remarkable progress had been made in product technology and quality. Therefore, an official report by the Chinese Light Industrial Association (CLIA) regards this period as the 'golden age' of the Chinese domestic household appliances industry (CLIA 2002: Chapter 1).

Towards the end of the restructuring of domestic industry in the mid-1990s, however, the 'golden age' of domestic white goods industry came to an end. The Chinese white goods industry has been affected by economic globalisation, and a growing number of foreign companies have begun to enter the Chinese market.

Going global

China's low labour costs and preferential tax policies have made it an attractive country for foreign investment. In addition, local governments extended support to foreign companies in order to persuade them to invest in their areas. Many manufacturers also regarded China as a huge potential market. Almost all the famous multinational household appliance manufacturers have come to China pushing up the production of white goods to unprecedented levels. Unit production of both refrigerators and washing machines approached to 16 million in 2002 (Table 4.4).

The entry of foreign capital resulted in changes in the ownership structure. Many SOEs and COEs were transformed into joint venture companies (JVCs). For instance, Electrolux set up a joint venture company in Tianjin to produce compressors and also invested $41.4 million to establish a joint venture company with the Changsha Zhongyi Group in 1995. Whirlpool carried out similar investments in both refrigerator and washing machine factories. Bosch-Siemens also set up joint venture refrigerator and washing machine companies in Anhui and Jiangsu provinces. Bosch-Siemens, in particular, has been offered preferential policies by the local government.

Table 4.4   Production of Refrigerators and Washing Machines in China, 1996–2002

	Output (000s units)	
	Refrigerators	Washing machines
1996	9,800	10,750
1997	10,440	12,550
1998	10,150	12,070
1999	11,190	13,420
2000	12,790	14,430
2001	14,390	13,340
2002	15,990	15,870

Source: CLIA (2002: Table 1-2; 5).

Bosch-Siemens, for example, purchased a state-owned enterprise. The local government officials considered the company, not only as a European company but as one that needed to be looked after as part of the industry in their province (Zhang 2002). Indeed, when the company laid off workers, it helped to deal with them.

However, in the early days of their operation, several joint venture companies were unsuccessful (CLIA 2002: Chapter 3). There were several reasons for this. For example, some foreign producers were not familiar with the Chinese market, its consumption patterns and styles of product, and this caused their products to under perform in the market. Then again, although many foreign companies took the form of joint ventures with Chinese home appliances enterprises, some of them failed in their dealings with the former managers of these enterprises and with local governments. Problems of management also impacted on production. It was, for example, with these sorts of considerations in mind that the local government promoted Bosch-Siemens Company to take complete ownership of the refrigerator and washing machine companies in Anhui and Jiangsu provinces in which it had previously had only joint venture status.

Concentration

As a consequence of the entry of foreign producers, the Chinese-owned white goods companies faced heightened competition. Compared to other industries, the household appliance industry is one of the most highly concentrated. One indication of this is that between 1995 and 2001 the number of brands of refrigeration appliances and washing machines fell from more than 200 to 20 (China Euromonitor 2002). In 2001 there were around 1,200 household appliance enterprises of various kinds (including foreign investment enterprises, though excluding non-state owned

Table 4.5   The Share of the Top Five Companies in Total Production in China, Refrigerators and Washing Machines, 1996–2002

	Share of top 5 companies in total production (%)	
	Refrigerators	Washing machines
1996	64	54
1997	68	62
1998	73	67
1999	72	69
2000	66	65
2001	66	73
2002	60	68

Source: CLIA (2002: Table 1-9, 13).

enterprises in which sales income was below \$0.6 million per year) but less than 10 per cent of companies controlled about 90 per cent market share (CLIA 2002: Chapter 3).

The course and extent of concentration differs between sub sectors. In the case of the microwave oven sector, manufacture began in the early 1990s. Before 1997, there were more than 30 local brands. Through drastic market competition, no more than ten enterprises still remain. The output of the top 5 companies accounted for 77 per cent of the total in 2002. The Glanz Enterprises Group Co. in Guangdong Province, the leader of the sector, had a 60 per cent market share in 2001 (China Euromonitor 2002). In washing machines, the 54 per cent of production accounted for by the top five companies in 1995 had risen to 68 per cent by 2002. By contrast in refrigeration whereas the top 5 companies (Haier, Kelon, Samsung from Korea, Xinfei, Meiling) had achieved a 73 per cent share by 1998, by 2002, their share had actually fallen, to 60 per cent of the total (Table 4.5). The contributing factor was that more and more foreign brands were now fighting for a share of the market. By the end of the 1990s, most foreign companies had completed their localisation processes and had become familiar with the Chinese retail network, production and market. Their predominance in technology, management and brands began to play a key role and their production and market share increased significantly (CLIA 2002: Chapter 1). Such developments at home were accompanied by growing exports.

Exports

Since the mid-1990s, exports have grown significantly, mainly to Asia, North America and Europe and Haier now has the biggest refrigerator sales in the world (Xiao 2002).

Table 4.6   Domestic Home Appliance Exports from China, Refrigerators, Washing Machines and Microwaves 1995–2002 (thousands of units)

Year	Refrigerators	Washing machines	Microwave ovens
1995	650	500	1144
1996	720	560	1496
1997	1230	710	2073
1998	1280	530	3244
1999	2293	654	5819
2000	3546	1008	8368
2001	4531	1615	12526
2002	6103	2267	20345

Source: CLIA (2002: Table 1-14).
Note: Domestic home appliances include refrigerators, freezers, washing machines and microwave ovens.

Between 1995 and 2002 refrigerator exports rose approximately nine-fold, washing machines almost five-fold and microwaves seventeen-fold (Table 4.6). Several factors contributed to the rapid growth in exports. Firstly, most of the Chinese white goods manufacturers had been affected by the oversupply of the domestic market since the mid-1990s. There were 87 refrigerators and 92 washing machines per 100 urban families in 2002 (NBSC 2002 a) and the penetration rate exceeded 100 per cent in some large cities. For instance, there were 107.4 refrigerators and 102.8 washing machines per 100 families in Beijing (Beijing Statistic Bureau 2001). Whilst the foreign companies began to expand into the market in China, some large domestic companies, such as Haier, Kelon and Meiling, also tried to expand overseas markets. The exports of refrigerators of the Haier Group, for example, accounted for nearly 30 per cent of its gross output in 2002. In the Xingxing Freezer Company, exports reached 36 per cent in the same year. (In order to gain more overseas markets, some Chinese companies are also setting up factories and research centres abroad, rather than simply exporting products.)

A second factor behind the growth in exports from China is to be found in the market strategies of the big multinationals. MNCs regarded China as an export production base as well as a huge market. For instance, 82 per cent of refrigerators produced in the Shanghai Sharp Company go for export. And 72 per cent of microwave ovens produced in the Suzhou LG Company owned by Korea go for export in 2001 (CLIA 2002: Chapter 1). The growing influence of foreign companies was not only evident in exports but also in the domestic market.

Domestic markets

Foreign-funded companies have taken up an increasing share of domestic markets in recent years. During the second half of the 1990s, the largest part of the domestic market was shared by four Chinese famous brands (Haier, Kelon, Xinfei and Meiling). Since then, however, some top world brands like Samsung, LG, Sharp, Siemens, Whirlpool and Electrolux have become well-known among the Chinese consumers and have begun to share much of the domestic market. Because of the increase in the foreign brands, some previously famous Chinese brands in domestic markets have started to disappear or lose market share. For instance, a leading world brand, Electrolux, replaced Zhongyi, a famous domestic brand. Likewise, Siemens eliminated Yangzi which was another major player in domestic markets until recently. In terms of sales, three (Samsung, LG and Electrolux) of the top 10 refrigerator companies were FIEs or JVCs in 2002, as were four of the top ten washing machine companies (CLIA 2002: Table 1-6).

Against this background, however, a growing proportion of domestically owned capital has also been poured into the white goods industry by both public and private sectors. For example, in 2003, the Greencool Company, partly financed by Hong Kong capital, bought stock in the Meiling Company, a famous state- owned enterprise in Anhui Province. This was regarded as an example of the Chinese government's policy of 'promoting the reform of state-owned enterprises and strategic cooperation with foreign and private capital' (Eastday 2003). In addition, several household appliance companies (which previously produced TVs and air conditioners and other products) have been moving in to white goods production. Sometimes this has been done by purchasing SOEs that are in difficulty and changing them into white goods plants.

The huge potential of the domestic market appeals to both foreign and domestic capital. Over the last two decades, the urban market has become almost saturated but the rural market not yet been tapped. China has more than 900 million rural residents in approximately 200 million families. Household appliance possession is very low. There were 13.6 refrigerators and 29.9 washing machines per 100 rural families in 2001 (Table 4.7). This was nearly equal to the penetration rate for urban families in 1986 (Yan 2002).

The inadequate level and growth of farmers' income has so far limited their spending. In 2001, for example, the income of rural residents rose by only 4.2 per cent compared to the 7.8 per cent growth rate of urban residents' income (Yan 2002). In addition, the insufficiency of the power network in the countryside has resulted in an unreasonably high electricity price. Farmers are forced to pay more than urban residents. Insufficient water supply and road transport have also limited the ability of manufacturers to expand in the rural areas. For all these reasons, manufacturers will find it difficult to expand in the rural market in the near future, despite its huge potential consumer base.

The entry of China into the WTO in 2001 is widely expected to lead to further changes. After WTO entry, import tariffs on household appliance products were unilaterally reduced and the Government committed itself

Table 4.7   Possession of Main Household Appliances in China, 1990–2001 (Units per 100 families)

Year	Refrigerators		Washing machines		Freezers in urban areas	Microwave ovens in urban areas
	Urban areas	Rural areas	Urban areas	Rural areas		
1990	42.3	1.2	78.4	9.12	*	*
1991	48.7	1.6	80.6	11.0	*	*
1992	52.6	2.2	83.4	12.2	*	*
1993	56.7	3.1	86.4	13.8	1.6	*
1994	62.1	4.0	87.3	15.3	2.3	*
1995	66.2	5.2	89.0	16.9	2.9	*
1996	69.7	7.3	90.1	20.4	3.5	*
1997	73	8.5	89.1	21.9	4.5	5.4
1998	76.1	9.3	90.6	22.8	4.5	8.5
1999	77.7	10.6	91.4	24.3	5.4	12.2
2000	80.1	12.3	90.5	28.6	6.0	17.0
2001	81.9	13.6	92.2	29.9	6.6	22.5

Source: CLIA (2002: Table 6-4).
* Not available

to the elimination of non-tariff barriers. In particular, it became easier for foreign companies to import capital in order to expand their presence in the Chinese markets. The desire to move into rural areas is likely to increase as competition among foreign and domestic companies stiffens in urban markets. In line with this, the Government has already decided to develop strategies in order to boost the purchasing power of rural consumers, and thereby, to sustain the long-standing economic growth of China (Kynge 2003).

ChinaCo

This section, based on the fieldwork in ChinaCo, a foreign owned refrigerator factory, considers changes in ownership (from a SOE to a JVC to FIE) and related changes in management strategy, the payment system, recruitment, change in workers' status and the role of the trade union, all of which developments can hopefully now be better understood in the context of the previously outlined Chinese economic reform and the wider development of the Chinese white goods industry. Our information derives mainly from interviews conducted with 50 workers, using the standard interview schedule, supplemented by further, longer worker interviews; from a questionnaire completed by 44 management and related staff, and further function- specific interviews with foreign and Chinese managers; and from interviews with trade union officials.

From SOE to FIE

Currently, ChinaCo, in Anhui Province, is owned by a European company, which is one of the biggest white-goods manufacturers in Europe. Located in East China, Anhui Province is one of the major agricultural and most populous provinces in China. Industrial restructuring in the province has resulted in the supply of the workforce outstripping demand. Compared with other provinces in East China, it is in the middle in terms of economic development level. In the mid-1980s, the provincial government decided to provide policy incentives in the hope of vigorously developing the household appliance industry. The main advantage of Anhui is the cheap labour they can offer. The average wage of employees in the province was 7,980 yuan ($964) per year in 2001, lower than the 14,040 yuan ($1,696) national urban average in China (Lin 2003) and lower still than the 17,764 ($2,145) average wage in the much more prosperous Shanghai (Ma 2002: 385). Apart from this, the convenient location and preferential policies of the local government as it attempts to emulate developments in the coastal areas have led several leading household appliance manufacturers in the world to set up factories in Anhui.

ChinaCo is situated in what is for China a medium-sized city with a population of about a million and a hinterland of a further 3.3 million people. There are few large enterprises in the city. Like other cities in China, the state-owned enterprises in the city are in the process of undergoing changes in ownership, and many of them are making losses. Labour supply is abundant. For instance, no more than few hundred thousand residents are employed in the work units or enterprises in the urban area. By 2002, there were approximately 40,000 enterprises, of which only about one per cent were large and medium-sized and the majority were small and labour-intensive. In 2002 there were about 20 large and medium-sized foreign-funded companies. ChinaCo is the only one in the city that is part of a world top multinational corporation.

The predecessor of the present company was a small state-owned iron and steel factory. In the mid-1980s, the factory imported a refrigerator assembly line from Italy and began to produce refrigerators. In 1992, when it had over 2,000 employees, it ranked No. 2 in China's cooling appliance companies in term of sales volume. By 1995, output had reached 0.6 million units and the brand had become popular among Chinese consumers. Given this, the managers decided to increase the scale of the company and they invested a great deal of money in air-conditioner and other products. Then in the mid-1990s, due to the level of competition in the household appliance market and management problems in the company itself, the company began to make a loss. At the same time, the European company was looking for an opportunity to invest in China. Following negotiations, the European company invested $82.25 million and took 70 per cent of the company's stock. Thus, in 1996, the operation became a joint stock company and its name was changed as well.

The new company was not successful during the period of the joint venture. In order to reach European production standards, the European managers sold almost all the old equipment at a very low price and invested substantial funds to upgrade the technology.

A serious problem occurred in the retail network. The European managers were not able to control the original retail network, which was informal and depended on personal relations. Sales volume decreased from approximately 0.5 million in the early 1990s to 0.2 million in 1998 and production costs could not be reduced without substantial changes in management and manning levels. Relations between the managers from China and Europe deteriorated. They differed significantly on the number and types of the product that the factory should be producing. The Europeans wanted to reduce output, improve quality and produce for the high end of the market, which they reckoned to be the profitable way forward. The Chinese managers wanted to keep up output and produce for the lower end of the market. The European managers also decided that they would use their European brand instead of the previous one. This decision worsened the relations between the two sides still further. The situation hit rock bottom at the end of 1998. The Chinese side could not afford the heavy losses. They had to sell all the stock cheap to the Europeans in order to repay their bank loans. In 2001, the company's name was changed again and it became a wholly European-owned enterprise.

At present, the company produces various models of refrigerators. There are three different cooling techniques: static cooling, dynamic cooling and non-frost cooling and both the top end of the market and the less expensive segments are catered for. Altogether the factory produces more than 20 different models to meet the requirements of different customers. The production capacity of the factory is 0.8 million refrigerators per year. It has maintained an annual output of more than 0.4 million units since 2001 and aims to expand production gradually. ChinaCo has a strong presence in the top end of the market, especially in the large cities. Since 2001, its products have been exported to East Asia and some European countries.

The company claims to produce refrigerators with the highest production and environmental standards. It also claims to have produced the first refrigerator in China with computerised temperature control. Managers are proud they have introduced the most advanced technology from Europe to China. The plan is to continue to achieve the highest production standard possible; to be the leader in technological development; and to increase market share.

The status of workers in the company

A special meaning attached to the status of workers under the planned economy. Chinese workers were regarded as the 'leading class' and the 'masters' of enterprises but as an old worker in the company commented:

> Did you ask me about workers' status? What a strange question you have asked me! I haven't heard the word for several years. Who still cares

about the workers' status today, in the 21st century? To be honest, it is not necessary to think about and answer the question. As a worker, the most important thing is to earn money and keep the job.

The average wage in the company is approximately $133 per month – half as much again as for the local area but only three quarters of wages in Shanghai. Compared with the other enterprises in the city, the workers' income ranked among one of the highest. For instance, the workers in the company earn almost twice as much as those who remain in the still existing part of the SOE to which the refrigerator plant once belonged. Many workers in the city are employed in small SOEs and COEs, the majority of which have made losses since the early 1990s. Workers in these enterprises have suffered financial difficulty. They have been laid off and lost their jobs as they went bankrupt or merged. Compared with those enterprises, ChinaCo, the largest foreign holding company in the city, holds a definite attraction for most workers.

The payment system has changed along with change in ownership. The SOEs' wage reform has been underway since the early 1990s (and as with other companies in China), a new payment structure – the skill-related pay system which took no account of seniority but gave more scope to the recognition of performance criteria, was implemented in the mid-1990s (Zhao and Nichols 1997: 88). Although total pay has increased since 1996, the basic part of workers' wages has declined. After the company took full ownership, a new payment system was introduced, which is still in force. This reduces the proportion of the basic wage and links pay strongly to performance.

There are three parts to workers' pay. A basic, fixed, part accounts for 40 per cent of the total wage. A further 30 per cent is based on performance at workshop level. The remaining 30 per cent is related to individual performance. In this way, assessment by managers potentially plays is a very important part in determining workers' income. Besides the wage, workers may receive subsidies in accordance with government regulations and a year-end bonus. In 2001 and 2003, the company made good profits. Workers' average wages rose five per cent each year. Apart from certain welfare benefits, local government regulations require that workers are provided with money to counter the effects of hot weather in summer and to help with heating costs in winter to a total value of about $22. During the three Chinese traditional festivals, $60 is paid to every employee each year. In addition, according to the Chinese laws and regulations, the company set up social insurance schemes for the employees (including old-age insurance, unemployment and medical insurance) and a housing fund. Besides the above, there are almost no other non-wage benefits in kind. This is in sharp contrast to the range of benefits available under the SOE.

Although 64 per cent of workers we interviewed are satisfied with their incomes, more than 20 per cent of workers consider some problems remain in the wage structure (which many believe, wrongly, to be the same that applies in the company's European operations). According to the chairman of the trade union:

> About 10 per cent of the workers are not satisfied with the wage system. The workers hope that the share of the fixed wage can be larger than it is now. Then their income can be guaranteed to a higher degree.

For the workers, there is an even more unsatisfactory part of the wage system than the low fixed element. This concerns the system of annualised hours. ChinaCo management has made working time flexible in relation to the production season. As a manager explained:

> One feature of refrigerator production is that it is based on different seasons. Every year we have busy season (from April to October) and low season (from November to March). In the busy season, the workers may need to work 11 hours a day and 7 days a week and there should be workers on shift 24 hours a day. In low season, we give the overtime working-hours back to workers. They may work 5–6 hours a day and 4 days a week. In any case, the work time isn't longer than that prescribed in the Labour Law [the 1995 Labour Law specified an eight hour working day].

Workers particularly resent the two shift arrangement (each shift works 11 hours) which makes them very tired in the busy season and for which they get no overtime pay. They have made several complaints about the annualised hours system and the trade union chairman has relayed their complaints to the general manager. But he is keen on retaining this.

Recruitment and the labour contract

There were circa 1,100 regular employees in the company in 2002, three quarters of whom work on the production lines. On average production workers are 30 years old and about two thirds of them are men. China has a vast rural population. However, the hukou system has meant that this particular generation of Chinese workers typically have urban origins. Nearly 60 per cent of those at ChinaCo have fathers who were themselves industrial workers. Almost two thirds of them have high school education and the company wants to employ more, better educated workers in future. Since the company established the joint venture with the SOE a double-track system has been used to train the new workers in order to get high-quality skilled recruits (students study theory and basic knowledge in class for two years and workshop practice for one year). The company recruits about 60 students at junior grades for this every year in conjunction with a local technical secondary school.

Besides the regular contract workers, the company has hired some temporary workers on three-month contracts in the busy season since 1997. The majority of these are laid off workers from the city's SOEs. These have an average age of 30 and are 80 per cent male. Most of them are engaged in less skilled work. They are paid on the bottom pay grade. At the end of 2003, in a new departure, about one hundred such workers were made contract workers. One of them was Li. His story underlines the importance of getting a contract job at ChinaCo. Thirty two years old, he had worked as a seasonal temporary worker on three month contracts for the previous five years. During this time, he said, he had always felt insecure but the contract that he now had – for one year only – might in future, he hoped, be extended to two years, which would make for relative job security, and as he also pointed out, this company paid wages on time and pension, unemployment and housing contributions. His wife works in a garment factory where it is common for workers to work 12 hours a day in order to reach their production quotas, which are impossible to meet in eight hours. In the light of this, he is 'definitely very satisfied with the job'.

Under the planned economy, workers were assigned to jobs by the government and almost all of them were permanent workers. The 1995 Chinese Labour Law promotes labour flexibility. As a consequence, more than half of the workers in the company are on two years contracts, only a minority of workers from the SOE having been offered open ended contracts despite their years of service.

The labour contract system had a serious impact on the workers' status. Firstly, it is possible for the number of workers to be readily cut. In 1999, the general manager of the company decided to cut 200 workers. When the workers' contracts expired, the company would not renew them. This redundancy resulted in a labour dispute. However, the company still did what it wanted. For the sake of political stability, the local government agreed to pay more than 600,000 yuan ($72,464) to the redundant workers in order to end the dispute (Zhu 1999).

Secondly, the contract system is an important means whereby workers can be controlled. The company only rarely terminates a contract at the end of the period. However, it is possible that the company will not renew it, either because of the market situation – or because of the worker's behaviour. As the HRM manager put it: 'Workers who are not competent to do their job or do not behave well will be selected out. The basic way is not to extend the contract'.

Because of the state of the local labour market and the relatively high income received by ChinaCo workers, most want to keep their jobs. This makes the labour contract an important source of leverage for mangers, even more useful than the 60 per cent variable element in the calculation of their wage. The logic is clear enough: 'We must work hard. Otherwise, the company may not extend our contracts'.

The fact that the company seldom fails to renew contracts is not the point. Workers know this. They also know it could decide not to renew them.

The implementation of management methods

The European managers aim to raise productivity and profits. Considering the role of modern management methods, the General Manager commented:

> The most important thing is to help the employees to understand that the company must make profit and operate regularly. The workers, even some managers might not know the names of management theories. But many theories have been used in the company. These theories have benefited both company and employees. Although the theories came from abroad, they are suitable for China. Since most of the theories have been successfully used in many companies in the world, why not in China? However, it is not easy to make the employees understand the methods at the beginning. For this reason, the company has not used 100 per cent of these methods. We implement new methods gradually.

Managers and workers in the company are aware of modern management methods to different degrees. Workers are clearly knowledgeable about total quality management, team working and just in time, which have all been implemented in the company. Other methods such as kaizen and flexible production are less well know, at least by name (see Table 4.8), though they have experienced their effects at first hand.

ChinaCo has its own quality-productivity package, which has been developed by the European parent company. It is regarded as an important part of the parent company's corporate culture. It stresses the importance of team working in the whole production process, with communication, cooperation and improvement being regarded as key elements. In 1998,

Table 4.8   Management Methods Known by Workers at ChinaCo (percentages)

	Workers
Team working	92
Total quality management	88
Just in time	72
Quality circles	56
Lean production	46
Kaizen	18
Re-engineering	16
Flexible production	16

a special section was set up in the Production Department. Two full-time staff are responsible for its work in the company.

The section organises work teams. Once a month, each team discusses the problems that should be solved next month. The discussion is held at shift handover. The manager of the Production Department and the two full-time staff hold a liaison meeting to exchange information once a month. The section also focuses on communication between the management and the workers in the workshop. Generally, the workers elect representatives to hold irregular meetings with the management. The representatives are expected to know workers' ideas and requirements, and to pass these on to the manager. This form of the meeting began in 1999. The section monitors the quality of goods from suppliers and seeks to link supplies to production in order to improve quality. It also promotes a suggestion scheme for employees. From 2002, a new field management tool named '5S' (sort, set in order, shine, standardise and sustain) was introduced. Most employees are of the view that both the special section and 5S have been useful in raising productivity and reducing errors during the production process. However, there are a number of workers who are dissatisfied with 5S. They complain that it has added to the pressure on them – a complaint that is made in other respects too.

Workers' views on their jobs and the changes in the company

As can be seen from Table 4.9, on the face of it, the majority of workers are satisfied with their current jobs. Around 65 per cent of them or more indicate that they are very satisfied or satisfied with a whole number of factors – pay, work prospects, fellow workers, physical working conditions, the way their section is run, the use of their abilities and the interest and skill in their jobs. Partly these results are a function of their expectations being set at a low level; partly they are a function of the related consideration, that these jobs are good compared to others on offer to them. Indeed, almost two thirds of them agreed that their jobs were good ones for people like them and in answering questions they would often begin by saying 'Compared to other workers' – and compared to most others in the city they are doing well. The following view is typical:

> As you know, I am 36 years old, with only high school education. It is difficult for me to get another good job. So many workers have lost their jobs or have been laid off, and their situation is not good. I have a job and can earn more than $120 per month, so I feel that the job is valuable for me. At present, you could not imagine having an easy job like we had in the SOEs in the 1980s. You have to work hard no matter what kinds of enterprise you are in. General speaking, to earn money and support my family is my aim. In the company, if you work hard, then you can earn money and keep your job.

Table 4.9   ChinaCo Workers' Satisfaction with Various Aspects of their Jobs
(percentages)

	Very satisfied	Satisfied	Dissatisfied	Very dissatisfied
Your usual take home pay	2	62	30	6
Your work prospects	2	65	31	2
The people you work with	22	70	8	0
Physical working conditions	2	72	19	6
The way your section is run	8	84	8	0
The way your abilities are used	8	63	20	8
The interest and skill involved in your job	10	63	22	4

Table 4.10   ChinaCo Workers' Assessment of Changes in the Company Over
the Last Five Years (percentages)

	Better	Worse	Same	Don't know
Right to make decisions	15	9	51	26
Workload	15	63	15	7
Pay	63	6	25	6
Stress	11	65	20	4
Satisfaction	29	18	42	11
Job security	38	17	27	19
Job prospects	23	15	25	38

Nevertheless, 94 per cent of workers told us that they would not like their children to do a job like theirs and they have mixed views on the transformation that has taken place in the company's ownership and its implications for them. A summary of their views on some of the changes that have taken place since the European company took over (five years before our interviews with them) suggests two things (Table 4.10). The key thing is that most see the pay to be better – but most also see this to have been at the cost of increased stress and increased work load, not least in the shape of the 11 hour long shifts of the peak season, which now extends for five to six months of the year. Few think that their involvement in decision making has increased. In fact, half the workers responded to the question we asked about this that they had not been involved in decisions under the SOE and that they were not now.

Generally, workers think more highly of the European managers (who occupy the top positions) than the Chinese ones, some of whom are referred to as 'traitors'. They are commonly said to be more concerned with data and rules than was the case for managers under the SOE and they are rated positively, mainly on the basis of the fact that their methods have delivered better wages. But the other side of this has been that work has got harder.

The trade union

The change of ownership and resultant disorganisation meant that the trade union ceased to exist for a period of about 10 months in 1997. When it was reinstated it retained its earlier organisational structure. The Chairman, who is a former SOE manager (which is not unusual in China) and who is also the Secretary of the Communist Party in the factory (which again is not unusual), was re-elected following the standard democratic centralist procedures and like the other two full time staff, the Vice Chairman and Secretary, is paid by the company.

At the end of 2003, union density stood at 99 per cent, but this excluded temporary workers, even though the ACFTU holds that all workers have the right to join trade unions. Following representations made to it by the trade union Chairman, from 2002 it became company policy that every regular worker would have five paid days holiday, which is a benefit not found in other local firms. Also in 2002, the company was persuaded to pay social insurance (for unemployment, retirement pension and medical insurance) for temporary workers as well as for regular workers. Other benefits that came about because of the union's involvement include a $0.50 per day lunch subsidy and a decision by the company to pay $3,600 per year so that workers can rent a venue to play sport. None of these improvements are subject to binding agreement but the trade union is highly rated by the city's trade union federation and its recognition as an advanced unit has been marked by a 'Multi-Love and Double-Rank' award. Difficult to translate, this award signifies, in the first part of the couple, 'Multi-Love', that the employees love the enterprises and that the enterprise loves the employees; the second part, 'Double-Rank', means something like 'Praise be to the good employees who love the enterprise; and praise be to the good employers who love the employees'.

One of the European managers told us that he had initially been doubtful about reinstating the trade union but he had come to appreciate it:

At first, I wasn't convinced. I knew the power of trade unions in Europe. They always fight for workers' interests. But I was told the main function of the Chinese trade union is so- called 'twin protection', that is, to promote the development of the enterprises and to protect the workers' interests. The union's staff keep in touch with workers in the workshop and let me know what they are thinking on a regular basis. I meet the Chairman once a month. So I can understand workers' opinions and deal with them. The trade union gives the company a great deal of help. Compared with a European trade union, I like Chinese trade unions very much.

All this is clearly no recipe for militancy. Indeed, there is no collective bargaining. The trade union has asked for collective bargaining rights many times but the General Manager has claimed that decisions about this cannot be made at his level and the trade union Chairman is in any case aware of another difficulty, for as he sees it, Chinese Labour Law is ambiguous, stating that a collective contract 'shall be' concluded by the trade union on behalf of the staff and workers with the enterprise, not that it 'must' be concluded. The management can get expert advice on how to deal with the trade union and how to interpret the law from a number of sources including the European parent company and its membership of a federation of foreign businessmen in China. It cultivates its relation to local government and can usually rely on it for support. The union officials are largely isolated and can get little help from the city's trade union federation, which thus far has little experience of dealing with labour relations in foreign enterprises.

The trade union Chairman emphasises that ChinaCo is a private company in which, partly for reasons of language, workers cannot communicate readily with managers, and that only the trade union can do this and represent their interest. He also claims that the trade union (compared with the trade unions of FIEs) is one of the best unions not only in the city, but also in the province. In this he may be right. Even so, most of the union's work is to transmit workers' views to management; wherever possible, which it is not for the most part, to improve workers' working conditions; and, in no small part, to help workers with whatever personal problems that they may have, including for example problems with the state bureaucracy. The effectiveness of the union basically comes down to the individual diligence and abilities of its officials, especially the Chairman, who knows that things are no longer as they were under the SOE:

> Relatively speaking, it is much easier to participate in the management in state-owned enterprises. Here, management make decisions by themselves. We get to know about things after they have been decided. Sometimes, we haven't known a decision has been made until a problem arises or workers have come to tell us. Then it's difficult to deal with. We are in a passive position.

The union has no impact on the key issues that concern workers – such as working time and labour contracts. The majority of workers, 77 per cent,

Table 4.11   How Good the Union and Managers are at Various Activities as Assessed by ChinaCo Workers (percentages)

Percentages 'very good' and 'good'	Union	Managers
Keeping everyone up to date about proposed changes	31	58
Providing everyone with the chance to comment on proposed changes	33	62
Responding to suggestions from employees	43	68
Dealing with work problems you or others may have	37	72
Treating employees fairly	37	58

said that if they had grievance they would take it to management, not to the union. One of them summed up the situation: 'the union staff are nice. I'd like to chat with them. But if I have grievance, I have to take it the manager. It is almost useless to take it to the union'.

Recognising the limitations of the trade union, about 40 per cent of workers still rate it (essentially meaning the Chairman and his fellow officials) as 'very good' or 'good' but most rate the company's managers higher on various criteria (Table 4.11).

Currently, the union's officials are doing their best to deliver workers' opinions and safeguard their interests. Nevertheless, their role and effectiveness is limited to what influence they can exert as individuals. Although there are about a dozen worker representatives, they have no role at shop floor level and are confined to making suggestions at the twice yearly workers' congress.

Conclusion

Generally, then, we have a situation in China in which the white goods industry – one of the first to be opened to market forces – has grown rapidly, along with the rising standard of living of the urban population and aided initially by the import of modern technology. This success, and of course cheap wages, has attracted foreign direct investment. It has also led to a situation in which Chinese companies have been rationalised through the force of foreign competition on their home territory and in which they, and foreign capitals, have entered the export market.

Workers like those at ChinaCo have had the historically significant experience of living through the shift to capitalism. In the specific case of ChinaCo, those who have remained in employment – and many have not – have experienced working in the same plant but, over the course of a limited span of years, they have undergone a change in status from 'masters' of the SOE, to employees in a joint venture, and then to being employees in a foreign owned private company in which they are dependent on short term contracts. The positive outcome of this exposure to market forces, from their point of view, was that they get better wages than were to be had elsewhere, and better wages than they had hitherto. Whether this continues to be the case remains to be seen. But even at the time of the fieldwork reported on here (2001–02), whereas workers had a certain appreciation of the professional competence that the foreign management has brought to bear in generating these wages, they were also very clear that this had a downside. The downside, which in the absence of collective bargaining, the trade union is in no position to substantially effect, is harder work, longer hours and increased stress. Better wages or not, workers have no desire for their children to follow in their footsteps.

Note

1 Collective owned enterprises (COEs) were an important form of ownership to be found in both rural and urban areas (concentrated on here). In principle, COEs rely on collective funds, are responsible for their own profits and losses, have democratic management and distribution according to work. The number and role of COEs has declined continuously since the mid 1980s.

References

ACFTU (2002) *Blue Paper on Chinese Trade Unions' Safeguarding of the Legitimate Right and Interests of Worker and Staff Members*, Beijing, Chinese Workers Press.

Beijing Statistic Bureau (2001) 'The Information of Citizens' Income and Consumption in Chinese Top Ten Cities', *Beijing Information Newspaper*, 16 February.

Bill, W. K., Chang, K. and Li, Q. (2003) *Industrial Relations in China*, Cheltenham: Edward Elgar Publishing Limited.

Chen, F. (2003) 'Between the State and Labour: The Conflict of Chinese Trade Unions' Double Identity in the Market Reform', *The China Quarterly*, 176.

Chen, S. H. (2003) *The Change of the Employment System from the Planned to the Market System*, Beijing, China Financial Economy Press.

China Euromonitor (2002) *White Goods in China*, GMID Report, http://www. eurmonitor.com/gmid/default.asp.

CLIA (2002) *The Report of Chinese Household Appliances Industry in 2002*, Beijing, Information Centre, Chinese Light Industry Association.

Ding, D. Z., Goodall, K. and Warner, M. (2002) 'The Impact of Economic Reform on the Role of Trade Unions in Chinese Enterprises', *International Journal of Human Resource Management*, 13 (3).

Eastday (2003) Greencool Company Held Stock in Meiling Company http:// qsy.eastday.com/epublish/gb/paper488/1/class048800001/hwz1147380.htm

Fan, L. X. (2004) 'The Developing History of the Yangzi Company', *The Report of the Economy in the 21ˢᵗ Century*, 11 May.

Haier Group (2004) http://www.haier.com.cn/chinese/about/index.html

Howell, J. (1998) 'Trade Union in China: The Challenge of Foreign Capital in *Adjusting to Capitalism: Chinese Workers and the state*. Edited by O'Leary G. Armonk, NY: M. E. Sharp.

Jiang, X. J. (2002) *Foreign Capital in China: Its Contribution to the Upgrading of Structure and Competition*, Beijing, Chinese People University Press.

Kynge, J. (2003) 'Can China Keep its Economy on Track?', *Financial Times*, 22 September.

Lin, L. (2003) 'Research in Industrialisation in Anhui', *China Information Net*, 24 March.

Ma, X. (2002) 'Social Life in Shanghai', *Shanghai Year Book*, Shanghai, Shanghai Year Book Press.

MOLSS (2001) 'Statistics Bulletin of Labour and Social Insurance in 2001, http://www.molss.gov.cn/index_tongji.htm

MOLSS (1993–2001) Statistics Bulletin of Labour and Social Insurance From 1993 to 2001, http://www.molss.gov.cn/index_tongji.htm

NBSC (1979) Statistics Bulletin of National Economic and Social Development in 1978, http://www.stats.gov.cn/tjgb/ndtjgb/qgndtjgb/t20020331_15372.htm

NBSC (1991) The Bulletin of National Social and Economic Development From 1986 to 1990, http://www.stats.gov.cn/tjgb/ndtjgb/qgndtjgb/t20020331_15385.htm

NBSC (1995) The Results of the General Survey of Industrial Sectors in 1995, http://www.stats.gov.cn/was40/outline?page=1&channelid=14522&presearch-word=%B5%E7%B1%F9%CF%E4

NBSC (1999) The Improvement of Living Standard of Urban Residents since the Reform, http://www.stats.gov.cn/tjfx/ztfx/xzgwsnxlfxbg/t20020605_21434.htm

NBSC (2002a) The Growth of the National Economy, http://www.stats.gov.cn/tjfx/ztfx/yj16da/t20021003_36771.htm

NBSC (2002b) The Situation of the SOEs, http://www.stats.gov.cn/tjfx/ztfx/decjbd-wpc/t20030909_107246.htm

NBSC (2002c) New Stage of China Opening to the World, http://www.stats.gov.cn/tjfx/ztfx/yj16da/t20020929_36630.htm

Xiao, J. (2002) 'Haier Is the No.1', *Chinese Industry and Business Times*, 13 November 2002.

Yan, X. (2002) 'Rural Market Failing to Spur Domestic Demand', *China Daily*, 20 August.

Zhang, Sh. (2002) 'The General Manager of Siemens Company Praises Chinese Investment Environment', *Anhui Daily*, 6 June.

Zhao, M. and Nichols, T. (1997) 'Management Control of Labour in State Owned Enterprises: Cases from the Textile Industry' in G. O'Leary (ed.) *Adjusting to Capitalism: Chinese Workers and the State*, Armonk, NY: M. E. Sharp.

Zhao, W. (2001) *The Changing Situation of Chinese Workers*, Beijing, Chinese Wujia Press.

Zhu, J. X. (1999) 'Report of Labour Dispute in a Foreign Company', *Anhui Workers Daily*, 16 July.

5

Taiwan: The Disappearance of the 'Golden Tale' – White Goods in a Changing Global Economy

Wen-chi Grace Chou, Theo Nichols and Surhan Cam

Introduction

Taiwan, with a population of little over 22 million, is renowned through-out the world for its strong rates of economic growth in the three decades or so up to the 1997 Asian financial crisis and for its pronounced export orientation. Most particularly, it is known for its OEM (original equipment manufacturing) of garments and textiles for American and other buyers in the 1960s and 1970s, including large retailers like K-Mart, and for its shift to the production, again for export, of second tier electronics products thereafter. Taiwan's white goods industry (we focus particularly on refriger-ators) has attracted much less attention, though it played its part in the country's early development, and is characterised, among other things, by two particular features that inform what we have to say here. One of these concerns the extent to which the industry has itself now gone off-shore from Taiwan, especially to China, so that China now substantially serves the Taiwan- based industry as an OEM producer, with consequent pressures on what refrigerator production that still takes place in Taiwan. The other concerns the implications of Taiwan's white goods industry having been dominated by Japanese companies and the extent to which employment in these companies – once highly regarded by Taiwanese employees for their wages and conditions of work (the 'golden tale') – are now themselves transforming under the perceived pressure of international competition.

In what follows we first outline what has been happening to the industry in Taiwan and its place in local-global relations and then turn to examine the case study. The case study company (TaiwanCo) received its first foreign direct investment from Japan in the early 1960s. This serves to remind us that although Taiwan is often referred to as a NIC (Newly Industrialising Country), outside the leading sectors its industry is by no means as uniformly 'new' as this might suggest. In the case of TaiwanCo, this has implications for the age-structure of its workforce, which in turn has financial consequences for the company because of retirement arrangements and seniority pay. Suffice to say, TaiwanCo has not only been in existence for a relatively long time, it has also seen better days. Managers recall that it used to be the case that 'one sale followed another'. Now, the prosperous past has gone. With the reduction of import tariffs in 1986 and the entrance into the WTO in 2002, the pressure to cut costs has become intense and employees, who used to seek the company out for its 'Japanese' employment practices, including its reputation for lifetime employment, now fear for their jobs.

The white goods industry in Taiwan's economy: locality and globality

The development of Taiwan's white goods industry

The domestic appliances industry in Taiwan started in 1949. Thus, the domestic appliance industry has been in existence in what is commonly regarded in the west as a 'Newly Industrialised Country' for more than 50 years. It is primarily centred on the home market. However, the domestic market has reached saturation point, added to which significant technological innovation has not been easy to achieve. Therefore, several domestic producers have started to set up new offshore production sites and expand their market abroad. As regards the total value of production, it was 1,464 million US dollars in 2002, down from 1,573 million US dollars in 2001 and 1,800 million US dollars in 2000. Between 1993 and 2002, the average growth rate was –3.6 per cent and in the last five years has been –7.8 per cent (Electrical Industry Yearbook 2003: 1–7).

In recent years, the domestic appliance industry has faced increased labour costs and difficulty in acquiring land. What is more, it has faced competition from both Japan and China, with the higher technology of the former and the lower labour costs of the latter, not to mention the rise of Korean branded products. Many different methods have been adopted to cope with increased global competition. At the company level, managers have downsized the labour force and attempted to reduce waste so as to promote efficiency. In seeking to retain the domestic market in Taiwan, they have emphasised enhancing the function of products, sales channels, after-sales service and the diversification of products. In terms of increasing production and sales, the strategies to increase competitiveness include outsourcing, cooperating with international producers and taking advantage of lower costs in China.

Taiwan white goods production in its international context

In January 2002, when Taiwan first became a member of the WTO, the average import tariffs for industrial products were 6.03 per cent. This was expected eventually to go down to 4.15 per cent. Refrigerators had an import tariff of 10 per cent for a 500–800L refrigerator, with a tariff for larger models of 5 per cent. These were expected to go down in 2004–2006 to 4.2 per cent and 4 per cent respectively. In addition a 12 per cent tax allowance was also removed, making for further difficulty.

Generally speaking, Taiwan's white goods have not performed well in international competition because they are faced on the one hand with cheaper products from China or the Southeast Asian countries and on the other with more advanced technology from Japan. Although the domestic market used to be dominated by the main appliance companies operating in Taiwan, the reduction of tariffs in 1986 and the entrance into the WTO in 2002 have meant more pressure. As a result costs and wages have been targeted, acquisitions and mergers have taken place, with increased diversification, overseas investment, attempts to increase exports and to supply the home market with imported rather than domestically produced goods. In 2001 for example, two firms, Tong-Yun and Sampo, merged to expand the scale of their enterprise and reduce costs. Sampo also attempted to make an agreement Grundig of Germany with a view to producing refrigerators and air conditioners under the Grundig brand name in the European and global markets (Taipei Times 2003).

Industry sources in Taiwan claim that labour costs amount to about 10 per cent of the total cost in the domestic appliance industry. The greatest expense is the key components, which account for about 80 per cent of the total cost. The remaining 10 per cent comes from the cost of land, marketing and management, etc. Taiwan imports some of the key components of domestic appliances. Forty per cent of the key components of washing machines and air conditioners are imported, as are 20 per cent of the key components of television sets and refrigerators. After joining the WTO and reducing tariffs, China was able to export cheap components directly to Taiwan. In the future, it is likely that many of the components for Taiwanese brands of appliances will be made in China and imported to Taiwan for assembly. Alternatively, complete machines will be made by OEM in China.

The impact of both China's and Taiwan's entry into the WTO is likely to be two-sided. On the one hand, Taiwan may have to prevent dumping from China. On the other hand, China is becoming Taiwan's 'backyard'. Sampo, for example, believing that WTO entrance would be permitted sooner or later, decided to get into China early on, for both production and sales, in the hope that its market share would be better secured. As we will see later, the openness of the market and the fierce competition among local producers in Taiwan and China has had a profound influence on local workers in Taiwan.

Refrigerator production, sales and major companies

The refrigerator market is mainly dominated by Sampo, Matsushita Electric Taiwan, Tong-Yun, Sanyo, Tatung, Kolin, Hitachi and others, all of these having connections with Japan, either in the form of investment or by means of agencies. Among them, Tong-Yun is the agent for many international brands; Kolin, in addition to its own brand, is also the agent for Samsung (Korea) and Mitsubishi (Japan); Sampo is the agent for Sharp Appliances (Japan); Tatung is the agent for Toshiba (Japan).

Sales of refrigerators are closely connected to the size of the replacement market, the marriage rate and the prosperity of the economy. With the increase of the national income and the gradual improvement in living standards, over 95 per cent of all households now have refrigerators. Many families now own two or more refrigerators. Most of them bear the names of domestic brands, which share 70 per cent of the total market followed by imported brands such as Samsung, Goldstar, GM, Whirlpool and Mitsubishi Japan. Recently, LG has taken a very active part in the Taiwan market, which it entered through extended TV exposure and big promotion schemes. Considering refrigerator production volume from 1991 to 2002 it can be seen that in 1995 the production of refrigerators reached its peak of 522,539 and then decreased to 409,573 in 2000, increasing to 493,565 in 2002. It can also be seen that although export volume increased sharply at the end of the period, unit prices have been in more or less continuous decline throughout (Table 5.1).

More refrigerators are imported than exported (Figure 5.1). From 1989, three stages in imports/exports can be discerned. First, there was a steady increase in exports and a decline in imports until 1997. Then, under from the impact of 1997 Asian financial crisis, exports experienced a decline and some stagnation until 2000. And recently, exports, though still at a low level compared to imports, have again tended to increase. In 2002, the total value of exports was 76.7 million US dollars compared to imports of 158.1 million dollars. Due to the maturity of the domestic market, local producers have had to increase their share of the export market.

In 1989 Taiwan's refrigerators were mainly exported to Japan, Hong Kong, the USA, Indonesia and Singapore (Table 5.2). By 2003, this had changed to China, the USA, Hong Kong, Singapore and Japan. Clearly, China has become the largest importer of Taiwan's refrigerators (15.4 per cent of them in 2003). This increase was not a gradual process but a jump. Before China's entrance into the WTO, its proportion of imported refrigerators was less than 2 per cent. But it suddenly increased to 7.2 per cent in 2002 and, by January 2004, it had reached 19.4 per cent. Collectively Middle East countries have also become an important destination for Taiwan's refrigerators, partly because the temperatures there are similar.

Imports from countries in the same region with lower labour costs have grown between 1989 and 2003, especially from Korea, China, Thailand and the Philippines, whilst the share of high-wage countries has declined, including USA and Japan (Table 5.3). Before 2000, the share of China's imports to Taiwan was less than one per cent. After 2001, it continued to increase, reaching 5.6 per cent in January 2004.

Table 5.1 Production and Sale of Refrigerators between 1991 and 2002 in Taiwan (US Dollars)

Year	Production Volume	Production Value	Unit Price	Domestic Volume	Domestic Value	Export Volume	Export Value
1991	388,828	175,123,394	430	388,680	176,706,303	27,166	2,017,273
1995	522,539	247,030,364	471	518,589	249,218,030	20,696	4,910,364
1996	465,806	231,316,273	494	486,020	249,020,303	31,391	6,795,788
1997	432,283	205,811,455	472	442,446	217,849,424	43,297	11,486,091
1998	455,359	206,826,970	453	472,470	222,138,970	40,270	10,296,939
1999	413,931	184,280,667	445	438,633	202,517,212	40,238	10,717,121
2000	409,573	151,971,424	376	456,798	176,981,424	49,841	13,668,939
2002	493,565	153,840,303	313	458,385	146,248,242	74,735	20,698,455

Source: Industry Technology Information Services (ITIS) Database.

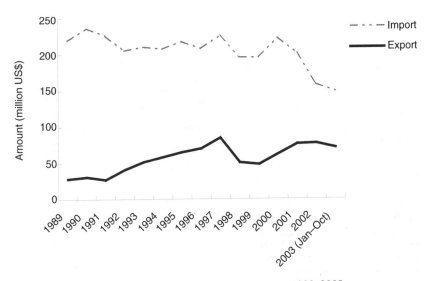

Figure 5.1   Imports and Exports of Refrigerators, Taiwan 1989–2003
Source: Directorate General of Customs, (DGOC), Ministry of Finance; Ministry of Economic Affairs, The Statistics of Trade, http://cus.moeaboft.gov.tw/cgi-bin/pbisa60.dll/customs/uo_base/of_start. (Product No.8418).

Table 5.2   Destinations of Refrigerators Exported from Taiwan, 1989 and 2003 (US Dollars)

1989		2003	
Country	total	Country	Total
Japan	7,264,212	China	10,549,571
Hong Kong	6,149,520	USA	8,078,701
USA	3,911,335	Hong Kong	7,423,882
Indonesia	2,653,787	Singapore	4,485,637
Singapore	1,321755	Japan	4,189,696
Thailand	1,083,629	Vietnam	3,688,668
Philippines	1,052,835	Philippines	3,445,413
Malaysia	485,926	United Arab Emirates	2,750,955
Australia	454,039	Israel	2,568,923
Pakistan	433,291	Malaysia	2,520,302
Korea	395,128	Kuwait	2,249,538
U.K.	382,856	Saudi Arabia	1,486,931
Total	28,350,255	Total	70,656,330

Source: Directorate General of Customs, Ministry of Finance; Ministry of Economic Affairs, re-calculated from The Statistics of Trade.

Table 5.3   **Countries from which Refrigerators were Imported to Taiwan, 1989 and 2003 (US Dollars)**

1989		2003	
Country	total	Country	total
USA	144,317,071	USA	53,741,578
Japan	29,416,231	Japan	28,850,441
Korea	15,104,707	Korea	26,559,837
Thailand	10,614,585	China	9,852,400
Denmark	5,342,745	Thailand	9,410,327
Sweden	3,090,405	Denmark	5,569,083
Netherlands	3,049,522	Philippines	2,648,875
Italy	2,949,497	Italy	2,305,695
France	1,153,665	Germany	1,848,387
Germany	939,234	France	1,509,056
Indonesia	527,441	U.K.	764,797
U.K.	522,600	Switzerland	658,437
Total	219,708,528	Total	148,500,220

Source: Directorate General of Customs, Ministry of Finance; Ministry of Economic Affairs, re-calculated from The Statistics of Trade.

Table 5.4   **Major Refrigerator Producers and their Use of Imports in Taiwan, 2002**

	Domestic production	Import	Total Domestic Volume	Imports as Percentages of Domestic Sales
Matsushita-Taiwan	65,237	2,124	67,361	3
Sampo	58,000	19,400	77,400	25
Sanyo	44,950	12,050	57,000	21
Tatung	44,500	0	44,500	0
Tong-Yun	28,700	36,200	64,900	56
Kolin	27,500	6,400	33,900	19
Hitachi	11,400	13,700	25,100	55
Others (Domestic)	5,500	0	5,500	0
Others (Import)	0	88,700	88,700	100
Total	285,787	178,574	464,361	38.5

Source: Information held by TaiwanCo (2002).

A sign of the weakness of Taiwan as a refrigerator producer is that almost four out of ten of the refrigerators sold by major domestic producers were actually imported by them from other countries (Table 5.4). Apart from Tatung (a Taiwanese owned company) and Matsushita-Taiwan, most producers in Taiwan import a significant proportion of the refrigerators they sell and two of these firms, Tong-Yun and Hitachi, import more than half of the refrigerators that they sell in Taiwan.

The top five companies share around 67 per cent of the market. But it is indicative of what has been happening that the largest selling refrigerator producer is not Matsushita Electric Taiwan, which has the largest share of domestic production, but the Sampo company whose imports constitute a quarter of all its Taiwan sales.

TaiwanCo

Historical background of the company and its transformations

TaiwanCo's origins go back to 1949 and the China-Japan Trade Treaty. In 1953, encouraged by a four-year plan for economic development, the company established a factory to manufacture radios and related components. In 1954, Regulations for Foreign Investment were enacted and the owner increased the output of the factory both in overall quantity and in the number of items through funding from US aid and bank loans. In 1956, the factory was enlarged and moved to Taipei County and thus, like other major appliance producers in Taiwan, gained proximity to the main domestic market. In 1960 and 1962, Regulations for Investment Encouragement and for Technological Cooperation were separately enacted, in the hope of benefiting from a link to Japan. TaiwanCo led the way, being founded as a joint venture with a Japanese company in 1962. Following this, many instances of foreign investment followed. The first refrigerator was made in TaiwanCo in 1965.

When TaiwanCo was formally established in 1962, the original capital investment was 0.3 million US dollars, which within ten years had increased significantly to 4.5 million US dollars. In 1970, the company made its one hundred thousandth refrigerator. Capital investment continued to increase for the next ten years – from 1973 to 1982 – 4.5 million US dollars rising to 20.6 million US dollars. Total accumulated capital reached 68.8 million US dollars in 1992. While at the same periods, the total number of employees increased from 2,431 in 1972 to 4,300 in 1982 and 5,995 in 1992.

TaiwanCo paid good wages and company welfare benefits. It also built up a very good image among employees. It was regarded as one of the best employers. Once employees joined the firm, there was no need to worry for the future, since TaiwanCo had the reputation of never making people redundant and of providing good quality welfare and training. As testimony to this, most of its workers stayed with the company a long time.

In 1989, TaiwanCo set up another company in Tao-Yuan County, one and a half hours away by car from the parent company. This started to operate in 1991. Altogether six factories were set up on the new site to produce refrigerators and other goods. Expectations were high. But after only a few years, in 2001, the Tao-Yuan factory closed and in its place the company built a new factory in Xiamen, China. One of the major goals was to improve and enhance cooperation between Taiwan and China. The company in Taiwan would mainly be responsible for making white goods, AVC and large products, while the company in China would mainly be responsible for producing motors and small domestic appliances (Company Newsletters 2002). As the management sees it, moving production off-shore in order to reduce costs is more advantageous than manufacturing in Taiwan, especially since high levels of severance pay and a lump-sum retirement payment from the employer can be avoided.

In 2002, TaiwanCo set up five main objectives in order to respond to market competition as a member of the WTO. These were: to ensure the company's market share in Taiwan; to cooperate with the parent company in technological development; to supply goods and materials for the Japanese market; to support the Great China business circle (a reference to the fact that the Japanese partner has now also invested in China and set up a China-Northeastern Asia headquarters); and to support the R and D of overseas companies in Eastern Asia. The already established so-called 'YKH/Half-size' mission is a major company programme to reduce 'waste' and boost innovation and it plays a major part in this. Although most company managers are not familiar with the term 'Lean Production' (as opposed to 'TQM' and 'QC') the similarity between aspects of lean pro-duction and YKH/Half size is marked. (YKH are the initials of the Japanese words whose original meanings are 'Rigorous', 'Start' and 'Innovation'. The 'Half size' speaks for itself.)

By now, TaiwanCo has been in existence for 40 years. The Japanese company – in effect the controlling power – has responded to the new global economy by setting up a China-North Eastern Asia headquarters, including Korea, Taiwan, Mainland China and the Republic of Mongolia, and TaiwanCo. It has established a global division of labour. The strategy is to import high-priced products from Japan directly or to have them part-made in Taiwan (also see Kawakita 1997: 81); to make mainly middle-priced products, which make up as much as 60 per cent of the appliance market, mainly in Taiwan, except for some components; and to make low priced goods in China.

Most of the higher level managers in TaiwanCo are appointed directly by the parent company. The general manager, who is directly responsible for the company and plant management is always Japanese, though the chair-man of the board is Taiwanese. A large proportion of the managing dir-ectors are also Japanese. Other executives, as a result, have to learn Japanese. The company, and others like it, are thus generally seen as having Japanese management.

In 2002, TaiwanCo employees totalled 2,869, of whom 412 were in the home appliance division and 168 were in refrigerator production. The home appliance division set up the goal of increasing sales (of which refrigerators production amounted to two-fifths) to 96.7 million US dollars, through changes in technology and manufacturing methods. The major production goals set up by the home appliance division were as follows. Firstly, it proposed to continue its three-year quality assurance system; secondly, it would reorganise production, moving away from a mixed assembly system. Finally, it would achieve the highest efficiency possible. To achieve the above goals in the refrigerator factory, the main changes included: enhanced productivity by such means as decreasing the defect rate; reorganising production; increasing productivity per person/per hour by 18 per cent; introducing sub line-systems; restructuring plant layout; introducing new equipment; and producing more large refrigerators for export.

In the past, the factory used a 'mixed production' system in which large and small or medium-sized refrigerators were assembled on the same mixed line. Under this, large refrigerators required 67 seconds Kosu[1] while small and medium-sized refrigerators required 41 seconds average Kosu. One assembly line needed 19 workers and the average inventory days stood at 22 (the latter being affected by severe traffic congestion). The average output of refrigerators per worker per day was 18.5, while on average 28 refrigerators were produced for every square meter of land. (Taiwan is a small country and maximum use of factory space is thus an important company concern.)

When the factory switched over to make large, small and medium-sized refrigerators on different assembly lines, it needed to set up sub-lines to allow production to flow more smoothly and decrease the use of 'Kosu'. It is estimated that this will reduce the total number of assembly line workers from 19 to 17 and the average inventory days from 22 to 20. The increase of productivity will be from 18.5 to 22 refrigerators per person per day, while the amount of land used would of course stay the same.

The refrigerator factory reduced the number of direct workers and indirect workers with a view to reducing their fixed costs. In 2000, the fixed costs were 27.2 per cent of the total production value, but through the reduction in the number of direct and indirect workers and in the other expenses, the fixed costs have come down to 20.2 per cent of the total production value. Over the two years between 2000 and 2002 the total number of direct workers employed dropped 16 per cent in two years with a reduction of 44 per cent of indirect workers. As well as reducing the total number of direct and indirect workers employed, the factory also aims to improve space utilisation. In the two years from 2000, the productivity of an average 'Pin' (a Japanese unit to measure land with one pin equal to 3.3057 square meters) has risen by 17 per cent.

The factory has discarded some production processes, such as painting. It has changed the layout and the flow of production. It has also reduced inventory. It has subcontracted out press work. In 1996, in order to comply with new CFC regulations for environmental protection, the company had already stopped producing its own compressors and started to import them from Singapore; this also impacted on the number of workers employed.

Through the above restructuring, although the total volume of refrigerators produced went down from 85,700 in 2001 to 77,863 in 2002, the capacity utilisation rate of production has increased and productivity has been increased (in terms of Kosu, the average output of each worker per day, the use of factory space, etc.) However, for some parts of their work, they have introduced new equipment from Italy to reduce the time spent on production (from 75 minutes to 15 minutes) and to enhance production efficiency.

TaiwanCo workers have suffered from the downsizing. Moreover, the factory has relied more on subcontracting and has started to deploy agency labour on the shop floor. All the changes have had a great impact on the employees' working experience and their working conditions, as will be seen in the following section.

The impact of corporate restructuring on workers: employment relations and working conditions

The changes in production organisation have had a serious effect on the experience of working, working conditions and employment relations. The following section will mainly focus on the changes in employment structure and employment relations to show how the 'harmony' that managers (and many workers) claim to have characterised TaiwanCo's relation to workers historically has disappeared and how insecure the workplace has become, subject as it is to greater diversification of forms of employment and an attack on seniority-related wages.

Looking at the refrigerator factory only, which is the main subject of the present research, the main parameters are that among the 51 workers interviewed, there were slightly more females than males and over three quarters of all workers interviewed were over 35 years old. Workers younger than 30 years old amounted to under 12 per cent and nearly 40 per cent of the workers interviewed had worked in the company for more than 21 years. A relatively 'old' workforce, this was also a relatively well educated one, nearly seven out of ten of which had graduated from a senior high school or better. The emphasis on educational attainment is increasing. A male worker commented, comparing his own background and first days at work twenty years ago with the situation at present:

> I have been here more than 20 years. Our company had a very good reputation when I was looking for a job in 1981. At that time, there were plenty of job opportunities. Now, the situation has completely changed. For example, the unemployment problem has appeared. My company still recruits new technical workers but they now have to have university and post-graduate degrees.

When asked whether they felt TaiwanCo was a good job for someone like them 60 per cent of the workers said 'yes'; 18 per cent said 'yes in part';

22 per cent said that it was not a good job. But when we went on to ask if they would like their son or daughter to work in the same job, 94 per cent said 'no'. They did not want their children to work in the factory as they had done.

Due to the meagre profits on refrigerators and increasing competition from other imports, TaiwanCo has downsized and rationalised its personnel significantly in recent years. Managers whom we interviewed claimed repeatedly that the last thing they wanted to do was to make Taiwanese workers redundant. However, they also indicated that a guarantee of lifetime employment is no longer applicable in today's conditions. Instead, early retirement and the transformation of the company's age structure is to be encouraged. In other words, their view is that, once a company is faced with operational difficulties, the policy of lifetime employment no longer holds and reductions in either staff or pay are inevitable. These managerial views and related practices are very similar to those found in Japan where long-term employment used to be the prevailing employment system (Higuchi 1997; Berggren and Nomura 1997; Ishikawa 1998; Kawakita 1997).

Some workers took a different view on the question of whether lifetime employment was a contractual term or not:

Lifetime employment is a spiritual symbol of our corporate culture. It is not a contractual term. We have given all our working lives to the company's development. They should not discard us when they do not need us. Furthermore, the company should not threaten us with closing down the factory, which relieves them of their redundancy or retirement requirements. Why should it always be we workers who suffer first and suffer most? It is totally unfair to us.

And:

In the past, lifetime employment brought no problems at all. The company asked us to 'regard our factory as our family' to enhance our commitment. Now, early retirement has to be taken. Faced with market competition, our company was not able to keep its obligations. However, it turned out to be we workers who suffered. No matter how much compensation the company offered, I just want to stay in my job. I have very little confidence that I will find another job. I am very scared and worried.

One of the top managers at TaiwanCo went out of his way to emphasise that lay-offs were the last thing to be considered to meet the needs of the restructuring. Sacking people, in his view, entailed loss of face. (The same idea was introduced by managers into discussions about resort to

OEMs in China. To rely on OEM, it was said, would entail loss of face. They preferred to produce their own products. Other companies might import refrigerators from LG or other foreign firms and put their own brand on them, but they would not.) However, the total number employed dropped by 50 per cent between 1996 and 2002 through early retirement schemes, redundancies, subcontracting out and reducing the number of foreign workers and school workers. Over the same years, agency workers (some of them being TaiwanCo's own retired workers) increased by 25 per cent.

Downsizing has gone through several phases. Before 1998, the first target was workers with an employment history of more than 25 years.[2] After 1998, the company speeded up the reduction in manning by lowering the relevant age and length of service criteria. To encourage workers to apply for voluntary retirement, the company often provided so-called 'Generous Retirement Programs' or 'Early Retirement Programs' (which are not, in reality, 100 per cent 'voluntary'). Age and length of service have become salient issues for workers. Considering the early retirement programme a female worker reflected:

> It will be a big shock to our middle-aged workers especially. It is very miserable. We don't possess high-tech skills. It is not possible for us to open a new business. In addition, similar work, which we could do, is not available and some of it has been relocated abroad. Should we move to another job? Junior and senior workers have different destinies. For junior workers, things would not be very different. But for senior workers, like me, I have stayed here for more than 20 years. It would be impossible to get the same pay as I get here, even if I got the same work. Basically, our wage is seniority-related. But things are changing. Sometimes we don't even get a wage increase.

Currently, retirement payments are non-transferable lump-sum payments paid by the employer, full eligibility for which requires 25 years of continuous service with the same employer. It has been proposed recently to change this into a transferable monthly pension since it has now become unrealistic for a worker to continue to work until retirement for the same company, especially in the case of a large proportion of small and medium-sized companies. However, this measure is still awaiting the approval of the Legislative Yuan and has done nothing for the many workers who have retired early already.

TaiwanCo was known for its policy of lifetime employment. This was an important part of its social prestige as a 'Japanese' company. The company has therefore conducted its retirement or redundancy programs very carefully. It has not only met the legal requirements but also offered better terms to ease 'the heart-rending difficulty of the task' – a term often used by their HRM director and section managers.

As well as seeking to bring forward the retirement of Taiwanese workers, the company has cut down on some workers employed under temporary labour contracts – students and foreign workers employed on fixed three-year labour contract , who lack any entitlement to redundancy payments, unlike their Taiwanese co-workers. The number of student workers and foreign workers has consequently fallen since 1996.

There are still some foreign workers. They are given the 3K jobs (so-called after the Japanese words *gemba-kiken* (dangerous), *kitanai* (dirty) and *kitsui* (stressful)). They work a 12-hour night shift and a contingent shift between the day and night shift. At TaiwanCo they are nearly all female Filipinos, who live in special dormitories, sleeping in bunk beds, several to a room. They typically not only hold higher educational qualifications but, according to interviews with managers, are easy to manage, unlike the Thai men workers who preceded them.

What is happening at TaiwanCo is in many ways recognisable from accounts of what has happened in Japan. For example, reduction in bonuses, decreases in new hiring, early retirements, increased use of non-regular workers and work transfers to dependant companies (Bernier and Mirza 2001). However, in so far as the practice of continuous employment within a single enterprise is slowly giving way in Japan to the practice of continuous employment within a group of enterprises (Sako 1997), this is a policy that cannot be pursued at TaiwanCo because the Tao-Yuan factory closed in 2001.

No matter whether redundancy is effected by 'generous retirement programs' or 'generous redundancy programs', it is clear that what workers really want is to continue to work in the same company. But the continual downsizing of their workforce has made workers realise that this is only a dream and not likely to come true. Now, they can only pray to receive better compensation. As workers, what will be their next destination?

The age and seniority structure in the refrigerator factory means that there are a number of workers who had entered the factory when they were young and now must leave, despite their considerable years of service, when they are in fact only middle aged. Due to the current labour regulations for seniority-related retirement and redundancy and other payments, these workers are very likely to face a hostile external labour market where few job opportunities are available, due to a bias against the employment of older workers. At the same time, unlike their own parents, older workers can no longer rely on the support of their children, which marks a major shift in inter-generational expectation. One worker commented that even when he retired from the factory, he would still have to work, explaining that:

> In the past, we may have had expectations from our children, with the slogan of 'Look after your children and they will look after you when

you get old'. But now we don't have these expectations any more. We had better run our own lives by ourselves. So, I may think of running a small business after I retire.

Internal factory transfer was another way for the company to rationalise personnel. In this process, workers have no choice but accept the transfer; otherwise they must leave the factory. One worker explained:

Due to the downsizing of our previous department, therefore, they put me in the department where I am now. If I hadn't accepted this transfer, I might have been made redundant. I consider my current job as a challenge. In the past, the company wouldn't make you redundant. It worked like the Japanese sort of lifetime employment. Now, you can be asked to leave – it's not hard [to be so invited].

When the economy gets up-graded, our down-market products are very likely to disappear. I don't think if I leave this factory I will be able to find the same kind of job again. So I will lose my retirement payment. I have my family to look after. There won't be any job with the same status. My kids are at school and I need to pay their tuition fees. So, I won't dare to take any risks. There is a joke going around. If you meet someone you know who works in the factory, you say – You're still here?'

Reducing the amount of subcontracting work is also a way of increasing the job opportunities available and securing work for the full-time workers in the company. Some managers claim that this was the reason that the number of subcontracting workers was reduced in 1998. But an interview with the director of the refrigerator factory revealed a change in policy, so that in recent years they had continued to subcontract work out to reduce the number of direct full-time workers and that they had also then deployed temporary workers and agency workers to reduce production costs.

When the firm that recruits TaiwanCo's agency labour takes on new workers the refrigerator factory can decide which workers it wants. And TaiwanCo's relation to its agency labour can be even closer than this. In November 2002, 20 workers were retired. But four of them were then taken on again as agency workers. TaiwanCo wants workers' accumulated skills and expertise; however, it wants to pay them less to save production costs. The current commission fees for agency labour are 15 per cent of the total monthly agency wages. However, TaiwanCo is currently dealing with only one agent. It is hoping to find another agency company to stir up some competition and reduce commission fees and thus production costs yet further.

Besides the increasing use of agency labour, some of the assembly work has been subcontracted to another company, but is actually carried out inside the TaiwanCo factory. The director of the refrigerator plant reflects that in the future this 'one factory but several employers' may make management more not less difficult.

In the words of the HRM manager:

> Our company is a Japanese joint venture company. We have always paid great attention to our workers' rights. When we have to rationalize personnel, we always think whether it is possible to first transfer them to other departments so they can continue to work in the company. If this finally proves unworkable, we will provide better retirement and redundancy programs to reduce our workforce. We feel very sad when this happens, since our workers belong to our big family. To expel family workers is a really disappointing thing.

It is in line with these claims that the company hopes to transform 'lifetime employment' into 'lifetime employability' for their workers (Company Newsletters 2002). They set up a training centre to help with this. They even proposed a program called the 'Follow-Up University'. The idea was to encourage workers to develop new skills in order to move between different departments or factories. However, the company now blames the government for a lack of support for this kind of in-job training and the scheme is not very successful. Without proper re-training schemes, even the director of the refrigerator plant was worried whether he could be re-employed after he retires (hitherto a common occurrence). He feared that, despite his considerable experience, he would be 'deskilled' and 'devalued'.

Looking at the changes over the last five years, workers generally believe that their right to make decisions has deteriorated, the pressure to retire 'voluntarily' to which they and their colleagues have been subject, no doubt play an important part in this (Table 5.5). Their responses to questions about job security and job prospects, stress and workload all also suggest deterioration, with no category we asked about yielding a majority response suggesting improvement. Further responses by workers to some

Table 5.5   Workers' Views on How Things Have Changed at TaiwanCo

N = 51 Percentages	Better	Worse	Same	Don't Know
Right to make decisions	12	71	12	6
Workload	20	51	24	6
Pay	33	35	29	2
Stress	18	57	22	4
Satisfaction	24	41	26	10
Job security	18	59	26	2
Job prospects	12	59	20	10

Table 5.6 Workers' Views on Their Job at TaiwanCo

N = 51 Percentages	Strongly Agree	Agree	Neither agree or disagree	Disagree	Strongly disagree
My job requires that I work very hard	20	53	14	14	0
I never seem to have enough time to get my job done	14	22	41	22	2
I feel my job is secure in this workplace	6	20	20	49	6
I worry a lot about my work outside working hours	12	61	22	6	0

Table 5.7 Managers' Views on How Things Have Changed at TaiwanCo

N = 51 Percentages	Better	Worse	Same	Don't Know
Right to make decisions	42	26	28	6
Workload	24	65	10	2
Pay	57	24	18	2
Stress	26	63	10	2
Satisfaction	22	53	24	2
Job security	14	65	16	6
Job prospects	4	34	10	3

standard questions that we asked reinforce this interpretation. Seventy three per cent reported that their job required that they work 'very hard'. The same percentage reported that they worried a lot about their work outside working hours (Table 5.6).

Managers also reported increased job insecurity, stress and workload, though interestingly they also report both increased right to make decisions and better pay, the former being in part the other side of workers' insecurity and the latter their reward for the effecting a tighter operation (Table 5.7).

At the time of the field study in 2002, unemployment in Taiwan had crossed the five per cent level – a historic high, excepting the 1970s oil crisis. This was a societal issue, which figured prominently in the mass media, and workers were fully alert to it. Despite the deterioration in their condition, the relatively good performance of the company, their seniority in the firm, which still carries some reward, and, for many of them, the threat, were they to leave, of the loss of their seniority-related advantage (in pay-off compensation and retirement payments) all contribute to the decision that most of them have made to stay with TaiwanCo as long as they can.

The company union

Labour unions in Taiwan are mostly enterprise unions. The TaiwanCo labour union is no exception. It was set up in 1965, three years after the company was established. Labour unions in Taiwan seldom become involved in collective bargaining to improve conditions for workers and most of the agreements at TaiwanCo were copied from the Labour Standards Law.

As should be clear already, the most serious problem in the company at present is that workers lack protection for their working rights, many who want to continue to work having been asked to apply for retirement or early retirement. Workers want to continue to work till they are 60, but the company asks them to retire before this. Union representatives sum up the situation like this:

> Three years ago, we had 6,000 workers. We have fewer than 3,000 workers now. However, if the company had not reduced its labour force, it might have had to shut down. Although the company has its own reasons for laying-off workers, those who have accepted retirement or redundancy workers complain 'Why me?'

When asked about the union's views on the employment of foreign workers and temporary/student workers, the union representatives told us:

> To be honest, from our standpoint it was a bad move to introduce foreign workers. Those foreign workers are a threat to our employment rights. How should we protect them? We have 100 or so foreign workers. A few years ago, we had more than 300 of them. We continued to nego-tiate with our company to reduce the number of foreign workers and as a result the company reduced the whole labour force, foreign workers and Taiwanese workers too.

The foreign workers are not members of the union, student temps are – or at least some of them were. But recently they have refused to pay their union fees, which are of no benefit when they go back to studying. TaiwanCo advised the union not to charge union fees to the students since they needed to take home as much money as possible, especially if their parents were unemployed. So, when the labour union increased the union membership fees from NT40 to NT60, they also stopped collecting such fees from the student temps. The workers had little solidarity with them and the major concern for the labour union is the situation of their own permanent workers. As far as the Taiwanese student temps were concerned, it made no difference to them whether they joined the labour union or not. They thus were unwilling to pay membership fees to it.

Of no use to foreign workers or student temps, the union is no use to agency workers either. Agency workers are not TaiwanCo 'employees' (or in the case of re-hired retired former employees are no longer formally so) and they cannot join the TaiwanCo union. Union officials realised that agency workers were severely disadvantaged. They were under a different contract and could not receive the major company benefits, or at least, not all the relevant seniority-related benefits. As regards the re-employment of the company's retired workers as agency workers, it was argued it was better for them to be able to carry on working after receiving their retirement payments; otherwise they could be unemployed at an age when it might be hard for them to find work.

The union is also in retreat on other issues that concern permanent workers. What were the union's views on seniority allowances, promotion and wage increases? According to a union official:

> Seniority allowances work as they did in Japan, but have gradually changed. Lifetime employment has broken down in Japan. In the poor economic climate, the company is anxious for most senior workers to retire in order to save costs. Promotion is no longer on the basis of seniority. It has now become 'performance-orientated' and 'performance dominated'. Lifetime employment may still exist for civil servants in the public sector. However, this may need to change in the future. In TaiwanCo, there will be negotiations with the labour union about the level of the wage increase, where the major principle is workers' performance.

He went on to give an example:

> We will have a certain rate of wage increase. But, within this level, the wage increase will be differentiated by different people's work performance and work appraisal – graded from A to D. For example, if the standard wage increase is 3 per cent, a worker graded as AA will have 4 per cent, while a worker with a C graded will have less than 3 per cent. It has become very difficult to ask more. Nine years ago, we used to have pay increases of 10 per cent.

As for early retirement, it is much the same, sad, story:

> Owing to the state of the economy, we have no choice but to accept early retirement. We cannot persuade our company to continue to employ all the workers, so all we can do is to help our redundant or retired members to have the best possible payoff. If we insist on keeping

these workers in the company and call for strikes, our company may not be able to survive and thus decide to close the factory and move offshore to China. This would be even worse. It's a very sad thing.

As the union sees it, the choice is a stark one. Either they accept redundancy or retirement programmes or 'All the workers will lose their jobs'. For the workers still employed, the union officials – like their managers – hoped that the company would get more high-end or high-tech orders from Japan. But final decision about this would be made in Japan at the Japanese company's headquarters.

As for the permanent workers they were generally disaffected with the union. The union received no strong support on a number of issues relating to how it served its members (Table 5.8) and this is not surprising since there was little reason for workers to suppose that it was 'their' union. As one of them put it:

There is very little interaction between the labour union representatives and us. I think that our union representatives do not have grass-roots support. It is only because they want to hold these positions and this is why they ask other workers to support them. They don't achieve anything at all. So, if I have the choice, I won't join this labour union, since at present it's useless. Our union representatives keep us at arm's length. They seldom come to us and discuss things with us.

Others point to the union as ineffective:

I think our labour union did a better job in the past. But things have changed. They do not care much about our working rights and working welfare. For example, when there was a big earthquake or a typhoon, as there was in 21 September, we should have been given time off. However, they expected us to come to work. Our unions did not argue very strongly against the company. They should speak for us or be our representatives and express our concerns to the company. Otherwise, I agree on the new changes in union law in Taiwan, because now I can decide on whether I am happy to join a union that is really standing up for me. I think the major problem of our current labour union is that they don't insist on their points. Before they consult with managers, they condemn themselves. They don't play their part properly.

Sako has claimed that 'Viewed through the Anglo-American lens, all enterprise unions suffer structurally from weak bargaining power, managerial interference and the inability to organise peripheral and retired workers. However, conceptually and in reality, enterprise unions have both weakness and strengths (e.g., access to managerial information) which industrial

Table 5.8   Workers' Views on the Company Union at TaiwanCo

N = 51 percentages	Very good	Good	Neither good nor bad	Poor	Very poor	Don't know
Keeping everyone up to data about proposed changes	2	41	39	14	2	2
Providing everyone with the chance to comment on proposed changes	2	24	43	22	8	2
Responding to suggestions from employees	2	26	51	18	2	2
Dealing with work problems you or others may have	4	28	47	14	6	2
Treating employees fairly	4	24	37	28	4	4

and craft unions lack' (1997:16). To have information is not necessarily to act on it, however. In the past few years, the company and factory have suffered major restructuring; no significant protests resulted. As a union official attempted to explain:

> We don't have strikes but we staged several protests. Maybe not exactly 'protests', more like 'negotiation'. They were about for instance the level of bonuses and wage increases. However, these are all dealt with at the bargaining table, so it is more like negotiation.

This is partly true. In their monthly factory-council meeting, the union representatives and other workers' representatives could be seen to continue to negotiate several issues which concerned them in and after the meeting. However, there is little doubt that the union is weak and workers are disaffected with it. This is not least because of its failure to protect jobs. Weaknesses are evident. Strengths are not.

The disappearance of the 'Golden Tale'

The white goods industry was introduced in Taiwan at the end of the 1940s and had a close relation with Japanese industry when it was first set up. In contrast to several electronic products, which were mainly export-oriented, it was categorised as an 'inner-demand' industry. However, the reduction of import tariffs in 1986, the saturation of the domestic market and the entrance into the WTO in 2002 have all put great pressure on domestic producers, who have to find ways to restructure their production and management. These transformations have had a major impact on workers' lives and experiences and have transformed the social relations of production.

Although Japanese practices, including lifetime employment and seniority allowances, were deeply embedded, TaiwanCo has started to abandon the former; to set up early retirement and redundancy programmes; and to implement performance orientation. It has flattened the management hierarchy. In addition, it has started to appoint younger managers and to speed up organisational reforms, including transforming the firm from a local production company into a regional research development centre.

Before reducing the number of Taiwanese workers on the grounds of seniority, we saw the management first reduced foreign employees and the subcontracting of work to others, in order to safeguard the job opportunities for Taiwanese nationals. This was done partly because of the requests from local workers and their labour union. But later on, early retirement, compulsory retirement and redundancy programmes were all deployed to downsize the labour force; and sub-contracting was increased too. In recent years, TaiwanCo has started to increase the use of agency labour in production. These changes brought workers (and managers) a high level of job insecurity. Workers also are unsatisfied with their labour union, largely because of the limited role which it has played.

What is described above has occurred in many other companies under the banner of 'restructuring' but, unfortunately from the workers' point of view, TaiwanCo used to be regarded as a 'model company' known for its better working conditions and lifetime employment; and it had a very good reputation in Taiwan as a 'Japanese' company. Its promotional video promises its workers 'Peace and Happiness through Prosperity' (PHP). Top managers claim that in the past they kept workers on as long as possible because they regarded them as family members. Now, they say, they have no choice but to reduce the number of long-serving workers as a way of surviving under the pressure of global competition. The workers' dream of staying in the factory for life is in ruins. The emphasis accorded to seniority has gone. The labour union has always been far from militant but now it is reluctant to ask for any improvements in wages or in company welfare. The 'golden tale' is a thing of the past. Workers lament the uncertain future, in contrast to former days when a job with a Japanese firm was really something.

Notes

1 Manufacturing operations can be divided between machine hours and man hours. Kosu refers to the specific man hours which it takes to process one unit of a product in a given process and is calculated by multiplying the number of workers involved in a process by the actual time it takes to complete the process and dividing that by the units produced. It is used as a measure of operators' productivity. Kosu reduction is one of the key measures of productivity improvement (Imai 1997: xxvi)

2 According to the Labour Standards Law, a worker who is in any one of the following situations may apply for voluntary retirement (Article 53: 1). When the worker attains the age of 55 and has worked for 15 years; when the worker has worked for more than 25 years. An employer shall not force a worker to retire unless any one of the following situations arise (Article 54: 1). When the worker attains 60 years of age; when the worker is incapacitated owing to mental defect or physical handicap, however, the age shall not be less than 55. One more important point is that, to fulfil the stipulated length of service, the workers must have worked for the same employer.

References

Berggren, C. and Nomura, M. (1997) 'Employment Practices: A Critical Analysis of the "Three Pillars"' in C. Berggren and M. Nomura *The Resilience of Corporate Japan: New Competitive Strategies and Personnel Practices*, London: Paul Chapman Publishing.

Bernier, B. and Mirza, V. (2001) 'Crisis and Strategies of Reduction of Labour Costs in Japanese Companies', *Labour, Capital and Society*, 34 (2).

Electrical Industry Yearbook (2003) published by Industry Technology Information Services (IT IS).

Higuchi, Y. (1997) 'Trends in Japanese Labour Markets' in M. Sako and H. Sato (eds) *Japanese Labour and Management in Transition: Diversity, Flexibility and Participation*, London: Routledge.

Imai, M. (1997) *Gemba Kaizen: A Commonsense, Low-Cost Approach to Management*, New York: McGraw-Hill.

Ishikawa, A. (1998) 'Changing Patterns of Japanese Industrial Relations' in A. Y. Hing, C. T. Chang and R. Lansbury (eds) *Work, Organisation and Industry: The Asian Experience*, Singapore: Stamford.

Kawakita, T. (1997) 'Corporate Strategy and Human Resource Management' in M. Sako and H. Sato (eds) *Japanese Labour and Management in Transition: Diversity, Flexibility and Participation*, London: Routledge.

Sako, M. (1997) 'Introduction: Forces for Homogeneity and Diversity in the Japanese Industrial Relations System' in M. Sako and H. Sato (eds) *Japanese Labour and Management in Transition: Diversity, Flexibility and Participation*, London: Routledge.

Taipei Times (2003) 'Sampo Purchases Control of Grundig', 2003, 10 January.

6

Turkey: The Development of White Goods in the 'EU Periphery'

Nadir Sugur and Theo Nichols

The Development of the White Goods Industry in Turkey

The post-war period witnessed the emergence of large scale Turkish private capital, which was mostly under family ownership. The presence of a big domestic market, a high rate of population growth, massive migration from rural areas and the emergence of middle and high-income groups in the cities all paved the way for a growth in demand for a wide range of consumer goods. As a result, large domestic private capital has invested in the white goods industry along with direct foreign investment and joint ventures.[1]

The first white goods firm, Arcelik, was founded in 1955 and is owned by the Koc Group, which is a major Turkish conglomerate. Arcelik produced the first washing machine in Turkey in 1959 with a Belgian license and the first refrigerator in 1960 with components mainly supplied from an Israeli firm, Amcor Ltd (Bugra 1998: 7). In the 1970s, however, despite the fact that Arcelik was enjoying growing demand for various white goods in the domestic market, it faced the problems of a low level of domestic savings on the part of potential customers and, on its own part, a lack of legal protection for sales made under hire purchase agreements. Arcelik overcame these problems by means of a highly informal system. This depended, on the one hand, on developing a relationship of trust between itself and its local dealers and, on the other, on developing such a relation between the dealers, chosen as people of probity and good reputation in their communities, and their customers (Bugra 1998: 14–21).

The company produced a wide range of white goods under licence from Bosch till 1986. After that, it set up a Research and Development Unit to develop its own designs and it produced white goods under its own brand name of 'Arcelik' in the domestic market and 'Beko' in the international market. Arcelik-Beko is currently the biggest private firm in Turkey, manufacturing electrical and white goods products ranging from fridges to cookers, microwaves, vacuum cleaners, washing machines, dishwashers, air conditioners, television sets, hi-fi systems and such like. It has now bought several white goods firms in England, Germany, Austria and Romania and has become an important player in the international arena.

In the early 1960s, a second Turkish firm, Profilo, started to produce white goods under licence from AEG. It continued to do so until 1996. Then in 1997, the majority of its shares were taken-over by a German multinational firm, BSH, with the Germans buying up the remaining shares belonging to their Turkish partner in 2003. BSH is now the second biggest firm producing various kinds of refrigeration appliances, washing machines and cookers in Turkey.

The third largest white goods firm, Vestel, started production in 1988. The firm entered into a licence agreement with the Italian firm Merloni in 1997 to produce fridges for the domestic and international markets. Vestel and Merloni have jointly set up a white goods production site in Manisa in the Aegean Region near Izmir. They now produce major white goods items and electrical goods in Manisa varying from fridges to cookers, washing machines, television sets, DVDs and VCDs.

There are also medium sized white goods firms in Turkey that produce a wide range of white goods, such as Teba and Auer. Teba has entered the UK cooker market very successfully in recent years and exports more than 50 per cent of its production to the international market. Other medium and small white goods firms have only a tiny share in the domestic market and little presence in the export market either. The big three dominate. Arcelik-Beko, BSH and Vestel account for 90 per cent of domestic sales. Arcelik-Beko alone accounts for 45 per cent of these (Figure 6.1).

White goods firms in Turkey usually use their own brand names in the domestic market. In addition to this, they also produce white goods for leading multinational firms through subcontract agreements. Many such brands are produced (Table 6.1).

In terms of both production and export revenue, white goods have been one of the fastest growing sectors in Turkey alongside textiles and cars. The

Table 6.1 Firms in Turkey Producing White Goods for Global White Goods Brands in 2000

Turkish Supplier Firms	Multinational Brands
Arcelik-Beko	Electrolux, Moulinex, AEG, Whirlpool
BSH-Profilo	Bosch, Siemens, Pitsos, Balay, Lynx, Coldex, Continental.
Merloni-Vestel	Ariston, Philco, Indesit, FTC-Frigidaire, Cosmos
Teba	Unimeks, White-Westinghouse
Auer	Goldstar-Candy

Source: http://www.igeme.org.tr/introeng.htm (Prime Ministry of Turkey Under-Secretariat of Foreign Trade Export Promotion Centre).

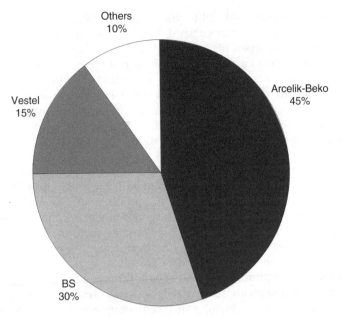

Figure 6.1   Market Share of Firms in Turkey, 2002 (sales volume)
Source: Beyaz Esya Sanayicileri Dernegi Dergisi (2003) No. 41.

State has made various efforts to boost white goods through the provision of a wide range of incentives such as tax exemptions and cheap loans. In the 1960s and 1970s, the state adopted an import substitution industrialisation policy, which was characterised by high protection achieved through tariffs, quotas and a set of incentives for firms producing consumer goods. The sector also benefited from subsidised inputs from SEEs (State Economic Enterprises). The aim was to create a strong domestic production capacity in consumer goods industries, including not only white goods but textiles, cars and a variety of electrical products. At the end of the 1970s, faced with economic and political crisis, and under pressure from the IMF, the state shifted its economic policy from import substitution to export promotion. The overall aim of the policy, which was pursued more or less simultaneously with the advent of military rule, and the severe weakening of the left and the unions, was to support the export of domestically produced goods through the provision of state subsidy such as cheap loans, credits and tax exemption.

Until the mid-1990s, the demand for white goods continued to expand in the domestic market and white goods firms enjoyed a high growth rate in a relatively state-protected market. In fact, in the 1960s and 1970s, the domestic market had been largely insulated from white goods imports. This began to change in the 1980s and the first half of the 1990s as the Turkish state gradually opened up the domestic market to international competition. The primary aim was to boost exports and then open up the domestic market to the importation of goods through reducing taxes and easing tariffs on imports.

In 1996 Turkey ratified a Custom Union Agreement with the EU. By that time white goods firms were, by and large, modern and competitive. By the mid-1990s, however, their increased production capacity threatened to outstrip the domestic market. By that time, 90 per cent of households had refrigeration appliances. Today, penetration rates are yet higher – 99 per cent for fridges, 75 per cent for washing machines and 70 per cent for cookers. This is so even though demographic and other factors mean that two thirds of the domestic sales of total white goods stem from first-time-buyers, with replacements making up only 30 per cent of the total sales (http://www.deik.org.tr/bultenler/2003320153551sectors-houseappliances-2002).

The Custom Union Agreement in 1996 aimed to integrate Turkish trade into EU norms. Under the agreement, both Turkey and the EU agreed to implement common tariffs on industrial goods and services by eliminating the import taxes imposed previously. Both sides also agreed to a significant reduction in existing export quotas on industrial commodities, which, amongst other things, opened up the EU market to Turkish white goods firms. The Custom Union Agreement came at the right moment for white goods firms in Turkey, which found them in need of a new market to sell their products. By lifting tariffs and quotas, and putting Turkey in an advantageous position as regards exports, it also attracted foreign investors such as BSH from Germany and Merloni from Italy. The Turkish private sector was also encouraged to invest more in white goods production, as did Arcelik-Beko of the Koc Group, or to set up joint ventures as Profilo did with BSH and Vestel did with Merloni. A further advantage accrued to white goods firms in 1996; they were exempted from VAT, previously paid at 18 per cent.

Whereas white goods production grew in the 1990s, it underwent a pronounced increase following the two Turkish economic crises of November 2000 and February 2001 (Figure 6.2). These crises forced the Turkish Central Bank to devalue the Turkish Lira against leading foreign currencies. The devaluation was substantial. For example, the Lira was devalued by around 75 per cent against the USD and Sterling. This made the white goods firms in Turkey even more competitive in the international market. It opened the door wide for white goods producers to make strides in the export market. They did. As of 2001, for the first time, total exports of white goods exceeded domestic sales. This growth in exports continued in 2002 when white goods production rose 41 per cent and exports rose 55 per cent. In 2003, white goods production and exports both continued to enjoy a high growth rate. In that year,

(thousand units)

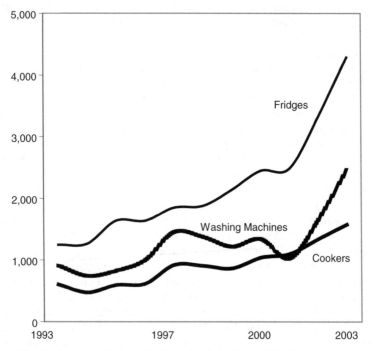

Figure 6.2   Production of Selected White Goods, Turkey, 1993–2003
Source: Beyaz Esya Sanayicileri Dernegi Dergisi (2004) No. 43.
Note: Fridges includes fridge freezers, refrigerators and deep freezers.

production grew 29 per cent and exports again grew faster than this, by 38 per cent. The production of fridges and fridge freezers has been the driving force in the Turkish white goods industry and thus these goods have the biggest share of white goods exports. In 2003 for example, fridges and related goods made up 50 per cent of total white goods production, capturing 45 per cent of domestic sales and generating 52 per cent of total white goods exports (Figure 6.3).

By the end of 2003, Turkish white goods firms sold around 70 per cent of their total annual production in the international market, a major shift to exports having been accomplished since the mid-1990s (Figure 6.4). In 2003 Turkey produced more than 8,300,000 million units of white goods and of these, 5,700,000 million were exported. Looking at the wider picture, again in 2003, white goods made up 13 per cent of total Turkish exports. The industry is Turkey's third biggest exporter, following textile and clothing (40 per cent) and automotive industries (17 per cent).

Turkish white goods firms aim to export, whilst also being competitive in the domestic market. Some firms, such as Arcelik-Beko, have looked

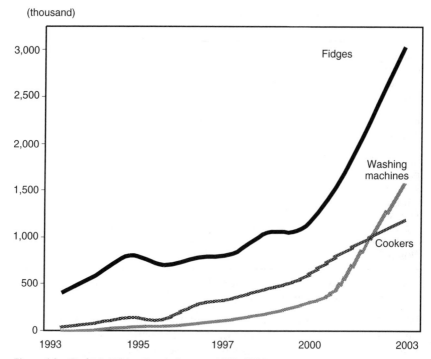

Figure 6.3   Turkish White Goods Exports 1993–2003
Source: Beyaz Esya Sanayicileri Dernegi Dergisi (2002).
Note: Fridges includes fridge freezers, refrigerators and deep freezers.

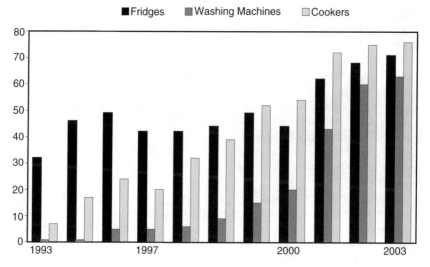

Figure 6.4   Percentage of White Goods Units Produced in Turkey that are Exported
Source: Beyaz Esya Sanayicileri Dernegi Dergisi, 2000a, 2002 and 2004.

Table 6.2   Turkish White Goods Exports by Destinations, 2002 (Percentages of Sales Volume)

Britain	16.9
Germany	11.4
France	10.1
Spain	6.0
Italy	4.8
Israel	2.6
Belgium	2.5
Greece	2.1
Bulgaria	2.1
Russia	2.1
Romania	1.9
Tunisia	1.9
Finland	1.8
Poland	1.6
Azerbaijan	1.6
Others	30.0

Source: Prime Ministry of Turkey Under-Secretariat of Foreign Trade Export Promotion Centre, http://www.igeme.org.tr/introeng.htm

beyond the EU and have successfully penetrated the Central Asian Turkic Republics and Eastern Europe (for the former of which Turkey is well positioned geographically as well as having some other advantages), and also some markets in Northern African countries. Nonetheless, countries inside the EU make up the biggest and the most important market. As of 2003, 80 per cent of Turkish white goods exports went to the EU (BEYSAD 2004). The leading destination was Britain, followed by Germany and France (Table 6.2).

Even after the 1996 Custom Union Agreement, imports made little impact on the domestic market (Figure 6.5). In 2003, white goods imports made up less than 10 per cent of total domestic sales, with China, Germany and Italy being the leading sources of white goods imports. Generally, German and Italian white goods imports targeted the high value end of the market, Chinese ones the low end. Nonetheless, devaluation of the Turkish Lira in 2001 made the import of white goods more expensive and thus the high income groups in Turkey saw a shift in demand towards domestically produced white goods. The import of white goods has declined gradually since 2001.

In short, white goods production in Turkey typically began under foreign licence. Both the large family style Turkish conglomerate and investment from foreign multinationals played a part in the industry's development and market share is highly concentrated. Above all, since the turn of the century, the industry has become export-oriented, with a particular focus on countries in the EU.

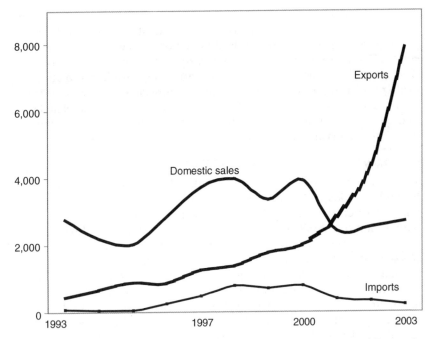

Figure 6.5   A Comparison of Turkish White Goods Exports-Imports and Domestic Sales (thousand units)
Source: Beyaz Esya Sanayicileri Dernegi Dergisi, various years.
Note: Data relate to refrigeration appliances, washing machines and cookers.

Factories and workers

Fieldwork research was conducted in the white goods industry in Turkey between 1999 and 2001. This was carried out in three white goods firms located in the Izmit triangle and its environs. The triangle, which runs from Istanbul at its apex to Izmit and Bursa, is at the heart of large scale industrial development and the area has attracted millions of new migrants since the 1950s. Pay and working conditions for manual workers are relatively better than elsewhere in Turkey and trade unionism is more common. The triangle holds almost a quarter of Turkey's 70 million inhabitants. The region contributes a third of GDP and over half of Turkey's exports (Istanbul Chamber of Commerce 2001). More than half of Turkey's top 500 enterprises are located in the triangle. The region's industrial development is dominated by car, textile, petrochemical products, cement, chemicals and white goods firms.

In all, about 150 white goods workers were interviewed (53, 50 and 50 in each plant respectively). All the workers interviewed worked in one of the main production departments. Two thirds were assembly line workers. The rest consisted of maintenance workers, quality control workers and packing workers. Information was obtained on the age structure of blue-collar workers from HRM managers and they were sampled on this basis. During the fieldwork, interviews were carried out inside the plants and further in-depth interviews were conducted with some workers outside the plants. Surveys were also conducted of about 50 managers and related staff in each plant, as well extended interviews being conducted with, amongst others, managers and trade union officials and representatives.

Cerkezkoy White Goods Factory (CerkWG)

The factory is located in Trakya (Thrace), 100 km west of Istanbul. It was initially a Turkish company which became a joint venture, and was then taken over entirely by its European partner in 2003. The factory as a whole employs 3,000 workers. More than 1,000 are employed in the refrigerator factory, where the fieldwork was carried out. The factory has over a third of the home market, producing around a million fridges annually. It exports over 50 per cent of them. Since the arrival of the European partner in the mid-1990s, which appointed a European managing director, the factory, which previously lacked investment, has benefited considerably from upgrades to its technology. The production site has also developed highly specialised R and D facilities for aspects of fridge freezer production with other aspects of fridge and freezer R and D being located in the corporation's factories in other countries.

The pace of technological change in this factory has been impressive and major investment continued despite the economic crisis at the turn of the century. Most pre-assembly line work in the paint section, in metal cutting and bending, in plastic cutting and in moulding, has been automated. There is generally a high standard of housekeeping. Nonetheless, in the final assembly line where the majority of the workers are located, work-tasks still remain labour intensive.

At CerkWG, 60 to 70 per cent of materials are outsourced, with variations according to particular cases. The main Turkish suppliers are in Istanbul and its environs with only about five per cent located in Cerkezkoy. The company policy is that no one contractor should carry out more than 30 per cent of its work for the company. The aim is to reduce the mutual interdependence of suppliers and CerkWG.

New management methods were introduced by the European parent company. Some managers have also been sent to Europe for training. After the takeover, the Europeans abolished quality circles. They are not against quality circles per se. But after the takeover, they decided that there were so many of them that they had become ineffective. A programme has been introduced to train workers and also suppliers. The new European management also stripped out the management levels of deputies and assistant managers. As a result, the bottom level of management now consists of team leaders, appointed by management and in charge of teams of between 9 and 45.

The company emphasises the importance of its continuous improvement process (CIP). It has a just-in-time stock control system and there is a suggestion system and 'total productivity maintenance' operating in the production process. By 2002, the company was running courses and seminars in Six Sigma for engineers and managers. Pareto diagrams and fishbone methods are used for problem solving and reducing defect rates.

Gebze White Goods Factory (GebzeWG)

GebzeWG produces washing machines and is owned by a Turkish conglomerate. The factory is situated between Istanbul and Izmit, a site of massive industrialisation which has increased since the 1980s as industry spilled out of Istanbul. The GebzeWG factory has occupied the production site since the end of the 1960s. It became a dedicated washing machine factory in the mid-1980s, and the level of technology has been upgraded significantly since then. In 2002, this modern and re-vamped plant was described by an international trade magazine in glowing terms as 'a modern manufacturing marvel' and the group that owns the firm regards it as a symbol of the company's rise as a regional manufacturing power. Turkey's youthful population, the growing number of households, massive migration from rural areas and what was initially a low level of penetration in such items as washing machines have all helped the company's growth. The company generated sales of 1.9bn US$ in 2003 and is expecting 2.3bn US$ sales and 1.1bn US$ export revenue in 2004. It is one of the biggest white goods manufacturers in Europe and the plant, which produces about one and a half million washing machines annually, has over 50 per cent of the home market. In 2003 it exported over 50 per cent of production.

A range of models is produced, stimulated by the presence on site of an advanced R and D unit. The GebzeWG plant employs around 1,000 workers in a well laid out modern plant, which has invested heavily in new technology since the end of a partnership with a European multinational in 1986 (like many Turkish companies, it had begun by working under license). Metal cutting and bending are highly automated and there are automatic devices and numerically controlled machines throughout the production process. In the powder paint unit, where metal frames are painted automatically, workers are largely reduced to pressing buttons when necessary. In the pre-assembly unit, most work tasks are highly automated through the use of CNC machines. In the final assembly unit, most of the work is carried out manually with a minority of women working side by side with the men. In the final quality control, the work tasks are again highly automated. Just over fifty per cent of parts are produced in Turkey with more complex electro-magnetic mechanisms being imported from abroad. The company seeks to maintain close relations with its domestic suppliers.

Bolu White Goods Factory (BoluWG)

BoluWG is an oven factory. It is situated 150 km from Izmit and is part of the spill over of industry from Istanbul that occurred in the 70s and 80s. BoluWG is part of the same conglomerate as GebzeWG. The factory employs just over 1,000 workers and produces over half a million ovens annually. A variety of models is produced for both the home and European markets and BoluWG has just over 50 per cent of the home market, with 50 per cent of production going for export in 2003. Part of the shop floor is set up for cellular production but this makes only a minor contribution to the output.

Of the three factories, BoluWG is the most labour intensive. Although the company began to upgrade its technology in the mid-1990s as it started to concentrate more on the international market, most work has not been highly automated, with the exception of the metal cutting and bending unit. On the shop floor there are a few computer controlled machines and CNC lathes. There are no women workers on the assembly line.

The plant was scheduled for a management re-organisation, but this had not yet occurred at the time of the fieldwork. The factory is located in a town which is itself situated in a predominately rural environment. This, combined with its paternalist tradition, lends it a distinctive character. One aspect of this tradition is the stance adopted by the plant's managers to the workers' religious practice. The BoluWG management provides buses for workers to go to-and-from a nearby mosque for Friday prayer. This stands in contrast to the determinedly secular stance of the managements of the other companies. Until very recently it also arranged for the circumcision of workers' children. The plant's vestiges of paternalism, the fact that its labour force is overwhelmingly of local origin, its lower level of technological development and the delay in introducing the same sort of stripped down management system as at the other plants, all mark BoluWG as different to the other two white goods plants.

Labour market formation, recruitment process and employment

Unemployment is high in Turkey. Official figures put the rate of unemployment at just under 8 per cent (plus underemployment of circa 6 per cent). Unofficial estimates put the unemployment figure as high as 20 per cent (plus 6 to 7 per cent underemployment). The majority of people in Turkey are employed in informal economic activities. This means that the jobs they do are characterised by low pay, job insecurity, temporary work, poor working conditions, an absence of trade unionism and a lack of social security rights. Thus, it is important for people to have a job in the formal sector, and it is to the top end of this that these plants belong.

In all plants, workers value their jobs highly. We asked workers: 'Is this a good job for someone like you?' Most workers were of the view that it was – responses ranged from 96 per cent in Bolu, 87 per cent in Gebze to 74 per cent in Cerkezkoy. Workers made comments such as 'This is the best job that I can get'. 'I'm lucky to get this job', 'It's good to work in here', 'I have become a proper man with a proper job'.

Workers told how they could not sleep the night before starting work because working in such a plant meant so much to them. Certainly, getting a job in these firms is an uphill struggle. All the plants advertise new jobs internally in order to minimise the massive number of applicants who would otherwise form lengthy queues outside the factory gate. They also require applicants to provide an internal reference. Competition for such jobs is stiff and it is important that applicants have a man inside or a worker who will guarantee that they are good, reliable and loyal people.

In all three factories it is still common for recruitment to operate through networks of family and friends and it can also be helpful to know trade union officials. To have such contacts does not guarantee a job, nor are interviews regularly dispensed with and sometimes performance (aptitude) tests are used. But all the firms require applicants to have a reference from inside and there are all kinds of connections that figure in workers' accounts of how they got in – and which figure yet more so in their accounts of how others did so. Some workers are quite open about having obtained their jobs by '*torpil*' (through someone on the inside) like this one at Bolu:

> I got in with torpil. There was someone close to the family, a deputy director, who worked here. He helped me. I think half of all the employees entered here with the help of someone

The range of possibilities is very large. At Bolu the tradition has been that a father can ask for his son to replace him when he retires. Everywhere there are brothers and fathers who already work in the factory and put in a word, and who tell future applicants about jobs coming up (which firms encourage by not advertising publicly). There are mothers who look after the children of managers, uncles who are trade union officials, fathers who are tailors and make suits for an important manager, cousins who are secretaries to managing directors, managers who one way or another can be got to by intermediaries who will put in a good word. In short, linking everything together is a dense web of friends, friends of friends and acquaintances, the web through which the ordinary citizen hopes to touch and be rewarded by the powerful. As a worker at CerkWG explained:

> It isn't possible to enter these kind of factories, especially the big ones by your own efforts. You have to have a man [a patron] to help you. This

man can either work in the factory or be outside, for example, someone who knows a director or a chief in the factory. Governors and kaymakam (the prime local government representative in the town) can help too.

Successful applicants serve a probation period lasting from 6 to 12 months. At the end of the probation period, if workers are judged satisfactory, they are granted permanent status. Only after this can they benefit from the formal sector's advantages. And once workers have got the job, they don't want to lose it. If they are dismissed, they will also lose a whole number of social and economic benefits provided by the firm.

Fringe benefits and other employment advantages offered by these firms differ very considerably from those offered in the informal sector in Turkey (Nichols and Sugur 2004: 25–42). Typical benefits include, high pay (paid regularly, itself an important consideration), bonuses, advances against pay, seniority related pay, redundancy pay, permanent contracts, trade union recognition, social insurance, Bayram (religious holiday) gifts, free meals at work, work clothes and boots, bus services to and from work, discounts on company products and more. Outside the factory, working in such a company endows workers with creditworthiness at local shops, gives them higher status in their neighbourhood, opens up a range of social activities and can even improve marriage prospects.

As can be seen from Figure 6.6, which presents the more general situation, the difference in gross pay between big firms in the formal sector and the minimum wage, which is the lot of many workers outside this, is consider-

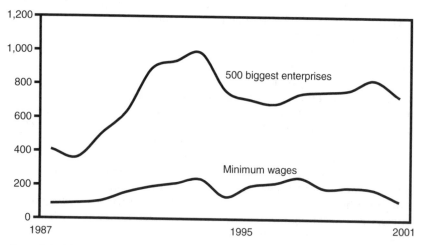

Figure 6.6   Minimum Wage and Wages in 500 Biggest Enterprises in Turkey 1987–2001 (Gross Wages at 1987 constant US$)
Source: Istanbul Chamber of Commerce 2002.

able. In all three of the plants reported on here the average monthly wage of workers with five years service was 650 USD in 2001, including fringe benefits. For workers employed in the informal sector, it was circa 160 USD.

In all the plants, physical working conditions are comparable to those found in many factories in the developed world and do not equate to those conjured up by conventional perceptions of third world factory labour, as for example depicted by Klein (2000). They are generally reckoned to be good by workers. Production workers in these plants are permanent and are a hundred per cent unionised by the same trade union, Turk Metal. All three plants are subject to the same collective bargaining agreement and all three of them provide the same pay and similar social and economic benefits to their workers.

There are some specific cases of temporary workers being hired. At CerkWG, for example, temporary workers are recruited to meet the increased seasonal demand for refrigeration products over the summer period but full-time permanent workers make up around 85 per cent of the direct production labour force. Also, in all plants, outside of the direct production workers, there are 'tacheron' workers, who make up approximately 10 to 15 per cent of the labour force.

Tacheron workers are employed through a subcontractor, usually for less than 11 months (their employer thus avoiding the legal obligation to pay compensation on dismissal) and they are only paid the minimum wage. They are not members of the trade union and have no holiday entitlement. However, the managements of these plants separate tacheron workers from permanent workers on the shop floor in order to avoid breaking the law. According to the Labour Law, employers are required to comply with the condition of 'equal pay for equal work'. Tacheron workers are recruited only to carry out non-production functions such as packing, warehouse duties, cleaning, refectory and security work. There are no tacheron workers engaged in direct production with the minor exception of CerkWG, where a few tacheron workers can be required to work on the production process in exceptional circumstances. Greatly disadvantaged as they certainly are, these workers therefore remained, at the time of our investigation, a small part of the labour force. They posed no direct threat to permanent workers, who in any case needed no further reminder of their own relative good fortune in the midst of the millions who worked in the informal economy.

Workers, managers and new management methods

The contemporary generation of Turkish managers has been more and more able to access international developments in management theory and practice, through the development of business teaching; through an increasing number of joint venture companies; through the emergence of management consultancy both internationally and, within Turkey, through new means of communication, including the web; and generally through the operation of what has been termed the 'cultural circuit of capital' (Thrift 1999: 42) and the many agents who form part of this and who produce and distribute prescriptions for business. The velocity at which new management ideas have been imported into Turkey has also increased considerably over the last few decades. For example, it took 30 years for F. W.Taylor's *Principles of Scientific Management* (1911) to appear in Turkish and much neo-human relations literature of the 1950s and 1960s seems to have remained untranslated. Nowadays, many of the outpourings of management gurus are available in Turkish within the year, with many Turkish senior managers being well able to read them in the original anyway (Nichols, Sugur and Demir 2002). Indeed, the top managers in these firms are as capable as those anywhere of 'talking the TQM talk'. For example the GebzeWG product development manager has spoken of creating 'a new revitalised organisation supported by fully motivated and empowered employees' and the MD at CerkWG is no less evangelical:

> Last year was Quality Year. It was a great success. We filled the big canteen and clapped each other. We are getting there. They are beginning to understand it's their company. Their company! In the beginning they were afraid of their managers.

We provided Turkish managers and related staff with a checklist to get a rough indication of which modern management techniques they were familiar with. Over nine out of ten claimed to be familiar with Total Quality Management (TQM), Quality Circles (QCs) and Team Working; seven out of ten with Just in Time (JIT), Kaizen and Flexible Production; six out of ten with Lean Production and five out of ten with Re-engineering. Some differences existed between the plants and these can be seen in detail in Table 6.3. In particular, there was a higher proportion of managers who were familiar with Kaizen at CerkWG and a higher proportion familiar with flexible production at GebzeWG. As can be seen from Table 6.4, the general pattern of response for workers is broadly the same as for managers.

As the tables suggest, TQM, QCs and Teams were the leading modern management techniques in the plants and TQM and these and related practices had largely arrived in the first part of the 1990s. The Custom Union agreement with the EU in 1996 put further pressure on domestic firms to increase quality levels in their products. In BoluWG and GebzeWG, the most used management techniques are team work, kaizen, just-in-time stock system, lean management, benchmarking and various problem solving methods such as Pareto Diagrams and suggestion systems. In CerkWG, management opts to use total quality maintenance, kaizen, Six Sigma, benchmarking and suggestion systems. In all the firms, total quality management techniques focus on the organisation of the

Table 6.3 Managers' Familiarity with Management Techniques in Three Turkish Plants

Percentages	TQM	Team Working	QCs	JIT	Kaizen	Flexible Production	Lean Production	Re-Engineering
Bolu (n = 51)	96	100	96	75	55	59	63	45
GebzeWG (n = 41)	100	100	100	66	73	90	73	59
CerkWG (n = 50)	94	98	88	80	86	68	52	48

Table 6.4 Workers' Familiarity with Management Techniques in Three Turkish Plants

Percentages	TQM	Teams	QCs	JIT	Kaizen	Flexible Production	Lean Production	Re-Engineering
BoluWG (n = 50)	98	96	100	50	14	14	14	8
GebzeWG (n = 53)	100	100	100	68	62	47	23	8
CerkWG (n = 50)	70	98	42	40	66	18	4	4

production systems and the systematic control of the labour process. As might be suggested by some of the statistical control techniques mentioned above, TQM implementation in these firms is generally applied through the 'hard' rather than 'soft' version.[2]

Some years ago, Kozan (1989: 795) argued that Turkish managers are apt to have a 'forcing style' with subordinates, and that centralised decision-making, authoritarian leadership and the display of power distance all make for a situation in which 'the handling of differences is brisk'. Another commentator on Turkish management, Wasti (1998), also asserts that Turkish managers in general have a highly developed sense of power distance, that employees lack autonomy and that they are afraid to disagree. Like several other management writers, she also suggests that TQM fits better in national cultures – including Japan – that have a high level of power distance (Katz et al 1998, Masters 1996, Scully 1996). It is in line with this that the aim of the management techniques implemented in these plants has been to make workers work very hard to minimise defects and to reduce the cost of production.

In all plants, workers can be held accountable for any defects discovered by customers. At GebzeWG, workers are monitored by electronic links between their workstations and a central computer. At GebzeWG, workers who fail to complete their tasks in the prescribed time are warned of this by an alarm, which also alerts management via the central computer system. Workers know that managers can monitor their performance in this way and in some plants they know that managers can do this from their homes too. As a worker at GebzeWG reflected: 'in the middle of the night, when you are on the night shift, after all the managers have gone home, you are still there to be watched over'.

Workers increasingly find themselves under pressure to improve their performance. Those who are members of quality circles are required to do overtime in order to finish their team work task. Management insists on getting more suggestions from workers, demands that they attend open-door meetings outside working hours and asks for ideas in so called brain storming sessions. Management does not typically ask workers for ideas on improving communications or career prospects. Issues concerning non-production activities are not dealt with or encouraged by the management in any of the three firms. Workers are increasingly subject to management agendas on solving problems at work. Teams have done little to alter this, in fact they are part of the same process. Studying Maquilas in Mexico, Helper has written of 'Kaizen from above' (Helper 1995: 270–1). Although there are attempts by managements to change the way they relate to workers, there are important respects in which the term that best suits these Turkish cases is 'TQM from above'.

In BoluWG and GebzeWG, there are two kinds of teams. One is a production team in a specific work area ranging in size from 7 to 150 workers. The team leader is usually appointed by management. The other is a quality circle. These were widely used in BoluWG and GebzeWG, consisting of 4–6 workers and lasting from 4 to 6 months. Quality circles are set up to solve a particular problem in the production process. As of 2000, BoluWG and GebzeWG had 15 and 14 quality circles respectively.

Teamwork is often thought an essential element of TQM. In this regard, various kinds of teamwork are expected to encourage workers to collaborate in order to increase the efficiency of production. One might also expect that quality circles and production teams inevitably encourage workers and managers to be collectively involved in decision-making processes and that teams set up in various forms might alleviate the problem of a lack of communication. However, the evidence from this study is not in line with this. For example, in the BoluWG and GebzeWG plants, quality circles are first organised and then team members selected from amongst the workers by the management. Membership of quality circles is determined by management and circles mainly consist of skilled and experienced workers. The workers make suggestions in response to management agendas, and management unilaterally decides what to do. Most workers found they had to do overtime to carry out the tasks assigned to their team. Some had to go to the factory during weekends in order to finish their work task. As one of workers put it 'I only have two hands, what more can I do?'.

In all three plants, the performance of quality circles is controlled, measured and monitored using a top-down method. Team members are required to give presentations at a pre-scheduled time. This puts intense pressure on workers to finish the work tasks in time. Members of quality circles are asked to hold meetings to discuss their work tasks and area managers usually attend these meetings to evaluate the team members' progress towards completion. In GebzeWG and BoluWG, there were various notice boards where all the teams' performance is boldly displayed. The management of BoluWG and GebzeWG select the best team annually in order to enhance competition among teams. In both plants, the decisive factor in becoming the best team is the material contribution resulting from a team's solution to the set problem. Though management emphasises during training and courses that it would welcome any solution to any problem at work, it actually compels workers to bring forward production related-solutions. A manager at BoluWG was critical of workers who tended to propose solutions that had nothing to do with the production process:

> Some workers come up and make suggestions like whether we could improve bus services or not, whether they could smoke whilst doing their work, etc. I hate workers like those who make suggestions for themselves only. What about work? Who is supposed to reduce the cost of production? Do your best for this company, you idiots.

Most workers are fully aware that the top down method of doing things has characterised Turkish industry more generally:

> They don't listen to the workers' voices. (GebzeWG)

> There is no dialogue between managers and workers in Turkey. They are not genuine. They don't treat workers with respect. They regard workers as inferior. (CerkWG)

> There is a big gap between workers and managers and there is no channel of communication. (BoluWG)

But in these particular factories there has been a measure of change. Looking back, a manager at CerkWG recalled how ten years ago:

> We applied these methods from above and forced workers to obey the rules and regulations without questioning them. At that time, we would set up teams of five workers completely instructed from above. We would instruct workers 'do this, do that'.

Similar observations were made by managers in other white goods firms. Partly, the change is a function of direct foreign influence. Child and Rodrigues (1996: 46) have argued that foreign direct investment (FDI) provides an extremely important potential vehicle for the transfer of managerial and organisational knowledge in developing economies, as well of course for the transfer of technology as ordinarily understood. In this respect, the foreign managers at CerkWG provided workers with a direct point of comparison. A worker there acted out for us the way the European and Turkish managers came onto the shop floor. First, he played the foreign manager. He entered, walking slowly, nodding to workers, greeting them, asking how they were, looking around him with interest as he went down the aisle and making occasional enquiries. He even smiled. The worker then played the Turkish manager. To do this he marched in, looked sharply from side to side, and barked commands: 'Ahmet!. Pick that up!. Put it over there! Mehmet! What are you doing? Go at once to the end of the section!' Such is the availability of information on modern management, however, that managers in these plants, or at least some of them, have not needed to be exposed directly to foreign colleagues in their own factories to pick up some of the less harsh mannerisms and practices of modern management.

Whatever the origins of a less harsh management style, some workers have come to take a jaundiced view of it and high hopes, often to the fore upon entering the factory, can get tarnished over time. As a GebzeWG worker put it:

> When I tell people that I work here they reply very positively. They say 'Well, what a good place to work'. However you see things differently

when you are on the inside. For example, there are regular meetings here. In these meetings, the managers always say 'Friends, we are having a hard time at present, but the future will be good for all of us'. Some of my work mates still believe them. I used to believe them too. But I don't trust them anymore, because when the time for a wage negotiation comes, we never get the money that we truly deserve.

If workers have not become subject to some new fangled managerial hegemony, however – and there are highly tangible prompts in their work environment to jar them out of any such temptation – not least a manager at CerkWG who told us proudly that he was 'the cock of the shop floor' – many do recognise that the managers in these plants are better than those in the general run of plants in Turkey and that, within the plants, managers are better than they used to be. Workers in these factories, like anyone else, would rather be treated with dignity than not and they would rather be recognised as human beings than be blandly ignored or scolded like children.

Moreover, as we shall see later, whatever remains of the top down nature of Turkish management, a clear majority of workers in all the plants also believed that their role in decision making (no doubt starting from a low base) had increased over the last five years.

We asked workers: 'In general, how would you describe relations between workers and managers here?' In every plant at least half of them rated the climate of relations as 'good' or 'very good'. However, these responses are far from providing a neat demonstration of the effectiveness of modern management methods because although the overall ratings are high, workers in the least developed plant in terms of management methods, BoluWG, scored higher (79 per cent) than workers in GebzeWG (58 per cent) and CerkWG (51 per cent).

There are a number of reasons why BoluWG workers rate workplace relations more positively than workers in the other two plants. Partly it is because of what their jobs offer them, compared to what they can expect elsewhere in the area. The importance of the local labour market in how BoluWG workers view their jobs is underlined by their high satisfaction with their job security and the fact that an astonishing 100 per cent of them stated that they are satisfied with their pay (Table 5). They live in an area where there are no comparable sources of work and where to work for a big company spells relative security.

These workers are in fact no more secure than those at the other white goods plants but they clearly feel that their jobs are secure compared to other jobs they might do. This belief is reinforced by the expectations of others in their community. Working for a big company – the only big company with a plant in the area – means that all the benefits associated with working in the corporate sector take on an added significance – the regular pay, social security rights, credit in the local shops and so on. In many ways, large or small, to work for BoluWG means an escape from the insecurity suffered by other manual workers in the area.

The pay rates at BoluWG are no better than in the other white goods plants. In fact BoluWG workers are subject to the very same collective bargaining agreement that applies to workers at GebzeWG and CerkWG. The agreement gives workers at these plants the same pay, but it favours those at BoluWG since they live in an area where the cost of living is considerably lower (an advantage augmented by the fact that having longer service on average they benefit from seniority pay). The main fact is that BoluWG constitutes a micro-zone of further advantage for workers employed in the large corporate sector, compared to those employed in the Izmit triangle itself. Thus, the BoluWG workers' advantageous position lets them project a more positive stance toward their plant and its management. Consideration of the BoluWG case indicates that workers' attitudes and behaviour in the different plants are a function of more than the extent to which modern management is practised (and it must be remembered that at BoluWG elements of paternalism persisted). In particular, an important role is played by the local context and, related to this, worker expectations. Relatively speaking, their jobs really are good ones for people like them, living where they do, and given the available opportunities. Their responses to a variety of questions in Table 6.5 reflect this.

Sometimes the identification of modern management as management-by-stress (Parker and Slaughter 1995) leads to the further idea that things are getting progressively worse, that continuous improvement in production efficiency and the greater demands on workers to contribute to this, mean there is mounting pressure on them. In some respects this is a fitting description of the GebzeWG and CerkWG white goods plants. From the point of view of the managers in these plants, the pursuit of

Table 6.5 Workers' Relative Assessments of Working in Three Turkish Plants

Percentages	BoluWG N = 50	GebzeWG N = 53	CerkWG N = 50
Agree or strongly agree that job is secure	78	34	28
Satisfied or very satisfied with pay	100	74	56
Agree or strongly agree job is secure in this workplace	78	34	28
Rate job as good one for someone like me	96	87	74
Against son or daughter working in the plant	26	64	86

ever decreasing defects is an unproblematic and logical activity. As a line manager at CerkWG explained:

> Our industrial engineers calculate how much time is needed to do a certain task by how many workers in the production department. So, if the workers do their work in the specified time, there is no problem. For instance, if you produce 400 fridges in a shift and if 400 fridges are passed through the band, if the worker doesn't make any mistakes, it means the work is going well. The defective products always return at quality checkpoints and we record these statistically. For example, we have nearly 250 error definitions. We are actually in a position to know where those errors are coming from and who is responsible. Since, everybody has got his own tasks; we can easily address it to the person who has erred. In this plant, it's always easy to know who makes a mistake and where the mistakes come from. Everybody can make mistakes once or twice, but if he's continuously making mistakes, it means that he is no good for us. I mean, if they accurately do their work without stopping the conveyor at the speed that we determine and are careful enough to reduce defects, these workers will have no problem in here at all.

In order to investigate the possibility that increased pressure from management to reduce defects and to comply in other ways has had adverse consequences for workers, we asked them whether stress, workload and their involvement in decision-making had got better or worse over the last five years. In all three plants seven out of ten and more workers who had worked in the plants for five years or more indicated that decision making had got better. But as can be seen from Table 6.6, about half or more of these workers in GebzeWG and CerkWG claimed stress had got worse, with generally lower proportions stating that workload had also got worse.

The lower proportions for workload makes sense since, as several workers reported, although the pressure to work had increased, mechanisation and automation had removed some of the physical labour.

Table 6.6 Changes over the Last Five Years in Three Turkish Plants

Percentage	BoluWG N = 39	GebzeWG N = 42	CerkWG N = 23
Decision making better	79	74	78
Stress worse	28	48	57
Workload worse	23	31	39

Note: Data relate to workers with 5 years or more service.

The nature of the trade union

Turk Metal is the biggest union in the metal industry, which has been a driving force in the Turkish economy over the last 20 years. As a union, Turk Metal is affiliated to Turk Is, which is the biggest trade union confederation in Turkey. Turk Metal is a far-right wing union. It has been well known in the past for its nationalist stance on various issues in Turkish politics such as standing firm against any political solution to the Cyprus problem and issuing a mission statement claiming that Turkey's place is not in Europe but in Central Asia (where the Turks originally came from) and in other Turkic speaking countries (described as 'our relatives'). To avoid misunderstanding it is important to make clear that not all the unions that are affiliated to Turk Is are like Turk Metal. There are, for example, unions such as Petrol Is, whose activities can be regarded as part of left wing unionism in Turkey. It is to Turk Metal, however, that these workers belong and to fail to understand its autocratic character is to fail to understand a widespread disaffection with it (clear exceptions being found among those politically aligned workers for whom it has found work in these factories).

Turk Metal lacks internal democracy and its structure is autocratic. The union's decision-making process is centralised and top union officials work hand-in-glove with the management. Turk Metal is in favour of new management methods and jointly organises seminars and workshops with the employer's union on TQM and related issues. The union has welcomed the adoption of teamwork, quality circles and the extensive use of TQM. For Turk Metal, new management methods are regarded unproblematically as the means 'to make the cake bigger.'

The union operates a closed shop in all the plants. Although this is illegal under Turkish Labour Law, the managements of the three plants have long made use of this practice in order to avoid taking on possible 'leftist' elements into their firms. New recruits are sent to the union office to sign on as part of the process of joining the company. In other words, the procedure is part of the standard practice. It is as unproblematic as going to the hospital to register for social security purposes – in fact it occurs as part of the same routine.

Workers in all three plants are critical of how the union operates. BoluWG:

> There is no communication with workers. They aren't interested in our problems. I haven't seen the face of the union president.

> I have no relationship to the union except for my membership.

> Our trade union is an employer's trade union and does what the employer says.

CerkWG:

> There's no difference if there is a trade union here or not. It's an employer's union.

> I have been here for six months. I haven't had any contact with the union.

GebzeWG:

> Our trade union is no good. They don't deal with worker's problems. They don't treat everyone the same. They are politically biased. They are not open to criticism. They don't tell us about elections for representatives. We don't know when or how they are appointed.

> For me there is no trade union here.

> The union isn't democratic. The representatives are appointed. The union must integrate with the worker. The workers must elect the representatives.

As these accounts make clear, most criticism of Turk Metal concern its lack of responsiveness to workers' needs, its lack of internal democracy and an absence of dialogue with workers.

Workers from all three plants have tried to leave the union, as have others elsewhere. In particular, thousands of workers broke away from Turk Metal and joined the left wing Birlesik Metal-Is when the union failed to live up to its promises in the 1998 bargaining round. According to Turk Metal, around 8,000 workers switched to Birlesik Metal-Is and then switched back. According to Birlesik Metal-Is, 40,000 did so. Whatever the true number, dissatisfaction with the union was considerable.

Turk Metal works in harmony with management in all three plants and management looks after Turk Metal, not least at times when workers attempt to leave the union. Labour Law plays an important role in preventing workers changing their union. According to Turkish Labour Law, to gain recognition, a union has to demonstrate it has 50 per cent plus one of a plant and – an important further obstacle – 10 per cent of the industry.

There are further difficulties that stand in the way of workers who want to leave the union and join another one. Managers (and the incumbent Turk Metal officials) have told them that their actions to join a new union will prove futile because of legal stipulations. Workers in these plants have been told that it is illegal for management to bargain with another union, since once an agreement has been made it remains enforceable for two years even if the workers leave the union and join another one. To this, it has to be added that if workers do leave, they fear the company will sack them. And, if workers do join another union surreptitiously and Turk Metal

Table 6.7   Turkish Workers' Evaluations of Management and Trade Union in Three Turkish Plants

How good managers and union are at	BoluWG N = 50	GebzeWG N = 53	CerkWG N = 50
keeping everyone up to date about proposed changes (% very good and good)			
Managers	78	54	32
Union	60	51	22
providing everyone with the chance to comment on proposed changes (% very good and good)			
Managers	63	35	36
Union	46	30	18
responding to suggestions from employees (% very good and good)			
managers	76	72	60
union	56	53	20
dealing with work problems you or others may have (% very good and good)			
Managers	94	77	76
Union	70	68	26
treating employees fairly (% very good and good)			
Managers	82	53	52
Union	66	62	28
average management score	79	58	51
average TU score	60	53	23
percentage difference in favour of management	+19	+5	+28

finds out, it has been known to pass the word to management and get them sacked.

In part, Turk Metal benefits from what, for workers, is the bureaucratised cage of Turkish labour law. In part the union benefits from flouting the law, for example by operating a closed shop. But in part, too, Turk Metal is sustained by the support of management. Managements have been complicit in Turk Metal's recruitment of its own political supporters. They have supported the operation of the illegal closed shop and they have also removed workers who opposed Turk Metal and tried to leave it. Managements favour Turk Metal because it leaves them free to manage. Yet in leaving management to manage, the union reduces its own usefulness and its appeal to workers. On a number of issues, workers rated management better than their union such as when dealing with workers' problems, treating workers fairly, involving the workers in decision-making process, etc (Table 6.7). This would seem to be the case for the union's performance in the Turkish car industry too (Nichols and Sugur 2004: 168, Table 8.1).

Many workers resent having to pay their membership dues. In future, they may be open to again seeking to defect from Turk Metal to join another union (difficult as they know this is). They may even be led down the non-union road, should management make this option sound attractive enough and decide to pursue it. Meantime, although it is sometimes claimed that Turkish trade union law (in requiring that a union must have at least ten per cent of the industry membership) has prevented the emergence of the enterprise trade unionism that is characteristic of Japan, it has fostered in the metal sector the yellow trade unionism of Turk Metal. It is quite evident that Turk Metal fails miserably as a democratic organisation.

Turk Metal owes its present prominence in the industry to the 1980 military coup and the preferential position it was accorded as the political Right consolidated its position in the early 1980s. So far managements have worked with it in order to keep other unions out but some managers are well aware of workers' disaffection and are concerned about this.

Coming in from the periphery?

It is to be hoped that in future these workers will be able to change their union. But other changes are on the way already that may impact adversely on what we have depicted, in some respects, as these workers' relatively advantageous position.

As we write, many people in Turkey are looking to the EU to set a date for the country's full membership. Relevant here is that in order to become a full member – and move in from the periphery of the EU as a political entity – Turkey has been required to come into line with EU norms. In several respects Government moves toward meeting these requirements have already helped to improve civil and human rights. It was in the name of this self-same, apparently civilised and progressive movement that a new Labour Law was introduced in 2003.

There is at least one important respect in which the new Labour Law does represent an important step forward. In fully implementing ILO Article 111, it specifically outlaws discrimination, not only on the basis of gender, but on the basis of language, ethnicity, race, political view, philosophy and religion. This has particular significance for the country's Kurds (who incidentally are rarely to be found in these factories). In one respect, there has also been a step forward in relation to tacheron labour. The new law prohibits employees of a company becoming tacheron contractors, which was not illegal before.

The new Labour Law was welcomed by TİSK , the employers' union, as introducing laws 'long-used in European countries' and 'the most advanced in the modern world' (TISK 2003 :5). This support is not surprising. To make the Turkish labour market acceptable for EU entry has been an important objective and part of this has been held to entail, as employers have seen it, an increase in '*esneklik*' – labour flexibility. In the pursuit of this, it is now legal for an employer who employs workers for at least ten hours a week to require him or her to work at times of the employer's choosing. It is now lawful for an employer to vary working hours unilaterally in the light of their assessment of economic conditions. Part time work is now legal and it is also legal to operate shift systems of more than three shifts per day. In ways such as these, previous legislation regarded by employers and their advocates as 'inflexible', 'unrealistic' and so on is being replaced and sometimes already existing practices that operate to the disadvantage of workers are being given legal authority.

Some of these and other changes – which the trade unions were unable to effectively oppose – may come to threaten the future position of workers in the formal sector, including workers in these white goods plants. A case in point – which would seem to owe everything to Japan and nothing to Europe – is that if an employer thinks this will increase his company's competitiveness he or she can lend their employees to another company in the group or to another company for six months, extendable to one year. Following the worker's return to the original company the procedure may then be repeated. It is also possible when workers have been lent to another firm for a few months for this other firm to lend these workers to yet another firm. All this is supposedly on the basis that the workers concerned agree but in reality workers' decisions will be constrained and as a manager remarked to us 'it's a wonderful way of getting rid of trouble makers'. In a further move that may also have implications for these workers, private employment agencies are also to be made legal for the first time in Turkey.

The new Law leaves workers subject to just the same disadvantages with respect to trade union recognition and, in the absence of a strong and democratic trade unionism, some of the above changes, including agency labour, should this now emerge on any scale, could undermine the advantages that presently accrue to the largely permanent, full-time workers in the white goods sector.

The Turkish white goods industry has become increasingly export oriented in recent years. This development began to speed up after the Custom Union Agreement between Turkey and the EU in 1996 and especially after the devaluation of the Lira at the turn of the century. As a consequence, foreign firms began to invest more in the white goods industry through joint ventures and takeovers and white goods firms in Turkey began to upgrade their technology and to further implement new management methods to make themselves more competitive. Through all this, whatever other problems they experienced, these white goods workers retained their 'proper jobs'. It remains to be seen whether they will continue to do so.

Notes

1 This chapter draws upon a larger study which provides considerably more detailed analysis of management, workers, unions and related matters in the white goods sector in Turkey as well as further accounts of the modern sector in Turkey more generally, including cars and parts of the textile industry (Nichols and Sugur 2004).

2 A hard version of TQM aims to increase the level of quality through systematic control of the production process; a soft version of TQM aims to win the 'hearts and minds' of workers (Wilkinson et al 1997: 800).

References

BEYSAD (2000a) Beyaz Esya Sanayicileri Dernegi Dergisi, No. 37.

BEYSAD (2000b) Beyaz Esya Sanayicileri Dernegi Dergisi, No. 39.

BEYSAD (2002) Beyaz Esya Sanayicileri Dernegi Dergisi, No. 41.

BEYSAD (2003) Beyaz Esya Sanayicileri Dernegi Dergisi, No. 41.

BEYSAD (2004) Beyaz Esya Sanayicileri Dernegi Dergisi, No. 43.

Bugra, A. (1998) 'Non-Market Mechanisms of Market Formation: The development of the Consumer Durables Industry in Turkey', *New Perspectives on Turkey*, vol. 19.

Child, J. and Rodrigues, S. (1996) 'The Role of Social Identity in the International Transfer of Knowledge through Joint Ventures' in S. R. Clegg and G. Palmer (eds) *The Politics of Management Knowledge*, London: Sage, 1996.

Helper, S. (1995) 'Can Maquilas Be Lean: The Case of Wiring Harness Production in Mexico' in S. Babson (ed.) *Lean Work, Empowerment and Exploitation in the Global Auto Industry*, Detroit: Wayne State University Press.

Istanbul Chamber of Commerce (2001) *Turkey's 500 Top Industrial Enterprises*, Istanbul: Istanbul Chamber of Commerce.

Istanbul Chamber of Commerce (2002) *Turkey's 500 Top Industrial Enterprises*, Istanbul: Istanbul Chamber of Commerce.

Katz, J. P. Krumwiede, D. W. and Wass C. M. (1998) 'Total Quality Management in the Global Marketplace: The Impact of National Culture on TQM Implementation', *International Journal of Management, 15* (3).

Klein, N. (2000) *No Logo*, London: HarperCollins/Flamingo.

Kozan, K. (1989) 'Cultural Influences on Styles of Handling Interpersonal Conflicts: Comparisons among Jordanian, Turkish and US Managers', *Human Relations, 42* (9).

Masters, R. (1996). 'Overcoming the Barriers to TQM's Success', *Quality Progress, 29* (5).

Nichols, T. and Sugur, N. (2004) *Global Management and Local Labour: Turkish Workers and Modern Industry*, Basingstoke: Palgrave Macmillan.

Nichols, T., Sugur, N. and Demir, E. (2002) 'Beyond Cheap labour: Trade Unions and Development in the Turkish Metal Industry', *The Sociological Review*, 50 (1).

Parker, M. and Slaughter, J. (1995) 'Unions and Management by Stress', in S. Babson (ed.) *Lean Work, Employment and Exploitation in the Global Auto Industry*, Detroit: Wayne State University Press.

Prime Ministry of Turkey Under-Secretariat of Foreign Trade Export Promotion Centre, http://www.igeme.org.tr/introeng.htm

Scully, J. (1996) 'TQM and Human Nature: Getting Beyond Organisational Misconceptions', *Quality Progress, 29* (5).

Thrift, N. (1999) 'The Rise of Soft capitalism', in L. Ray and A. Sayer (eds) *Culture and Economy After the Cultural Turn*, London: Sage.

TISK (2003). *İş Kanunu Tasarısı,* Istanbul: TİSK Yayın No. 231.

Wasti, S. A. (1998) 'Cultural Barriers to the Transferability of Japanese and American Human Resources Practices to Developing Countries: The Case of Turkey', *The International Journal of Human Resource Management, 9* (4).

Wilkinson, A. Godfrey, G. and Marchington, M. (1997) 'Bouquets, Brickbats and Blinkers: Total Quality Management and Employee Involvement in Practice', *Organisational Studies, 18* (5).

http://www.deik.org.tr/bultenler/2003320153551sectors-houseappliances-2002

http://www.igeme.org.tr/eng/Turkey/Ekonomy.pdf.

7
Brazil: Between Global Trends and National Politics – Restructuring and Workers' Responses

Angela Maria Carneiro Araújo, Leda Gitahy, Alessandra Rachid and Adrianna Marques da Cunha

Introduction

The internationalisation of the Brazilian white goods industry in the 1990s raises a debate on the restructuring processes of its major firms and their consequences for employment, work conditions, as well as for industrial relations, especially with regard to trade unions.

This chapter will discuss the question of what the internationalisation of this industry means to labour. Within this objective it will focus on the technological and organisational changes in a cooker factory located in the Campinas Metropolitan Area, State of São Paulo, and their consequences for the workers and the union. It will examine the impacts of the firm's restructuring on the size and composition of the labour force, on working conditions, on the workers' perceptions of the changes and on the trade union's action.

The firm chosen for the case study is the main Brazilian cooker company (BrazilCo), whose market share is around 40 per cent of domestic sales. It is a distinctive example of the recent changes in the development of the Brazilian white goods industry. BrazilCo's restructuring has been affected by internationalisation through a cross-border acquisition and technological and organisational changes aimed at production efficiency and cost reduction.

The study is based on secondary data about the Brazilian white goods industry, the evolution of employment in the sector and the metalworkers' characteristics in the Campinas region. Fieldwork data were collected in the first semester of 2002. In the cooker factory interviews were conducted with managers from sales, production, logistics, quality and human resources to obtain information about the restructuring process. A survey was also made with the administrative staff (48 persons, 41 men and seven women, including directors, managers and supervisors) and with 53 production workers (41 men and 11 women) from different areas of the factory (stamping, enamelling, painting, assembly lines, maintenance, tool shop, and stock) to evaluate their perceptions of the changes.[1]

The first part of the paper shows the development of the Brazilian white goods industry, emphasising its denationalisation and performance in the 1990s. The second part presents the company studied and the technological and organisational changes implemented. The following section analyses the impacts that the firm's changes have brought to the structure of employment, the division and content of work, the working conditions and to the characteristics of its labour force. Workers' perceptions of the changes are discussed in the fourth part. Finally, the context of industrial relations in Brazil and the role of the Metalworkers Union are explored.

There is clearly evidence of globalisation in the Brazilian case, in particular foreign ownership dominates. There is also evidence that outsourcing has increased, so too labour productivity, pressure on numbers employed, stress and RSI. However, our argument is that in the Brazilian case, national politics counts both for the development of the white goods sector, and for the kind of consequences management strategies have on employment relations. Economic and industrial policies were important for the way this sector was reshaped by capital concentration and internationalisation and by technological and organisational innovations. Labour market regulation, political difficulties the government faced to flexibilise labour law, and the political orientation of the union can explain why in this case study a strong flexibilisation and precariousness of working conditions and an important change in labour relations were not observed.

The Brazilian white goods industry

The white goods industry was introduced in Brazil at the end of the 1940s, during the initial phase of the import substitution policy adopted by the Brazilian government. It followed in the wake of demographic and urban expansion in Brazil, as well as the creation and development of a large consumer market in the urban areas of the country. There was a significant increase in the Brazilian population in the period from 1940 to 1970 with growth rates of roughly three per cent per annum. Brazil also saw a steady increase in the concentration of its population in urban areas starting in the 1940s, mainly in the large cities. In 1940, 31 per cent of Brazil's inhabitants were city dwellers. This percentage climbed progressively from 36 per cent in 1950, 45 per cent in 1960, 56 per cent in 1970 and 68 per cent in 1980 to 78 per cent in 1996. The portion of the Brazilian population that lived in cities with over 500,000 inhabitants rose from 11 per cent in 1940 to 36 per cent in 1996 (Camarano and Beltrão 2000).

The international scenario was of increased household appliance production and consumption after the Second World War. At that moment, the main Brazilian producers in the segment of white goods for refrigeration were founded. It is worth recalling that the Brazilian producer of gas cookers under study in this chapter (BrazilCo) had already been founded in the 1930s at the very onset of the creation of a metal-mechanical sector in Brazil. The limitations in the country's capacity for producing electric energy at that time may be linked to the noted predominant demand for gas cookers, due to the high costs of electricity. The electric cookers have been directed towards the high end of the Brazilian consumer market.

In the 1970s and 1980s this industry came to be characterised by the existence of a reduced number of large national family-owned businesses and by the presence of two large national groups that controlled the major companies in the sector (Gitahy and Cunha 1999). The entry of foreign groups during the 1990s played a role in reshaping the industry's structure of financial control, chiefly as a result of the acquisition of leading national companies (including the household appliance producers and some of their suppliers, as the main Brazilian producer of hermetic compressors).

The leading world groups entered the Brazilian White goods industry mainly through the acquisition of its major firms, with eyes on the size and growth potential of both the internal and regional markets (Mercosul) as well as on the previous existence of a structured production chain. That chain was characterised by the development of important links among its different levels, by the presence of strategic suppliers (like the suppliers of the main component for refrigeration appliances: hermetic compressors) and by a strong external commercial insertion.

The Brazilian white goods industry is still an oligopoly, though now dominated by large internationalised foreign groups that directly or indirectly control the major companies. The four largest companies in Brazil (Whirlpool, Electrolux, Bosch-Siemens Hausgeräte and General Electric) accounted for about 72 per cent of the total revenues of the industry in 1997 (Cunha 2003). The foreign groups that control Brazilian companies are the four main conglomerates within the world's white goods market.

Technological maturity represents a key feature in the white goods industry. Technological opportunities are to be found in the possibilities of incremental product and process developments. Product innovations have been related to changes in consumers' tastes, habits and needs, innovations that stimulate a sense of product obsolescence. As far as gas cookers are concerned, it is interesting to observe that their features and design certainly change if the product is directed towards the high or the low end of the Brazilian consumer market. Bigger and more sophisticated (with more features and different design) cookers are directed towards the high end of the market and smaller and simpler products towards its low end. Besides, in general, cookers' size has been reducing due to the shrinking of Brazilian families and of their houses or apartments. Still, one can observe a growing preference from Brazilian consumers to buy more sophisticated and expensive cookers for esthetical and social reasons (even if they don't cook their own meals very often). In turn, process innovations have been associated with the dissemination of microelectronic automation and new techniques for the planning, organisation and management of production and quality. They are aimed at reducing both costs and stock levels and at increasing flexibility.

In the 1990s, the leading companies in the Brazilian white goods industry underwent productive restructuring processes, especially after their acquisition by the main worldwide producers and clearly following an international trend. White goods firms closed plants with traditional technology and opened new technologically updated ones. Besides, they bought new equipment and introduced new managerial methods seeking the modernisation of production and cost reduction. Moreover, they developed a higher quality supply chain. This restructuring process has been extended to domestic suppliers, both national and foreign.

During the last decade, Brazilian companies produced the entire range of white goods and introduced market segmentation according to income groups. They began to shift their production focus to the international market, especially stimulated by agreements with, or acquisitions by, foreign companies. Yet the production of these companies was predominantly aimed at the internal market. The major Brazilian supplier (one of the world leaders) of hermetic compressors began an important productive internationalisation before its acquisition, through external investments, involving the building up of production plants in foreign countries, the acquisition of foreign firms and the development of joint ventures, especially with Asian firms. It made also a significant effort aimed at the improvement of its external commercial insertion, including the expansion and diversification of its exports' destination.[2]

The Brazilian white goods industry was responsible for generating revenues in the order of roughly US\$ 2 billion[3] and for providing jobs for 22,422 workers[4] in 2000. The average annual growth rate of revenues in the industry during the 1990s was quite modest (only four per cent) and employment fell by four per cent per annum between 1994 and 2000 (Cunha 2003). Sales had reached a peak of 12.9 million units of white good appliances in 1996, 4.4 million cookers and 4.0 million refrigerators. In the year 2000, internal sales stood at 9.6 million units (3.6 million cookers and 3.2 million refrigerators).[5]

The performance of the Brazilian white goods industry has always been closely linked to the direction defined by the macro-economic policies adopted by the Brazilian government.[6] The economic recovery witnessed in Brazil from 1994 to 1996, mainly after the Brazilian government adopted a plan aimed at maintaining prices stable (known as the 'Plano Real'), brought about high levels of annual growth in the consumption of white goods. This expansion in sales (as well as in the revenues of the companies in the sector) occurred due to stable inflation, which led to increased real incomes, combined with a drop in interest rates and expanded credit lines to consumers, generating a higher demand for products from those with lower incomes. Sales also rose because of the demand of high-income consumers seeking more sophisticated products, whose internal availability had been increased by lower import tariffs (as a result of a policy to implement free trade adopted in the beginning of the 1990s by the Brazilian government) and by a foreign exchange policy directed towards increasing the value of the national currency (which started with the adoption of the plan for stabilisation set off in the middle of the 1990s).

The rising trend in sales of white goods changed abruptly after 1997 in the wake of a phase of deterioration in the country's economic situation. This period was characterised by increased unemployment, more cases of default and higher interest rates, not to mention the crisis in the retail sector. Revenues and job openings started to show a recovery in 2000 with respect to the previous year (they presented, respectively, increases of roughly 24 per cent and two per cent).[7] Nevertheless, at the end of the decade revenues had only managed to reach the level registered in 1992 and the number of job openings failed to reach the levels at the beginning of the decade. This trend clearly demonstrates the problems that the sector was facing, especially during the second half of the 1990s, problems which also produced a high level of idle capacity.

The penetration rates for some traditional white goods, such as cookers (98 per cent), and refrigerators (85 per cent), reveal a high level of saturation amongst Brazilian consumers. Saturation levels for other types of appliances, such as freezers (19 per cent), washing machines (34 per cent), clothes dryers, dishwashers, microwave ovens and air conditioners, are much lower.[8] This can be explained by the consumers' perceived necessity for such appliances and the income level of the consumer population. The future expansion in white goods sales in the Brazilian market will be based on the demand for appliances that have very low levels of saturation, which will depend particularly on the evolution of the population's buying power and on the replacement rate of appliances that have high levels of physical saturation.

As far as foreign trade of white goods is concerned, it is possible to affirm the following: First, exports and imports of final products have not played a significant role in the revenues of the Brazilian white goods industry. Exports and imports reached, respectively, an average annual stake of roughly eight per cent and one per cent of revenues in the 1990s.[9] Secondly, imports of components have not had a significant impact on this sector – the percentage of national content is high.[10] Thirdly, the persistence of a trade surplus highlights the fact that the industry is more an exporter than an importer. Finally, the trade surplus has increased approximately 80 per cent from 1990 to 2000, revealing that the firms are interested in sustaining their export performance after the period of ownership denationalisation (Cunha 2003).

The Brazilian cooker company's restructuring process

The firm studied, BrazilCo, is a Brazilian cooker company of long standing, founded at the onset of the import substitution period and located in the region of Campinas, State of São Paulo. The company remained a family firm until the beginning of the 1990s, when a process of administrative modernisation changed the way the company worked. The Company was purchased in the middle of the decade by a North American Multinational (NAMN), whose goal was to enter the Brazilian market to produce the whole line of white good appliances in the country.

In 2000, BrazilCo had around 2000 employees, a total revenue of US\$ 170 million[11] and it sold around 1.3 million cookers, which represented a little more than one third of all domestic sales in that year,[12] making it the main Brazilian cooker manufacturer. In 2002, the factory had an output of around 8,500 cookers per day, which represented something close to 65 per cent of its daily production capacity.

The company's sales were initially focused on small cities, outside of the state of São Paulo. This strategy allowed its products to become very well known in the country. Nowadays, the company continues to target domestic production and sales to the internal market, but it also imports appliances made by the group in other countries. The BrazilCo brand name is used for simple models of cookers directed towards lower level income groups and the NAMN brand name is used for cookers with features directed towards higher-level income groups. The company's main clients are medium-sized and large retailers, with the top 100 retailers being responsible for 70 per cent of the company's sales. The share that supermarkets have held in sales has increased from 1997 on, when some of these establishments began to sell household appliances. As far as exports are concerned, they make up around 20 per cent of the company's total revenues and are destined to approximately 50 different countries, mainly Argentina, Mexico and Chile.

BrazilCo initiated a process of modernisation in the 1980s, following a general trend observed in the Brazilian white goods industry. Changes at that time involved investments in new equipment for the stamping, painting and enamelling sectors and for the transport of pieces and an attempt to implant a kanban system that didn't succeed.

The restructuring process was intensified with the acquisition by NAMN in the middle of the 1990s. It included changes in the firm's organisational structure, in its production and work organisation and in inter-firms relations through downsizing and outsourcing. The downsizing led to the reduction in the firm's hierarchical levels. According to a manager interviewed, the organisational structure was flattened in order to decentralise its decision-making processes and to increase its capacity to respond to the constant changes in the market's competitive scenario.

The main changes in production organisation included investments in new equipment, the change of some parts of the plant layout, the formalisation of the quality system and new forms of relation with suppliers.

The company adopted new equipment to automate the assembly lines and make them more flexible. Nevertheless, they have not yet achieved very high levels of automation. Assembly is one of the most difficult stages to automate in the cooker production process, because various types of thin metal sheets have to be joined. Despite these difficulties, its automation is considered a priority due to the introduction of new NAMN's models and mainly due to the necessity to reduce the incidence of Repetitive Strain Injury (RSI)/Osteomuscular Work-Related Disease (OWRD). However, some of the interviewees noted that the plant uses equipment that is not found in any other cooker factory in the country, such as the progressive tools that are used to make the cook tops and the equipment used to produce the gas tubes.

The changes in the plant layout were not so significant. There are few cells in metal stamping and there have been no great changes in the positioning of the machines. The layout of the factory continues to be predominantly functional, with separate sections for stamping, enamelling and so on.

During the 1990s, BrazilCo conducted a gradual formalisation of its quality system, and this enabled the company to obtain the ISO 9002 certification, which is particularly important to export activities.[13] At the end of the decade, BrazilCo adopted the Six Sigma program, following instructions from its foreign headquarters, which imposed the adoption of Six Sigma to all companies belonging to the group. Six Sigma's objective is to attain a smaller number of errors per million operations in all sections of the company. The term 'Six Sigma' was coined by Motorola and has been used to denominate a managerial package involving the combined use of various techniques, which already existed. In BrazilCo, the programme includes problem-solving methodologies, Statistical Process Control (SPC), Failure Mode and Effect Analysis (FMEA), Design of Experiments (DOE) and 5S or housekeeping.

The Six Sigma program has a specific manager who is responsible for its implementation and co-ordination and is called 'Black Belt Master'. The employees that have already been trained are called 'Green Belts' and they take part in groups responsible for generating improvements, reducing costs and developing projects geared towards quality. These groups are formed ad hoc for trouble-shooting regarding a specific problem or for improving a specific process or product.[14] The groups are made up of people from all levels that can bring contributions to the issue under study, such as managers, engineers, project designers, technicians and shop floor workers, when deemed necessary.

As part of the restructuring process, many activities have been outsourced, although, an interviewee considers it one of the most vertically integrated cooker factories. Indirect activities outsourced include product design, final product movement in the factory, tool and mould construction. Direct activities outsourced include bobbin cutting, the production of wire parts, the stamping of drawn steel parts – a labour intensive activity – and part of the silkscreen and enamelling processes.

The outsourcing process led to changes in the relationship between BrazilCo and its suppliers. The company uses an external just-in-time[15] with its suppliers, which must deliver parts daily or, in some cases, several times per day, and it usually keeps enough stock for two days' production. This system permits a more flexible response to clients, which is of utmost importance in a sector plagued by constant changes in their clients' demands, which derive from the lack of stability in the demand for domestic appliances. The company is training its suppliers as part of its quality programme, and now many of them have also received the ISO 9000 certificate.[16]

These changes in production organisation did not lead to major changes in the work organisation. Most of the employees are stationed in the assembly line area, where they appear to work very intensively. The performance of tasks along these lines is governed by pre-determined time frames, within which workers must work. Short cycles of these repetitive tasks make up their working day. Even in the production stages with cellular layouts, each worker still carries out just one operation. Yet there is job rotation within cells and in the assembly lines every one or two hours, another change introduced in order to reduce the incidence of RSI/OWRD.

The company's main programme at the time of the research, the Six Sigma, rarely involves shop floor workers in its groups. To obtain their commitment to quality objectives, a suggestion program was specifically designed for them, which rewards individuals or groups if their suggestions are accepted and carried out by the managers and if they generate cost reductions. However, if a suggestion is accepted its copyright is transferred to the company, allowing it to patent it. The worker, therefore, automatically loses the property of his (her) creation.

Restricted workers' participation can also be observed in the training program for Six Sigma, which was only attended by managers, supervisors and others holding positions of responsibility. The Six Sigma manager, for instance, took part in a five-month training program in the US, having then received the title of 'Black Belt Master'. The 'Green Belts', who take part in the Six Sigma projects groups, also received intensive training, but they were mainly from the engineering and technical areas. Shop floor workers, on the other hand, had only become acquainted with this new method either through a primer containing general information or through posters on the plant's walls.

Most of the time, workers just receive incentives to finish middle or high school. However, the majority of them had attended some training course, the total provision for workers' training being around 36 hours per year, according to the Human Resources Manager. The training programmes for production workers were generally directed more towards operational issues, involving aspects such as safety in the workplace, preventive maintenance and quality control, many of these programmes aiming to transfer more responsibility regarding quality over to the workers. These courses were generally short ones, which take a few hours, some of them being offered on the job.

The firm usually invests in the behavioural training of shop-floor workers in order to develop their responsibility and commitment. Many of the workers interviewed mentioned they had attended speeches and meetings with managers and supervisors whose main aim was the changing of attitudes.

Although BrazilCo does not adopt team working, the workers' knowledge about work group (Table 7.1) reveals its importance in terms of behavioural improvement. All of those interviewed affirmed that they work in groups for they related it to mutual help and a good work relationship. Some said they work in groups just because they rotate between working stations – that is, to avoid RSI. Only one of them associated the work group concept with autonomy.

Table 7.1 Management Methods Known by BrazilCo's Managers and Workers

Management Method	Managers percentages (n = 48)	Workers percentages (n = 53)
Total Quality	98	100
Certifications	96	96
Work groups	98	89
Six Sigma	96	85
Preventive maintenance	79	72
Quality Control Circles	71	38
Flexible production	73	23
Lean production	54	23
Internal just-in-time	90	15
External just-in-time	85	9
Re-engineering	79	9
Statistical Process Control	73	9
Kaizen	60	2

The firm invests far more resources in the training of managers, supervisors and administrative personnel than in that of shop floor workers. That is one of the reasons why some of the workers were not so familiar with the management methods, compared to the managers (Table 7.1). Most workers (47 from the 53 interviewed) knew that BrazilCo was introducing the Six Sigma program, but they didn't have much information about it. Some had become aware of it because 'there are some posters in the company'. One of them said: 'we don't have free access to it'. It was very different for most of the managers, who knew it well. Many of them had already taken part in a Six Sigma group.

Impacts of restructuring on employment and working conditions

The consequences of this process of restructuring, for workers as well as for managers, have been of great significance. In the case study, as in the white goods industry and in the metal sector as a whole, the introduction of technological and organisational changes has affected the structure of employment, the recruitment policy, the division and content of work, the working conditions and the characteristics of the workforce (Araújo et al 2002).

The intensification of the restructuring process in the metal and in white goods sectors during the 1990s together with a persistent economic crisis caused a significant reduction in employment alongside increased productivity for local companies. The loss of jobs was directly associated to organisational and technological changes and also to outsourcing. The move towards outsourcing productive activities and the related redefinition in the division of labour amongst companies in the supply chain have contributed to trigger an important loss of jobs, specially of shop floor workers, as well as an increase in productivity and a change in the distribution of employment amongst companies of different sizes (Araújo and Gitahy 2003; Araújo et al 2002; Gitahy and Cunha 1999).

The metal manufacturing sector of the Campinas region employed 71,095 workers in 1989. The number of jobs in this sector decreased steadily during the 1990s, reaching a level of 43,798 in 1998. However, in the last few years, due to the set up of new factories in the region, a slight increase in the number of jobs has been witnessed in this sector, which reached 49.000 in 2000 and employed roughly 45,000 workers in 2002.

Employment in the white goods industry fell between 1994 and 2000 by 25 per cent for Brazil as a whole and 30 per cent for Campinas. Similarly, at BrazilCo, the restructuring process led to a significant reduction in the number of workers. Dismissals increased towards the end of the decade, due mainly to the changes introduced after the acquisition. In 1996, there were 2,600 employees in the plant. This number was reduced to around 2,100 employees in 2000 and, reduced once again, to around 1,750 in 2001. This represents a reduction of 33 per cent in the total number of employees between 1996 and 2001. Moreover, there was a reduction of 28 per cent in the number of shop floor workers in less than two years (Table 7.2)

The reduction of jobs also reached administrative and management staff due to the flattening of hierarchical structure and to the decentralisation of functions. Initially, the number of technical, administrative and managerial positions was reduced, but in recent years, there has been some growth in the number of staff involved in administration and planning.

The introduction of technological and organisational changes has also affected the company's recruitment policy. BrazilCo, at the time of the study, required that the applicant should have completed at least elementary school (i.e. eight years of schooling in the Brazilian schooling system) and it favoured candidates who were not very young and married. Immediately after the acquisition by NAMN, preference was given to single young workers, with a higher schooling level. However, in the last years this policy was changed for the company felt that married and more mature workers, who were in the age bracket between 35 and 45 years, had a greater sense of responsibility and a greater willingness to get involved with the company's goals.

Another way to ensure that hired workers would have a sense of responsibility and that the company would be able to obtain a stronger commitment from them was through using inter-personal networking. In over half of the sample the workers had some relative who was working in the company and 34 of the workers had got the job through relatives and/or friends.[17]

At BrazilCo, shop floor workers work a standard 44-hour working week and are permanent workers. According to the labour legislation, established since 1943 (The Consolidation of Labour Laws – CLT), workers have first a probationary three month contract and after this they become, automatically, permanent workers. The legislation guarantees 30 days paid holidays, one day of rest per week, eight hour working day, minimum wage, sick leave, retirement, special female rights (as paid maternity leave), a Christmas bonus (equivalent to one month wage) and a sum paid as compensation when a worker is dismissed.

When the company needs to increase production for seasonal reasons it still uses overtime or contracts temporary workers through an agency. These contracts last for only three months and can be renewed for no more than another three months. BrazilCo could not take advantage of temporary contracts and annualised hours to adjust its production to demand fluctuations because of the opposition of the Metalworkers Union. Thus, precarious forms of contracting were not used inside the company although it sought to flexibilise its production organisation mainly through personnel reduction and externalisation of productive activities, via outsourcing.

Table 7.2 White Goods and Related Employment in Brazil, 1994–2000

	1994	1995	1996	1997	1998	1999	2000	2001	1994–2000 percentage change
White Goods Industry – Brazil*	29,990	23,758	26,623	26,393	22,093	22,093	22,422	–	(–25)
White Goods Industry – Campinas*	4,835	5,041	2,424	4,646	4,224	3,557	3,406	–	(–30)
Metalworkers Campinas*	55,059	49,570	43,919	46,390	43,798	43,698	49,102	–	(–11)
BrazilCo employees	–	–	2,600	–	–	–	2,100	1,750	(–33) 1996–2001
BrazilCo production workers	–	–	–	–	–	–	1,800	1,290	(–28) 2000–2001

Source: *RAIS Data base/Ministry of Labour – Brazil.

Concerning the division and content of work, those changes, on the one hand, have facilitated the execution of tasks and have reduced the risks of accidents, through the acquisition of new computerised machines (such as presses, for example) and the use of automatic tooling in the assembly lines. On the other hand, they have led to the quickening of the pace of work through the transfer of responsibilities and new tasks to shop floor workers, such as cleaning the workplace, visual inspection of parts and minor procedures in machine and tool maintenance. Besides, the requirement of a greater involvement of the workers and the pressures for the reach of quality and productivity goals together with inadequate conditions of the work environment have brought negative consequences to workers' health.

According to one of the managers interviewed, one of the problems that the company was deeply concerned about was how the workers' hearing capacity could become impaired or even lost, for this could occur even when protective equipment was worn, because of the very high noise level in the factory. Regarding the issue of impaired hearing or deafness, the factory was starting to measure the hearing capacity of new recruits in order to monitor any hearing impairment. The other and most important concern was the rise in the number of cases of RSI/OWRD at the firm, particularly in the last seven years. This had been due to the addition of new tasks to existing jobs, greater controls on breaks ('wasted time') and the general intensification of what was essentially repetitive work. Data from the firm suggested that around 10 per cent of the shop floor workforce was suffering in some way from the effects of repetitive strains.

The firm's major preoccupation in that respect was on how to find a solution to the problem within the assembly lines. Job rotation was performed within the few existing cells in the metal stamping sector and in the production lines every one or two hours, and ten-minute gymnastics classes were also being offered on a daily basis. In addition, projects and studies were being carried out, with the aim of improving the ergonomic conditions at the workstations.

Discussions with managers from the Production and Human Resources areas suggested that there were two main reasons for the firm's concern with those occupational health issues. Firstly, the local union had made health risks at work a very visible theme. Secondly, there was a need to reduce costs related to the job stability guaranteed to workers who got RSI, which was an agreement that had been established with the union.

Around 80 per cent of both male and female workers said they were satisfied with their conditions of work. This may be related to the fact that the firm had introduced technological changes in some sectors (for instance, in the stamping and painting areas) and incremental changes in many pieces of equipment, improving the performance of a large number of tasks on the shop floor. In addition, the cleanliness of the workplace, the creation of spaces to rest and meet colleagues, may well have contributed to that positive evaluation of the work environment.

Nevertheless, around 59 per cent of those interviewed affirmed that they felt frequent physical discomfort at work in the month before the interviews, the main complaints being of backaches and pain in the legs. The discomfort caused by dust in the air was an issue brought up by 28 per cent of the interviewees, who worked in some specific sectors of the factory (in the painting sector, for example). The conditions in terms of temperature, mainly excessive heat, were mentioned by roughly 38 per cent of the workers as a factor that caused frequent discomfort.

The intensification of restructuring in the firm led to a significant change in workforce composition. We can observe that the workforce became better educated and stable, and the trend also shows the permanence of older workers, with a longer time on the job. The overwhelming majority of both managers and workers (more than 80 per cent) were male, married, had children and came from other towns (77 per cent of the workers and 65 per cent of the managers had been born in other cities), hence, being migrants. The average amount of time that the employees had been working at the company was quite high among the workers (an average of 10 years). The worker who had been the longest time in the company worked there for 23 years. In contrast, among the managers, there was one group that had been working there for a reasonably long time. Yet many of them had been hired after the company's acquisition.

Against the trend observed between 1989 and 2000 in the region's metal industry, where women's participation increased constantly (Araújo and Gitahy 2003), BrazilCo presents the reverse process. According to some women workers interviewed, the firm ceased to hire women for production in the second half of the 1990s. They became reduced to eight per cent of the total number of employees and to an even lower proportion in the shop floor. According to some managers, although the firm adopts a policy that forbids any kind of discrimination, the decrease in the number of women was due to the high incidence of RSI among them, for they were concentrated in the assembly lines and in the more repetitive tasks.

Data in the tables below show the characteristics of BrazilCo's workforce in relation to age, schooling, sex and wage levels. Analysing Table 7.3, one can see that most of the workers had concluded their high school studies or had reached even higher levels of schooling and, with regards to age, most found themselves in the age bracket ranging from 30 to 39 years old (the average age being of 34.5 years old). The greatest portion of the workers with higher ages (those between 40 and 49) had lower levels of schooling. Among the 11 people who fell into this age bracket, only three had finished their high school studies and 1 worker was attending university. On the other hand, the group of younger workers (those with ages ranging from 20 to 29) had a higher level of schooling, for the majority had already obtained their high school diplomas.

Table 7.3   Age and Level of Education of BrazilCo Workers and Managers

	AGE	Incomplete Elementary Schooling[1]	Concluded Elementary Schooling[2]	Incomplete High School Level[3]	Completed High School Level[4]	Incomplete University Level[5]	Completed University Level[6]	Total (%)
Workers	20–29	3	1	1	8	3	0	16 (30)
	30–39	2	4	3	16	1	0	26 (49)
	40–49	3	4	0	3	0	1	11 (21)
	Total	8 (15%)	9 (17%)	4 (8%)	27 (51%)	4 (8%)	1 (2.0%)	53 (100)
Managers	20–29	0	0	0	0	0	2	2 (4)
	30–39	0	1	1	3	1	13	19 (40)
	40–49	1	0	0	6	3	12	22 (46)
	50–59	0	1	0	1	0	3	5 (10)
	Total	1 (2%)	2 (4%)	1 (2%)	10 (21%)	4 (8%)	30 (63%)	48 (100)

Notes: (1) less than eight years of schooling; (2) eight years of schooling; (3) from nine to ten years of schooling; (4) 11 years of schooling; (5) from 12 to 14 years of schooling; (6) bachelor's degree or beyond – 15 years or more of schooling. The levels of schooling in this and the following table start from first grade on (not including the number of years of nursery school nor kindergarten attended).

Table 7.4 shows that the workers were concentrated in a salary bracket ranging from 5.01 to seven minimum wages. Women were concentrated from 4.01 to five minimum wages (55 per cent) while the majority of men found themselves between 5.01 to seven minimum wages (52 per cent). Among the women interviewed who had already completed their high school studies, the majority (60 per cent) was receiving less than five minimum wages, while among the men of the same school level, 60 per cent were receiving more than five minimum wages.

Women are paid less, partly because at BrazilCo they are concentrated in the assembly line and in the allegedly less skilled jobs.[18] However, if we compare the wages of males and females who worked in the less skilled positions and had the same level of schooling women remain disadvantaged despite the policy of no discrimination adopted by the company after the acquisition. This is only one example of the wage inequality between sexes that exists in large scale in the Brazilian economy due to the fact that the legislation instituting equal pay for equal work is not actually enforced.

As noted by the BrazilCo Production Manager, shop floor workers' salaries were established through a collective agreement signed annually with the union.[19] Nevertheless, compared to other companies and also to the declining wage average among metalworkers in the Campinas metropolitan area, BrazilCo pays relatively higher wages. This is, in part, due to the greater length of service of the majority of its workforce, which, in the past, had seniority pay. As an indicator of the purchasing power and the standard of living of these workers and managers, it is interesting to note that 83 per cent of the workers and 90 per cent of the managers interviewed were homeowners and 70 per cent of the workers had their own cars.

However, workers at BrazilCo, at the time of the field research, did not receive individual or group performance-related pay nor did they still have seniority pay. According to the law, they have the right to a premium for participation in results. This premium amount is negotiated between the union and the company and at least part of it is related to the general achievement of goals.

Furthermore, the workers had few chances of being promoted. According to the Human Resources Manager a new plan was being discussed to redefine positions and compensations. However, it is important to emphasise that the company had a policy of in-house recruitment. Only those positions that could not be filled by people inside the company were advertised and preference was given to applicants who had already worked for the company.

The lack of a career plan was a cause of dissatisfaction mainly among the managers, but among the workers as well. Among the interviewed workers, some, having been in the company for quite a long time, affirmed that they still held the same position that they had when they entered the

Table 7.4 BrazilCo Workers' Pay According to Level of Schooling and Gender

	Salaries (in multiples of the minimum wage)	Incomplete Elementary Schooling	Concluded Elementary Schooling	Incomplete High School Level	Completed High School Level	Incomplete University Level	Completed University Level	Total (%)
Men	3.01 to 4	0	1	1	3	0	0	5 (12)
	4.01 to 5	4	2	0	5	1	0	12 (29)
	5.01 to 7	2	4	2	11	3	0	22 (52)
	7.01 to 10	0	1	0	1	0	0	2 (5)
	10.01 to 15	0	0	0	0	0	1	1 (2)
	Total	6 (14%)	8 (19%)	3 (7%)	20 (48%)	4 (10%)	1 (2%)	42 (100)
Women	3.01 to 4	0	1	0	1	0	0	2 (18)
	4.01 to 5	2	0	1	3	0	0	6 (55)
	5.01 to 7	1	0	0	1	0	0	2 (18)
	7.01 to 10	0	0	0	1	0	0	1 (9)
	Total	3 (27%)	1 (9%)	1 (9%)	6 (55%)	0	0	11 (100)

company's service, which is clear proof that the lack of perspectives for promotion for the production workers had not changed due to the process of restructuring undergone by the company.

Nevertheless, workers did receive some benefits in the form of indirect salaries. BrazilCo provided a restaurant, transportation, a health care plan, life insurance and time off for specialised training courses (if so required by company training programmes) to its production workers, even if the benefits provided were fewer than those granted by other companies in the sector.[20] In addition, many benefits were only extended to managers, such as performance related premiums or bonuses, grants for courses, expense accounts, fitness classes and a company car.

Workers' assessments of changes in the firm

How do workers assess the changes in work conditions and what explains their attitudes in the face of the transformations just described? Table 7.5 displays the answers provided by workers to the following question: 'Compared to five years ago, how have things changed for you in the following respects?'

The majority of the workers felt that their satisfaction and right to make decisions had improved. Although this right is actually limited by the strong presence of the department's supervisors it is appreciated by the workers compared to the previous situation. 70 per cent of the interviewees also considered that their workloads had got better or remained the same, which seems in conflict with the fact that for 78 per cent of them their levels of stress had increased or had not changed. Nonetheless, the introduction of automated presses and new tools in the assembly line could explain why 28 per cent of the workers observed a reduction in their workload comparing with five years before. Moreover, many of those who said that their workload did not change acknowledged that the pace of work and their functions and responsibilities increased. It is also interesting to note that the right to make decisions increased along with stress, which

Table 7.5   BrazilCo Workers' Assessment of Changes Last Five Years

	Workers percentages (n = 53)			
	Better	Worse	Same	Don't Know
Right to make decisions	57	6	34	4
Workload	28	23	47	2
Pay	51	15	32	2
Stress	21	38	40	2
Satisfaction	49	15	34	2
Job security	34	25	38	4
Career prospects	36	23	36	6

can be explained by the association, in the workers' assessments, of that right with the heightening of their responsibilities.

In order to analyse the meaning of the answers given by the workers, we organised the interviewees into five groups, whose members had some characteristics in common, in order to better explain the meaning of their answers and their attitudes towards the changes that had been occurring in their jobs:

1. employees who were 'handicapped' by RSI (11 per cent of the sample);
2. workers that had come from rural areas (17 per cent of the sample);
3. those 'looking forward to retirement', or who felt they had very low chances of improvement in their careers (21 per cent of the sample);
4. 'workers with good chances of improvement in their careers' or who were confident of good prospects in their careers (40 per cent of the sample) and
5. 'workers who wished to change their type of professional activity, or to change to a different field of work' (11 per cent of the sample).

The first group of workers suffered from RSI, which had brought them a very high level of dissatisfaction, with regards to their working conditions as well as to their lives. Their ages varied from 26 to 43, and their salaries were concentrated between five to seven times the minimum wage. The members of this group had been working in the company for periods ranging from five to 23 years. Their complaints repeatedly registered their dissatisfaction with regards to their pace of work, the difficulties that they faced and the discrimination that they felt from their colleagues. The workers in this group were the ones who expressed the highest levels of dissatisfaction, even though they took into account that they were happy to have a job, for, due to their illness, they reckoned that their chances to reach good perspectives in their careers were very slim.

The workers in the second group (those of rural origin) declared they had begun to work early, when still children, helping parents to run farms. For the large majority of them, their jobs at BrazilCo had been their first 'formal' (contracted) job. Their ages varied from 28 to 47, the amount of time they had been working at the company ranged from five to 23 years, and their levels of schooling went from those having completed an elementary school level up to one member who had finished a university course, the largest concentration being of workers who had finished high school. Over half of these workers had taken a special course (called 'supletivo', i.e., accelerated courses for teenagers and adults to reach either elementary or high school level equivalency) while they were working at the company. The largest portion of them received salaries from five to seven minimum wages.

This group presents the highest levels of satisfaction with work conditions in the firm, their satisfaction being linked to the fact of having a 'formal' job and also being related to their improved standards of living. These people had come from rural areas to work in the company through indications they received from relatives or acquaintances, already at work in the firm. These workers were satisfied with their wages and with their career prospects in the company, due to the possibilities linked to in-house recruitment. For these employees, the chances of improving their living conditions derived from their jobs, and their acknowledgement of this fact made them grateful for the opportunity they had been given, and that explains their high levels of satisfaction.

The characteristic common to all members of the third group are that they couldn't see any career prospects and their plan for the future was 'to look forward to retirement'. Their ages varied from 35 to 45 and their salaries ranged from four to seven minimum wages, most of them having been in the company and in their positions for more than eleven years. This group consisted of some of the workers who had worked the longest period of time for the company and that had the lowest levels of schooling. Their assessment of their working conditions seemed to be associated to their own amount of initiative and their own competence (which they considered to be low).

In general terms, they held a positive view regarding their jobs, relating their jobs to their ages and to the fact that they had low levels of schooling. They associated their satisfaction to the analysis that they made of the labour market (in which they identified scarce opportunities for professional growth, both within and without the company) and also linked it to the fact that they held a guarantee to be able to make a living. Regarding the changes that had taken place in their working conditions, they considered that improvements had occurred with respect to machinery and also with respect to the prevention of accidents. Nonetheless, they pinpointed worsened conditions with respect to incentives linked to salaries and to the pressure felt regarding productivity. Rather than actually feeling satisfied, they seemed to be resigned to their work situation in the light of the unfavourable conditions perceived in the labour market.

The fourth group is a type of antithesis to the former. They (19 men and two women) believed they had good career prospects and they showed interest in investing in themselves, through improving their professional capacity. The majority of them were attending (or planned to attend) technical or university courses with the aim of moving up in their careers in or outside the company.

The members of this group were distributed in different age brackets (ranging from 25 to 42 years old) and held different levels of schooling: three were attending university courses, 14 had concluded high school and four had finished or were finishing their elementary schooling. The salary bracket, where these workers concentrated (11 of them), was that ranging from 5.01 to seven minimum wages. The length of time working for the company varied considerably among them: one year and eight months being the shortest amount of time and 23 years being the longest.

With regard to their working conditions, some of the members of this group said that they were satisfied with their salaries or, even, just with the fact of having a job, while others complained about the scarcity of opportunities on the labour market both outside and inside the company. They also dwelled upon the ever-increasing pressures placed on them for higher degree of schooling and skills' improvement in order to keep their jobs. These workers took upon themselves a great part of the responsibility to look for improving their qualifications.

The workers encompassed in the fifth group had, as a common feature, a plan to change their line of work and envisioned the possibility of opening up their own businesses or of passing an exam for a position as a civil servant. Their ages ranged from 31 to 40 and their salaries varied from three to 10 minimum wages. Most of them had completed their high school education and only one of them had not completed the elementary school level. The amount of time that they had been working for the company varied from five to 15 years.

With regards to the changes that had occurred, they believed that they currently faced more pressure and more demands from the company and that, on the other hand, they received very little reward for any extra efforts that they had put in. The dissatisfaction of this group of workers was linked basically to the fact that their skills were not being used effectively by the company and to the lack of opportunities. A commonly heard statement was that they couldn't see any prospects for themselves at BrazilCo. This perception was leading them to seek other alternatives of work outside of the company. This dissatisfaction also led them to put more focus on the aspects that they considered negative about the changes that had occurred: higher levels of demand, an increased pace of work and pressure regarding productivity.

Analysing the comments of the interviewees, we observed that the issue of career prospects is the key factor to explain the levels of satisfaction, this perspective depending on the interviewee's perception of his/her situation within the labour market, in times of adverse conditions. For many workers, just the fact of having a job was a conquest in itself. This possibility, in turn, came up related to the issue of professional skills/training, being seen both as a chance to grow inside the company or outside it or as a barrier, for they perceived access to jobs as being conditioned by professional and training background.

Those with lower levels of schooling ended up blaming themselves for not having studied enough and were trying to increase their levels of schooling, either through accelerated 'fast track' courses or in regular school programmes. They felt insecure but they felt that whatever job security there might be was directly linked to their performance in their jobs and to their qualifications. 'Job security, you're the one that can guarantee it.'

All groups thought that the pace of work had increased quite a lot over the last five years. They attributed the quicker pace to an increase in the amount of responsibilities and in the amount of functions that the workers had to carry out, which, according to their testimonies, had contributed towards raising levels of stress. The increased responsibility was viewed both as a complaint as well as an opportunity to learn more (to become more multi-functional), linked to a chance to increase one's opportunities in the labour market.

The Metalworkers Union

The workers at BrazilCo are represented by the Metalworkers Union of Campinas. This is the largest and most important trade union in the region.[21] It is an industrial union, which currently represents 45,000 unionised and non-unionised workers in collective bargaining and it covers around 1,500 companies from different sectors in the metal branch[22] in an area that includes nine municipalities in Greater Campinas. This union has 20,358 paid members.[23]

Since 1984, this trade union has been largely staffed by activists linked to the Young Catholic Workers Organisation (Juventude Operária Católica) and to the Catholic Pastorate for Workers (Possan 1997). The majority of the executive members were affiliated to the Socialist Forum (Forum Socialista), a left wing sector within The Confederation of Labour Unions (CUT).[24] This political orientation led the Metalworkers Union to adopt, in the 1990s, a critical position with respect to the moderate majority within CUT.

During the 1980s, the union movement in Brazil grew and became stronger, in contrast to the crisis in union membership being witnessed in Europe and in the United States. During the process of political re-democratisation, pressed by the intensification of strike movements, the function and role of the unions were altered with the progressive liberalisation of State control over their activities and with the replacement of 'complacent officials' by more active leadership. However, this did not alter the trade union's corporatist structure, which was established by the State in the 1930s. This structure's main characteristics, still in use, are: the necessity of union's recognition by the Ministry of Labour, the representation monopoly of all the workers of one industrial sector within a specific territorial remit, and compulsory union tax paid by all workers whether unionised or not. The legislation conferred some privileges upon union officials such as job security for the length of their term but did not recognise the right of union representation in the workplace. During the military dictatorship, established in 1964, state control over the unions was increased through the rigid use of the law's coercive mechanisms, such as state intervention in the unions, replacement of elected officials and union closures. These measures were complemented by discretionary decrees and the repression against leftist and also independent union leaders.

Although keeping the same old structure but acquiring more autonomy, Brazilian trade unionism experienced a significant expansion and internal diversification in the 1980s. Strikes and the practice of collective bargaining were the main instruments of reconstructing the labour movement and of redefining labour relations in the country. The right to strike, the unionisation of public servants, the recognition of national confederations and the elimination of the mechanisms of state control were guaranteed by the Constitution of 1988. Nevertheless the main characteristics of the unions' corporatist[25] structure were retained.

The political, economic and social changes of the 1990s contributed to the weakening of the Brazilian union movement, breaking down its unity and disturbing the articulated processes of collective bargaining, which had been built up during the 1980s. The changes experienced by the union movement were visible in the decreasing number of strikes and in the difficulty of mobilising workers. Weakened by growing unemployment, falling membership and by sharpened political divisions among them, many metalworkers unions adopted a defensive posture and were not able to react in an articulated way against this scenario. This meant that in the 1990s the metalworkers unions fought to maintain what they had already obtained in the past decade and they had to make concessions to company representatives, negotiating flexible working hours, the profit-sharing programs[26] and the programmes of voluntary dismissals, among other issues, to avoid large scale layoffs and prevent factories from closing their doors. After 1998 these unions faced their worst collective bargaining positions and were unable to avoid the loss of many important advantages.

However, in spite of the predominance of neoliberal ideas and policies and of the weakening of the union movement, there were neither substantive changes in the unions' structure, which kept its corporatist characteristics, nor in the mechanisms for solving collective conflicts. Even in the face of collective bargaining fragmentation and with the predominance of firm or sector negotiations depending on the strength and ability of the union, annual collective bargaining in an industry basis continued to occur in the 1990s.

Despite unfavourable conditions for the labour movement, the Campinas Metalworkers Union maintained a more resolutely combative stance than many other Brazilian metalworkers unions, especially in view of the level of unemployment occurring within the metal sector. The political affiliation of its executive led this Union to adopt, in the last decade, a critical position with respect to the moderate majority within CUT. It sought to provide a base of support for metalworkers in the region as a whole and this may have been vindicated by the fact that they did manage to maintain a fairly stable unionisation rate (41–43 per cent) during a period when employment in the sector fell quite significantly (37 per cent between 1989 and 2002).

In recent years, there was a fall in the level of unionisation, dropping from 46 per cent in 1995 (23,000 members) to 36 per cent in 1998 (14,230 members). This drop derived from the reduction in the number of workers, from outsourcing and also from the company's involvement/participation policies. Nonetheless, there has been a turn-round in this trend, which started in 2000, with a relatively significant growth in the number of union members, which reached 20,358 in 2002 (45 per cent).[27]

The political stance and direction adopted by the executive have had important repercussions in the way the union has approached the consequences of the restructuring process. According to union officials, the union's priority has been to criticise the ideology involved in restructuring and its more perverse effects on workers. They have therefore resisted processes such as downsizing, outsourcing, flexibility and factory closures – in an effort to defend workers against flexibilisation and the reduction of their rights.

With regards to outsourcing, as the union could not stop it from happening, it has directed its actions towards fighting for the workers employed in subcontracted companies to have the right to be represented by the same union as the contractor's employees. As this target was not reached, the union has taken up the position that those workers should have the right to the benefits that have been obtained through the collective bargaining of the metalworkers.

The Metalworkers Union has taken a firm stand against neoliberal policies adopted by different governments in the 1990s, which favoured the deregulation of the labour market. Until the middle of the decade, the resistance of the labour movement and the opposition of the left wing parties – mainly the Workers' Party (PT) in Parliament prevented a reduction of labour rights. Although there was strong pressure from employers' associations and from right wing political parties for the flexibilisation of labour legislation it was only under the government of Fernando Henrique Cardoso (1995/2002) that it began to become more flexible. Employment contracts and the eight hours working day were the first to be altered with the approval of a law allowing fixed term contracts of between six and of 18 months along with the alteration of the length of the working week through the establishment of annualised hours.[28] In both cases the new conditions could only be implemented if they were agreed upon by the unions.

The Campinas Metalworkers Union has strongly refused to sign agreements that included dispositions that dwell on these two issues. This steadfast position has brought positive results for the metalworkers for, up until the present moment, no agreements establishing flexible working hours have been approved nor temporary contracts in companies anywhere in the region where the union is present, despite the huge amount of pressure coming from the company owners and their representative associations. This shows that the union has been able to stand its ground and to impose some restrictions to the flexibilisation of working conditions, minimising, in this manner, some of the perverse effects that the new management methods can have on the workers.

With respect to programmes involving workers' participation, this union has fought the participation of workers in suggestion schemes and also the linking of profit share to productivity and quality targets established by the companies. The reason is that union officials believe that to accept such conditions would jeopardise the workers' position, making them subject to the company's objectives and to its management.

Following a national trend, a significant number of negotiations by the Metalworkers Union in Campinas now occur at company level, although this organisation tends to favour collective bargaining on an industrial basis (Araújo, Cartoni and Justo 2001). However, the majority of issues negotiated are still related to wages and working conditions. Another group of issues has to do with the consequences of restructuring, including the issue of job retention that appears most frequently (e.g. temporary job security, suspension of layoffs, reintegration and guarantees to laid off workers). The issue of indemnifying workers with RSI was negotiated only in 1997 and even then in only four companies in the region.

The workers at BrazilCo have a high level of unionisation (59 per cent) when compared to the level at other large companies (e.g. in auto parts producers, like Eaton, Bosch or Wabco, the union membership varies from 36 to 44 per cent, according to information provided by the trade union) and also if compared to the average rate of unionisation in the whole metal sector of the Campinas region (roughly 45 per cent). This fact can be explained by the high level of activities that the union has carried out in the company since the 1980s. Union density did not change significantly after the process of acquisition of the company by the NAMN and the adoption of a new management culture.

This high rate of unionisation at the company suggests that the union is active, visible and well represented in the factory, a fact which is well recognised by the managers interviewed. One of the union officials[29] works at BrazilCo, and the union can also count on the support of worker's representatives within the Internal Health and Safety Committee (CIPA) which is a bipartite body, established by law, including representatives of both management and workers whose jobs are guaranteed for the duration of their term.

According to the Human Resources and Production Managers, up to the moment of the company's acquisition, relations with the union had been laden with conflicts as the company refused to start up dialogues or negotiations with union representatives. They believe this has changed since the company is aligned with the requirements of the NAMN, has been attempting to improve relations between directors, managers and factory workers, and to achieve a better dialogue with the union.

Interviews with union officials between 1998–2003 have confirmed the turbulent history of the union at the firm; but they have also confirmed that, in the last few years, communication and relationships with managers have improved. However, union officials still thought at the time of the interviews that BrazilCo was one of the most difficult companies in the region with which to negotiate. In any case, nowadays, the company seems to be maintaining a channel open for communicating with the union, although questions concerning conditions for profit-sharing, flexibility of working hours and outsourcing are subjects guaranteed to lead to strong conflicts. In these cases, the firm has tried to avoid situations of confrontation, often by avoiding negotiations. When the firm adopted flexible hours for administrative staff, negotiations were informal and established directly with the employees. The effects of outsourcing were also partially hidden by spreading employment losses across various parts of the firm.

Despite the apparent apathy of the workers and the strategies of involvement and co-optation adopted by the company, latent conflicts finally emerged when a strike broke out in 2002, motivated by disputes around the amount to be paid in the profit sharing programme. This strike, which lasted four days, resulted in the dismissal of 51 workers, among them the union leader. Almost all of them had obtained job security due to work related diseases or because they were members of the CIPA. The company had to go back on these dismissals soon afterwards due to a judicial decision. However, claiming many different reasons, once again it dismissed the union leader in August, 2003.

The serious condition of the workers health, due to the high incidence of RSI/OWRD led the union to dedicate a key part of its work at the company to this issue demanding the adoption of preventive measures and defending the rights of those workers suffering from these illnesses. These actions brought important gains for the workers such as the re-hiring of those who had been dismissed after getting RSI or after suffering an accident and the payment of compensation relative to the wages they had failed to receive during the period they had been out of the company. However, for both the company's management and the union leaders, the issue, which brings the greatest friction in negotiations, is that of job security for workers suffering from RSI/OWRD up until their retirement. This is because BrazilCo, as well as the rest of the entrepreneurial group in the metal sector, has been trying, constantly, during the last few years, to eliminate this right in all collective agreements being discussed.

The Metalworkers Union of Campinas has given priority to minimise the negative impacts of production changes on workers and it has taken great steps in this direction. Nevertheless, it is striking that the intensive trans-formation occurring inside companies has not been reflected in collective bargaining. Throughout the decade not a single clause relating to the new issues raised by restructuring was incorporated into the agreements.

The lack of negotiations regarding the restructuring of the company may stem from the absence of union organisation in the workplace that in turn has made it difficult for its representatives to obtain information regarding management strategies and innovations during their phases of implemen-tation. Hence, the absence of shop stewards is a major obstacle to the capacity of the union to influence the changes introduced by the com-panies that directly affect the members it represents. The strategy adopted by the Campinas' Metalworkers Union to make up for the non-existence of representatives in the workplace was significant, namely to have one union official working at the company and to count on the CIPA's elected members as the union's spokespersons in the shop floor. However this strategy did not seem to have a very wide-reaching impact for establishing closer ties between the union and the workers as well as for increasing the contact of the union with the shop floor's reality. Besides, the difficulties encountered by the union in increasing its influence are related, in great measure, to the fear of unemployment that predominated among workers.

Despite all the difficulties that it has been facing, the union received a positive evaluation from most of the workers interviewed. As all the inter-viewees were shop floor workers, the level of unionisation among them (67 per cent) is much higher than that of the whole group of BrazilCo´s employees. There is also a striking difference in the number of unionised workers among those who have worked at the company for more than seven years (81 per cent) and for those who were hired after its acquisition by the NAMN (48 per cent). This data show that the union has had more difficulties trying to recruit people who were hired more recently.

The trade union was positively evaluated by the majority of the workers interviewed, both men and women, with men more likely to be positive, and also by those who were not union members. How people judged the union varied according to the worker's age and length of service in the company.

The view of the union was much more negative among the workers aged 31 to 35, (73 per cent) than among those of other age brackets, in which a striking majority (70 per cent) had evaluated the union's perfor-mance positively. Besides, data from the questionnaires suggest that older workers (over 35 years old), who had been working at the company for more than seven years and in the more labour intensive jobs, such as in the assembly lines and in the metal stamping, tended to have a more positive view of the union. One might suggest that this could be in part due to these workers having witnessed the battles taken up by the union in the 1980s and the beginning of the 1990s, when many benefits for the workers were won.

Having analysed the comments made by the workers to explain their views on the union, it could be seen that some of them had reservations towards aspects of the union's practices. Among the interviewees who gave a positive evaluation of the union almost 30 per cent had some type of criticism to make. Another group (39 per cent) expressed their criticism and stressed negative aspects more emphatically. The positive view of the union was attributed, in many cases, to the role the union had been playing in defending the interests of the workers and, particularly, of those suffering from work-related diseases. Among those who criticised the union, some (15 per cent) questioned the background of the union leaders and their lack of qualification for exercising their functions on the shop floor. Others (10 per cent) stressed the distance that existed between shop floor workers and union leaders and the fact that the workers' voices were not being heard by them. This perception of distance also appeared in the criticism made by around 30 per cent of the sample regarding the lack of adequate communication between the union and the workers. It is noteworthy that this was the complaint that most frequently appeared among all criticisms made.

Although important critical views existed regarding the union's actions, workers at BrazilCo clearly recognised the need and the importance of the union as an instrument to defend their rights. None of the workers interviewed affirmed or suggested that the union had lost its role in these new times of flexibilisation and labour market deregulation.

Conclusions

The white goods industry was introduced in Brazil at the end of the 1940s as part of the import substitution policy. Until the 1980s this industry was characterised by a falling number of large national family owned companies. The entry of foreign multinational corporations in the 1990s, which followed the opening of the economy and the policy of establishing a common free market between the southern countries of Latin America (Mercosul), reshaped the industry's structure and ownership, as a result of the acquisition of leading national companies.

The entry of leading world groups is explained by their intention of taking advantage of the size and potential of internal and regional markets, as well as by the existence in the country of a previously structured and complete productive chain and by its strong international presence. It is worth noting that, while the largest part of the main companies' production is aimed at the internal market, exports grow steadily and the sector's trade balance after the acquisitions presents positive results.

Since the 1980s, BrazilCo initiated a process of modernisation that was intensified after its acquisition by the NAMN. This process included investments in new technology and changes in the company's organisational structure and work process through the introduction of new management methods. These changes, driven by competition and cost reduction are very similar to the ones that are observed in other white goods multinational companies in Brazil.

They have meant both reductions in the labour force and a requirement by management that workers should have a higher level of education. They have led to new tasks for shop floor workers, an intensification of labour, increased productivity and an increase in RSI.

The frequency of RSI (around 10 per cent of the labour force) in this company is explained by the association of the increase in the pace of work to the use of assembly lines with fixed positions and very repetitive tasks. The size of the problem has led to the introduction of prevention measures, to the reorganisation of labour process and to the automation of some lines. One should keep in mind that these changes occur in a context of increasing unemployment and wage reduction in the labour market as a whole.

In this context, it is interesting to note workers' views on the changes in their work conditions. The majority of workers declared themselves more satisfied or as satisfied as five years before. The key factors for the satisfaction level are the improvement of the take home pay, which was considered better for almost 50 per cent of the workers, and also the idea they have of their career prospects, either within or without the firm, which derives from the analysis they make of the labour market (increasing unemployment and growing barriers to entry and permanence, through professional training and demand for more schooling). Job security is seen as having disappeared and as depending on individual effort (both as hope and as guilt), and staying employed is seen as a triumph in itself.

On the other hand, there were not important changes in the labour contract and in industrial relations. There is still annual collective bargaining on an industry basis and agreements at the company level too. Moreover, the Brazilian labour law did not change that much. This was because, in the general context of the country's democratisation and of the growth of social movements from the 1980s on, the workers' movement was able to set limits to changes in labour laws and to prevent a still higher flexibilisation in labour contracts. Thus, a new law allowing the establishment of temporary contracts and flexible hours – but only through agreement with the unions – was passed only recently.

This is an important feature of the Brazilian case, mainly because the union movement, most specifically in the metal sector, although it was weakened in the 1990s, is still strong and active, having political influence both at the national and regional levels. For this reason it plays an important role in setting limits to outsourcing and to the flexibilisation of the working hours as well as in keeping labour rights and guaranteeing jobs and benefits for those workers suffering from occupational diseases.

Besides, in this case study, the political orientation and legitimacy of the Campinas Metalworkers Union and its strategies in relation to this specific cooker plant can explain why the latter was not able to avoid negotiation with the union, neither to increase the use of casual or agency labour, nor to establish flexible hours and to eliminate job security for workers with RSI/OWRD. Thus, workers acknowledge the role played by the union, on the one hand, but on the other, show a high level of job satisfaction. The contradiction is only apparent if one keeps in mind the context characterised by growing unemployment, informalisation of the labour market and generalised wage reduction.

In this sense, one can say, from the Brazilian case, that in a globalisation context, with the industry's internationalisation, national politics counts both for the development of the sector and for the kind of consequences management strategies have on employment relations. Economic and industrial policies were important for the way this sector was reshaped by capital concentration and internationalisation and by technological and organisational innovations. On the other hand, the democratisation process and the political importance of union action have a substantial influence on labour conditions and relations.

Notes

1 The interviews were carried out within the factory, in a room where the researchers could stay alone with the interviewees. Nevertheless, the supervisors of each area chose the workers that would be interviewed. To avoid workers' resistance and fear that this could be a company sponsored study, we assured them of the confidentiality of all the information we were collecting. We are aware that, although this option can minimise distortions in the workers' answers due to the conditions of the interviews, it cannot eliminate them completely.

2 Embraco has been presenting a remarkable export performance during the last decades. The firm's exports accounted for around 70 per cent of its revenues in 1999 (Cunha 2003).

3 This estimate was reached through data supplied by The Brazilian Electrical and Electronics Industry Association (ABINEE).

4 Source: Data base RAIS (Social Information Yearly Report)/Ministry of Labour and Employment (MTE), Brazil.

5 Source: National Association of Manufacturers of Electronic Appliances (ELETROS).

6 It is worth noting the importance of the tax incentive policies taken up by some state governments to lure certain companies of the white goods sector to set up installations in their states, as well as policies for financing investments for production plants to make their facilities more modern and/or to expand them, policies implemented by government agencies, such as The Brazilian Bank for Economic and Social Development (BNDES).

7 Source: ABINEE and RAIS.

8 Source: National Sample Survey (PNAD) / Brazilian Statistics Bureau (IBGE), 2001.

9 Source: ABINEE and Brazilian Foreign Commerce Secretary (SECEX).

10 It is worth noting the importance of exports for the main component of refrigeration – hermetic compressors. In 1999, the top two Brazilian producers of hermetic compressors – Embraco and Tecumseh do Brasil – together exported US$430.2 million, holding respectively the 29th and 60th ranking in the list of main Brazilian exporting companies in that same year (SECEX).

11 Source: *Gazeta Mercantil* (2000) – one of the leading Brazilian business newspapers.

12 Considering total sales of the cooker manufacturers, which are ELETROS' members.

13 The firm does not intend to seek the ISO 14000 certificate, because it was in a process of certification in the same international environmental, health and security certificate held by the NAMN parent body, which seems to be more comprehensive.

14 Also due to influence exerted by NAMN, a system was introduced regarding the development of new products, the New Product Introduction (NPI). It is a method used to introduce new products to the market. 'It spans the entire product life-cycle from initial identification of market/technology opportunity, conception, design and development through to production, market launch, support, enhancement and retirement' (GDP Program 2003: 1).

15 Just-in-time (JIT) is a management system created in the Japanese car industry to adjust input demands and production, reducing stocks, and costs of production. It can be used within the firm (internal just-in-time) or between client firms and suppliers (external just-in-time).

16 A widespread trend identified in the reorganisation of the relationships between client firms and suppliers is the tremendous pressure from client firms to formalise product quality from suppliers. This marks a clear-cut trend reflecting rising demands to introduce documentation and procedures related to production quality, parallel to rising pressures to trim costs. These demands are reflected in regular assessments and audits by the client firm companies and, to an increasing extent, pressures to obtain ISO 9000 certification (Gitahy 2000).

17 It is worth mentioning that this is a BrazilCo's traditional practice, which was not modified after its acquisition.

18 Of the 11 women interviewed only one worked in the department of logistics while the male workers interviewed were distributed in the following departments: Logistics: 3; Maintenance and Tool making: 3; Assembly line: 13; Painting and enamelling: 13; Stamping and general production: 10.

19 The minimum salary for metalworkers in the state of São Paulo varied throughout the 1990s – from 2.5 minimum wages/per month (for small and medium-sized companies) to three minimum wages in large firms. However, with the devaluation of the Real (the Brazilian currency), a drop in minimum wage levels was witnessed. The Brazilian minimum wage had been worth US$100.00 in 1995 and was worth around US$60.00 in December 2002.

20 Even companies in the region, which were smaller in size, offered benefits such as dental care, a nursery and financial aid (through loans and advances).

21 This union went through a significant process of renewal and strengthening, which began in 1984, when the opposition, which had been active in the union since the late 1970s, won the elections.

22 The metal-mechanical branch, as defined by the Ministry of Labour, includes companies with operations in the following sectors: metalworking, car manufacturing

(assembly and auto parts plants), machine and electrical-electronic manufacturing, electrical equipment, foundry and non-iron metal sector.

23   According to an interview with one of the union's officials on March 26th 2002.

24   There was also a minority of union officials affiliated to other small leftist groups represented within this Confederation. CUT is the largest Brazilian labour confederation.

25   According to the literature the Brazilian union structure is corporatist. We use the definition of corporatism given by Phillippe Schmitter (1974) and Alfred Stepan (1980). Many Brazilian authors (Erickson 1979; Araújo 1998 and 1998a; Rodrigues 1990; Boito Jr 1991, for example) consider the monopoly of representation along with the union tax as the main characteristics of the Brazilian union structure. The monopoly of representation means that when a union is recognised by the Ministry of Labour as representing, for example the metal workers of Campinas, the workers don´t have the option to choose another union. All metal workers in this city, unionised or not, are represented only by this union – whether they like it or not – in collective bargaining with companies, in relations with the state and in the labour courts.

26   The Constitution of 1988 established the right of workers' participation in enterprises' profit. Since then the unions included in collective bargaining the demand for the establishment of profit-sharing programmes. These programmes were widely adopted by companies during the 90s. Usually they mean an annual bonus for the workers which is related to the company's productivity and output. The amount of the bonus in general is determined by meeting productivity and quality goals. CUT unions oppose to the establishment of these goals as a condition for the amount of the PS bonus to be granted to the workers.

27   This relative stability in the number of union members, despite the unfavourable conditions, may be due, in part, to the fact that this union has been developing systematic campaigns to promote unionisation at factory doors and inside the companies. Union representatives, in compliance with the Brazilian legislation, have the right to enter the factories to carry out recruitment. According to Brazilian legislation, all of the employees in a company can become members of the union that represents their workers, be they production (blue collar) workers or administrative staff (white collar workers). The union has been able to recruit a greater number of members among shop floor workers. Nevertheless, the agreements established with the companies are also valid for the administrative staff. In general, professionals with higher levels of schooling – such as engineers, economists, physicians – have their own unions. Different unions also represent the workers of subcontracted companies that render services such as cleaning, security, catering and information technology services, among others.

28   The compensation scheme eliminated the payment of extra hours but could not surpass the average of 44 hours per week. For a detailed analysis of recent changes in the Brazilian labour legislation see Galvão (2003).

29   The company pays the salaries of the union leaders that remain working in it. Others, who get leave from their jobs, are paid by the union and cannot be fired until one year has expired from the date of the end of their term (which is in general of three years).

References

ABINEE (Brazilian Electrical and Electronics Industry Association), cited 2002 (www.abinee.org.br).

Araújo, A. M. C. (1998) *A Construção do Consentimento: Corporativismo e Trabalhadores* nos anos 30, São Paulo: Scritta.

Araújo, A. M. C. (1998a) 'Building Consensus: the implementation of corporatist unionism in Brazil during the thirties'. Working Paper 21, Manchester: International Centre for Labour Studies, Manchester, pp. 1–35.

Araújo, A. M. C. and Gitahy, L. (2003) 'Reestruturação produtiva e negociações coletivas entre os metalúrgicos paulistas' *Idéias*, Ano 9 (2)/10 (1): 65–111.

Araújo, A., Cartoni, D. M. and Justo, C. (2001) 'Reestruturação produtiva e negociação coletiva nos anos 90', *Revista Brasileira de Ciências Sociais*, vol. 16, no. 45, February.

Araújo, A., Cunha, A., Rachid, A. and Gitahy, L. (2002) 'New management strategies and labour: a case study in the Brazilian white goods industry'. Paper presented at The International Congress on Sociology (ISA), Brisbane, Australia.

Boito Jr., A. (1991) *O Sindicalismo de Estado no Brasil*. São Paulo: Editora da Unicamp/Hucitec.

Camarano, A. A. and Beltrão, K. I. (2000) 'Distribuição Espacial da População Brasileira: mudanças na segunda metade deste século' in *Texto para Discussão*, nr 766, IPEA, Brasília.

Cunha, A. (2003) *As Novas Cores da Linha Branca: os efeitos da desnacionalização da indústria brasileira de eletrodomésticos* nos anos 1990. PhD Thesis, Institute of Economics, UNICAMP, Campinas.

ELETROS (National Association of Manufacturers of Electronic Appliances), cited 2002 (www.eletros.org.br).

Erickson, K. P. (1979) *Sindicalismo no Processo Político no Brasil*, São Paulo: Brasiliense.

Galvão, A. (2003) *Neoliberalismo e reforma trabalhista no Brasil*, PhD Thesis, Institute of Philosophy and Human Sciences (IFCH), UNICAMP, Campinas.

Gazeta Mercantil, *Balanço Anual 2000*, São Paulo.

GDP (Good Design Practice) Program *New product introduction (NPI)*. University of Cambridge and Royal College of Art (site www.betterproductdesign.net/npi/ visited in August, 2003).

Gitahy, L. (2000) 'A New Paradigm of Industrial Organization. The Diffusion of Technological and Managerial Inovations in the Brazilian Industry', *Comprehensive Summaries of Uppsala Dissertations from the Faculty of Social Sciences* 93, Acta Universitatis Upsaliensis, Uppsala.

Gitahy, L. and Cunha, A. (1999) 'Redes y flexibilidad: reestructuración productiva y trabajo en la industria de línea blanca' in Montero, C., Albuquerque, M. and Ensignia, J. (eds) *Trabajo y Empresa entre dos siglos* (ed.) Nueva Sociedad, Caracas, pp. 79–103.

IBGE (Brazilian Statistics Bureau) – PNAD (National Sample Survey), 2001.

Possan, M. (1997) *A Malha Entrecruzada das Ações: As Experiências de Organização dos Trabalhadores Metalúrgicos de Campinas* (1978–1984), Campinas: Área de Publicações CMU/UNICAMP (Coleção Campiniana, 14).

RAIS/MTE (Social Information Yearly Report/Ministry of Labour and Employment) Database, Brazil.

Rodrigues, L. M. (1990) 'O sindicalismo corporativo no Brasil', in *Partidos e Sindicatos*, São Paulo: Atica.

Schmitter, P. (1974) 'Still the Century of Corporatism?' in Schmitter, P. & Lehmbruch, *Trends toward Corporatist Intermediation*, Beverly Hill: Sage.

SECEX/MDIC (Brazilian Foreign Commerce Secretary – Ministry of Development, Industry and Commerce) Database, 1990/2000.

Stepan, A. (1980) *Estado Corporativismo e Autoritarismo*, Rio de Janeiro: Paz e Terra.

8

Labour in a Global World – Some Comparisons

Theo Nichols and Surhan Cam

Certain broad tendencies about the white goods industry are evident from the preceding chapters. As we have seen, despite the continued relevance of logistic and supply chain considerations and the specific needs of local markets, the shift from established to low wage production sites is taking place in many parts of the world: for example, in North America with reference to Mexico and China; in South Africa with reference to Swaziland; in the EU countries with reference to the European periphery; in Japan with reference to China; in Taiwan, once known for its status as an OEM producer with reference to OEM production in China. Then again, lower trade barriers and related measures have had their effects everywhere. They have put producers with plants in South Africa and Taiwan under considerable pressure. In Turkey, they have created opportunities for increased exports, though in the period reviewed, powerfully aided by currency devaluation. In China, they have both aided exports and, through an inflow of new foreign producers, they have led to severe reductions in the number of domestic Chinese producers. Similarly, the massive influx of steel into China in order to sustain its industrial expansion has had knock-on effects for white goods producers in all the countries reviewed.

There has been a search for new markets – in China and India and Eastern Europe – but the promise of expanding into markets in the vast rural areas of China is frustrated by lack of electrification or adequate gas supply and, not least, lack of disposable income. It is the same story in South Africa. Markets do not simply 'open up'. As the case of Turkey makes clear, markets also require institutional supports, including a satisfactory way through which those who finance the debt out of which white goods are often purchased can recover their money.

However, we put a good deal of the emphasis in Chapter 1 on markets. Suffice to say here that a common problem for most large white goods producers in most countries has been price erosion. This has contributed to mergers and acquisitions, to reductions in the labour force; and to the widespread adoption of management methods – TQM, Quality Circles and their derivative forms and Six Sigma – intended to increase quality (and thus enhance or conserve product value) and reduce waste. It is on the production side of things that we want to comment selectively here. First, we consider briefly some common features in the meaning of work for workers in the factories investigated; then, issues relevant to management-worker relations, trade unions and the impact on workers of the more or less common set of changes that have come with the new management methods; then, the nature of the factory regimes in which white goods have been produced in these countries.

The meaning of work

The workers in the factories reviewed in previous chapters are not all of one gender. They are not all the same age. They are not all the same colour or the same ethnic origin. Some are rural-born, others not. It is certainly possible to make distinctions between them – with respect to their rural or urban origins and educational level for example (such an intra-firm sociology is produced by our Brazilian colleagues in Chapter 7). An inter-firm comparison is offered with respect to Turkey in Chapter 6 (in the case of Turkey a further extensive examination of the possible significance of age cohort differences between workers in this and other sectors is provided in Nichols and Sugur 2004: 185–200). However, there is reason to suppose that workers in all these factories will become more alike in future, at least with respect to their educational experience. Managements are seeking out better educated workers, usually those with high school education. Also, these workers already have in common that the jobs they hold are highly prized. (In fact, the workers in China, Taiwan and Turkey (though not in Brazil) had a relatively good opinion of foreign companies.[1] This goes against the grain of some anti-globalisation rhetoric (Nichols and Sugur 2004: 25–42) but is understandable in view of the fact that the foreign /joint enterprises we have considered are relatively large ones, with substantial resources, which are there for the long haul and which tend to pay better than average wages).

It is a common feature of all the factories that the jobs these workers do – predominately assembly and related tasks – tend to be internally advertised or at least require an inside connection; and that when jobs are externally advertised they attract massive queues of applicants. Such jobs are often an escape from the informal economy and they tend to carry with them, for permanent workers, relatively good wages and other advantages (workforce segmentation and some of the differential benefits associated with this are examined in the later discussion of Factory Regimes).

Most workers in these factories, whatever the country, think these jobs are good ones for people like them. But even though the physical conditions in these factories are often on a par with many in the more highly industrialised countries of the west, these workers are also fully aware that

Table 8.1   Worker Expectation, Experience and Aspiration – ChinaCo, TaiwanCo, SKoreaCo, Turkey3Co and BrazilCo

	ChinaCo	TaiwanCo	SKoreaCo	Turkey3Co	BrazilCo
Percentages agree and strongly agree					
Good job for someone like me	64	60	68	85	90
Could not work at this pace until 60 or think it unlikely	60	65	55	75	65
Not a job wanted for son/daughter	94	94	60	61	75

their work takes its toll on them. The majority, in all countries, believe that they will not be able to do such work when they are 60. No doubt related to this is the view of the majority of workers, again in all factories,[2] that they do not want their sons and daughters to follow them into jobs like theirs. In short, because of their relative expectations – their assessment of what else is available – workers do appreciate working in jobs in the big corporate white goods sector in these countries. But, the relative value placed on the job is one thing; experience of the job is another; aspiration for one's children is yet another (Table 8.1).[3]

Management – worker relations

To summarise: Outside of South Africa, where the position is less certain and which is excluded from the following discussion, it can be fairly said that these plants do not represent 'the industrial revolution over again' but an industrial revolution with modern technology and modern management methods (a theme already advanced in Nichols and Sugur 2004). Relative labour costs affect the mechanisation of particular processes and the development of local and national infrastructure affects how much of the production process is out-sourced. However, the technology is broadly comparable across all these plants. Similarities arise from: multinational corporations transferring work designs, methods and processes; a high level of knowledge of competitors' plants and production processes; and a limited number of suppliers of machinery to whom manufacturers can resort. As a reading of the various chapters makes clear, similar presumed best practice management methods have been diffused to all these plants – Six Sigma and more generally TQM – usually under American influence, though in TaiwanCo with a bias to Japan. All these plants have HRM departments. All their management structures have now been delayered. All factories except BrazilCo operate annualised hours systems.

The statistical control aspects of the new management techniques have major implications for how production is organised. The stress on the reduction of variance in performance is apt to be understood by managers in technical terms. For workers, it often translates into the intensification of their labour. On the other hand, although this is often forgotten today, even F. W. Taylor, the father of scientific management, emphasised that a 'mental revolution' was necessary if his methods were to have the desired effect (Bendix 1956: 276). Modern management methods, such as TQM and its near-relative Lean Production, are also sometimes interpreted as imbued with the same idea, though generally expressed in terms of 'empowerment', employees being urged to believe that they are each others 'customers' or that they 'own the company' or 'the problem'. This is not all hocus-pocus. Managers who are committed to reliable and high quality output and to the dream of continuous improvement have something to gain from workers acting as if they did 'own the problem' and in encouraging workers to do so. The question therefore arises: do workers recognise any movement toward their involvement in decision-making? Do they think that their opinions are asked more frequently?

Given authoritarian management traditions, and indeed a recent history of military rule – as has been the case in Turkey, South Korea, Brazil and Taiwan – the significance of a sense of recognition and dignity, albeit as assessed from a low initial base, is not to be discounted, and there is some evidence that, in most countries, workers in these factories believed that they have been more involved in decision-making over the past five years. At a minimum level, workers took note that managers recognised their existence and spoke to them. They also appreciated to some degree the sometimes relatively small extent to which factory managements solicited their views and at least went through the motions of being open to their influence in decision making. It would seem that changes in this direction have recently occurred in all but one of the companies (Figure 8.1).[4]

Previous work in Turkey provides clear examples of cases where workers have developed a cynical view of managers precisely because they question their sincerity or resent the pretence that they have been accorded any independent role in making decisions (Nichols and Sugur 2004: 133–40). The magnitude of any change should not therefore be exaggerated. In China, indeed, half the workers responded to a question we asked about this that they had not been involved in decisions under the SOE and that they were not now. Even so, the direction of change, as opposed to its magnitude, is not in doubt.

In so far as workers did report an increase in their involvement in decision making, however, they also reported an increase of another kind – in stress (Figure 8.2). The suggestion is that the management methods practised in these companies may have led to some increased involvement by

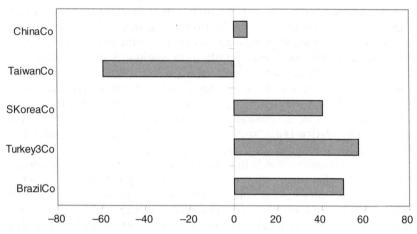

Figure 8.1   Direction of Changes Last Five Years – Right to Make Decision; Balance of 'Better' over 'Worse' Responses ChinaCo, TaiwanCo, SKoreaCo, Turkey3Co and BrazilCo (Percentages)

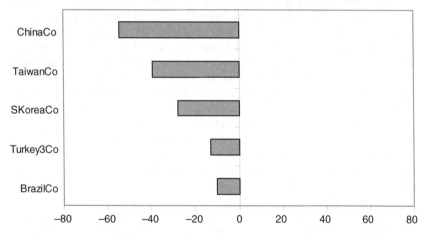

Figure 8.2   Direction of Changes Last Five Years – Stress; Balance of 'Better' over 'Worse' Responses ChinaCo, TaiwanCo, SKoreaCo, Turkey3Co and BrazilCo (Percentages)

workers in the process of production but that the price for this has been increased stress.

Most workers also worried about their jobs outside work. In fact by asking a question about this that derives from the British Work Employment Relations Survey (WERS 98) three interesting things are suggested (Table 8.2). The first is that although in the UK, and in many other highly

Table 8.2 Worry a Lot about Job Outside Working Hours – ChinaCo, TaiwanCo, SKoreaCo, Turkey3Co, BrazilCo and Some UK Comparisons (Percentages)

Percentage	ChinaCo	TaiwanCo	SKoreaCo	Turkey3Co	BrazilCo	UK comparator	UK Manufacturing
Strongly agree / agree	52	56	72	49	27	26	20
Neither agree nor disagree	32	23	30	7	6	22	20
Disagree or strongly disagree	16	6	17	43	55	52	60
DK	0	0	0	1	2	0	0

Table 8.3 In General, How Would You Describe Relations between Managers and Employees – ChinaCo, TaiwanCo, SKoreaCo, Turkey3Co, BrazilCo and Some UK Comparisons (Percentages)

Percentages	ChinaCo	TaiwanCo	SKoreaCo	Turkey3Co	BrazilCo	UK comparator	UK Manufacturing
Very good / good	34	37	71	59	61	23	44
Neither good nor bad	48	49	25	28	20	27	30
Poor / very poor	5	6	4	10	16	50	26
DK	14	8	0	3	4	0	0

industrialised societies, much is to be heard about 'stress' and related issues, the levels reported in these less developed countries are generally higher, at least when compared to levels for manual workers in UK manufacturing as a whole or for workers in the WERS sample who worked in a white goods company.[5] The second is of course that the Brazilians were the least worried. Note, though, that they were rivalled in this by British workers. The third is that the responses from SKoreaCo are different.

There is evidence that SKoreaCo was indeed characterised by a different level of worker commitment to the rest. Workers in all the firms tended to have a higher level of appreciation of 'climate' as assessed by a standard WERS question (Table 8.3) than would seem to typify British manufacturing or the comparator British white goods factory but workers at SKoreaCo had an even higher level of appreciation. A similar finding resulted when, in an attempt to pick up evidence of any strong worker commitment to their company, we asked which statement workers most agreed with; either 'Lunch break is a good time for us to get together as a team to go over things and solve problems' or 'Lunch break is our personal time, it shouldn't be a time for company business'. Less than five per cent of workers in ChinaCo, TaiwanCo, Turkey3Co or BrazilCo chose the pro-company option. By contrast, 49 per cent of SKoreaCo workers did. As we shall see, it is too easy to attribute the Korean workers' responses to some timeless, different Korean culture. To invoke 'culture' in this way is inadequate partly because it fails to take into account the exceptional lengths to which SKoreaCo's managers have gone to secure the commitment of their workforce and partly because such efforts, on the part of management, were a reaction to exceptional militant action by these workers. Some other qualifications also need to be entered which have to do with the contractual composition of the workforce and the fact the data reported for SKoreaCo is based on *de jure* (permanent) employees (excluding agency workers, to whom we will come in due course).

The idea that in at least one of these companies, SKoreaCo, the management has apparently made important strides in winning the 'hearts and minds' of its permanent workers raises the question of trade unionism. Does the trade union command workers' loyalty in these factories? As can be seen from the relevant chapters, unions are recognised by management at all of these plants and trade union membership is high. Prima facie, it is difficult to be sanguine about the chances of these trade unions winning these workers hearts and minds however. In ChinaCo, the history and nature of the state formation mean that the union is a creature of the state apparatus and is not a free or independent union. In SKoreaCo and TaiwanCo the unions are company unions. In Turkey, the trade union is authoritarian in its practice to its membership and fascist in its orientation to the wider world (pan-Turkic and anti-Kurdish). Only in Brazil is the union democratic. In none of the countries, though, does the union have the equivalent of an effective or independent shop steward representational system and, as our Brazilian colleagues make clear in Chapter 7, although the union officials who deal with BrazilCo are committed to democratic values, the non-existence of representatives in the workplace is a significant problem.

Unions are sometimes criticised nowadays for having become 'service organisations' (at its narrowest, providing reduced rates for private medical care and various consumption goods for example). This raises many questions about what, if anything, a union essentially is. But one thing that is clear is that unions are unlikely to serve workers' interests in a wider sense unless they keep them up to date, encourage them to comment, respond to their suggestions, deal with their problems and treat them fairly. Table 8.4 tabulates the responses to a number of questions that we asked in each of the companies about workers' views of trade unions and their managements. Our interpretation of these results is that they do reflect the main reality. They reflect the more positive view of the union's commitment to workers that workers held in BrazilCo; they also reflect the disheartened state in which workers at TaiwanCo regard both management and union as they face the 'end of the golden tale'; but, more generally, they suggest that managements are rated somewhat more highly than unions in most of the companies.

In a way, the strength of this finding is its weakness. On the one hand, it lends a comparative dimension to the findings on particular countries. For instance, in Chapter 7, our Brazilian colleagues are sensitive to the lack of shop floor organisation at BrazilCo but they have not been in a position to see the situation in, say, TaiwanCo – nor are they in a position to see that there is a general tendency for management to be rated more highly than unions in all the other plants researched. On the other hand, the idea that these managements were rated more highly than unions raises a question about the yet wider comparative landscape – is it possible that such indications that management is winning a battle for hearts might be found much more generally? that they are not only a function of the particular structure, function and ideology of the unions considered here? It is a good question but we know of no research that bears directly on this. It does merit note, however, that two things in which trade unions would be expected to do better than management are dealing with workers' work problems and treating workers fairly. In each case, it is only in BrazilCo that workers assessed trade unions doing these things better than managers.

We want to turn now to a more particular consideration of the three East Asian factories in order to explore one of their distinctive features that can easily get lost sight of when worker subjectivity becomes the almost exclusive focus of discussion, as in modern social science it so often does. To this end, we will use Michael Burawoy's *The Politics of Production* (Burawoy 1985) as our jumping off point, so a little background is necessary.

Table 8.4 How Good Unions and Managers are at Various Activities – ChinaCo, TaiwanCo, SKoreaCo, Turkey3Co and BrazilCo (Percentages)

Percentage very good and good		ChinaCo	TaiwanCo	SKoreaCo	Turkey3Co	BrazilCo	Averages
Keeping everyone up to date about proposed changes							
	Managers	58	31	68	55	82	59
	Union	31	43	52	44	71	48
Providing everyone with the chance to comment on proposed changes							
	Managers	62	20	64	45	59	50
	Union	33	26	44	31	78	42
Responding to suggestions from employees							
	Managers	68	28	66	69	71	60
	Union	43	28	52	43	69	47
Dealing with work problems you or others may have							
	Managers	72	45	64	82	69	66
	Union	37	31	46	55	82	50
Treating employees fairly							
	Managers	58	37	58	62	69	57
	Union	37	27	52	52	76	49
Average Scores							
	Managers	64	32	64	63	70	58
	Unions	36	31	49	45	75	46
Percentage difference in favour of management		**+28**	**+1**	**+15**	**+18**	**-5**	**+12**

Factory regimes

Burawoy's book provided many social scientists with the broad parameters of their understanding of what happened to factory labour following the increased dominance of capital over the last quarter of a century. In it, he distinguished three factory regimes. The first of these to appear historically is market despotism. The concept clearly owes its theoretical origin to Marx's dictum that anarchy in the market leads to despotism in the factory. But there are further assumptions that are no less important. One is that workers are both free to compete in the labour market and to work for capitalists of their own choosing and free in the other sense; they are bereft of any other means of livelihood (are free to work or free to starve). Another is that workers lack the ability to effectively resist arbitrary coercion. In such a regime coercion prevails over consent, especially of course in the absence of collective forms of organisation.

The second type of factory regime is the hegemonic regime. Here some departure from perfect competition may be assumed but of key importance is that the choice 'work or starve' is modified to the benefit of labour. This is achieved by workers' dependence on capital being reduced by state social insurance and by state labour legislation facilitating resistance to arbitrary coercion. In such regimes consent prevails, though as Burawoy makes clear this is never to the exclusion of coercion. As he also makes clear, the specific character of this and other regimes varies with the specific forms of the labour process, competition among firms and the degree and form of state intervention.

The third type of regime is hegemonic despotism. Such regimes rise out of the contradictions of hegemonic ones. The hegemonic regime entailed constraints on the deployment of capital, whether by tying wages to profits or by creating internal labour markets, collective bargaining and grievance machinery (1985: 263). Under hegemonic despotism, labour's vulnerability to capital's national and international mobility leads to a new despotism, built on the foundations of the hegemonic regime. Workers face the loss of their jobs not as individuals but as a result of threats to the viability of the firm. Management turns the hegemonic regime against workers, relying on its mechanisms for co-ordinating interests to command consent to sacrifice. Concession bargaining and quality of work-life programmes are two faces of this hegemonic despotism. In other words, where labour used to be granted concessions on the basis of the expansion of profits, it now makes concessions on the basis of the relative profitability of one capitalist vis-à-vis another. This is the 'rational' tyranny of capital mobility, a hegemonic despotism which workers collectively work within. Quality Circles and other such innovations signify management's attempts to invade the spaces created by workers under the previous regime and to mobilise consent to increased productivity (1985: 150).

Labour Control Issues

Modern management methods; workplace autonomy and control: empowerment versus intensification, deterioration/amelioration of work conditions, cultural control, team working; fear versus commitment

Material Support Issues

Wages
Level in relation to local labour market
Composition–proportion that is
basic/variable

Influenced by:
State
Market
Collective Organisation

Non main wage material support
Employer/state/family/community/
& other waged jobs

Contract Issues

internal and external contract, permanent, temporary, part time work

Figure 8.3   Labour Control, Material Support and Contract

There are some queries and qualifications that may be directed at Burawoy's schema. Relevant here is how far the posited shift from hegemonic to hegemonic despotic regimes relates to the unravelling of the post war settlement in Europe and North America and how far it can be validly applied elsewhere. And is it always necessary for hegemonic despotic regimes to be preceded by hegemonic ones? Such criticisms are not our main concern here. Two different things interest us: that there are elements in Burawoy's thinking that tend not to figure so prominently in the thinking of those who invoke the idea of 'hegemonic despotism'; and that there is an important aspect of factory regimes which Burawoy himself tended to neglect. Before going further, is helpful to discuss these matters with respect to the three sets of issues presented in Figure 8.3.

Labour Control

Arguably, the recent and current social science literature that is most often thought to resonate well with the concerns of Burawoy's hegemonic despotism is that which explores the balance of coercion and consent in studies of new management methods. Much of this literature is concerned primarily with issues related to labour control, rather than with issues related to material support or to type of contract. The labour control issue of commitment versus compliance (Cole 1979; Lincoln and Kallenberg 1990) has played an important part, either implicitly or explicitly, in steering many studies of team work, Total Quality Management, Japanisation, Toyotaism, Lean Production and so forth (Womack et al 1990; Elger and Smith 1994; Berggren 1993; Babson 1995; Danford 1999). Often the underlying question is: 'does this teamwork/ TQM/ or whatever really work?' and the test of it working is equally often 'does it actually elicit commitment?' For example, Stewart et al (2004) argue against 'the champions of lean production', who make claims about 'empowerment' and emphasise instead that 'lean has more to do with establishing a new model of cultural control in the workplace'. It might well be said, indeed, that management writers want to argue, and tend to conclude, that such techniques 'work' and that generally radical writers want to argue that they do not – or that, to the extent they do, they have adverse consequences for labour. In this respect, there is a certain amount of common ground between them. They are both concerned with issues of labour control and their consequences.

To the extent that the significance of Burawoy's work is commonly understood to relate to labour control – in particular to commitment/consent – this is disappointing because Burawoy is sensitive to a range of social relations much greater than those that usually figure in attempts to establish whether this or that management technique 'works' with reference, say, to workplace autonomy versus control, empowerment versus intensification of labour or, in the widest sense, the success or not of management projects for cultural control. Admittedly, the term 'labour control', into which we bundle all the above issues, is not entirely satisfactory (after all, most things that management does in production have implications for labour control). It does, however, help to distinguish two further dimensions – material support and contract.

Material support

This most obviously concerns wages but whereas wages may constitute all the means of material support they should be regarded initially as only one such means. For varied in structure (as well as level) as wages themselves can be, additional material support may be forthcoming from several other sources. Workers may do other jobs. They may have other sources of income, from family, from land and elsewhere. Also pertinent is that non-wage welfare benefits may be made by the same employer, thus increasing dependency, or by the state, thus reducing it.

Burawoy himself has always devoted considerable attention to wages (Burawoy 1976; 1979) but in *The Politics of Production* it is very clear that he is fully aware of the importance of that particular sort of freedom which spells the freedom to starve. It is vital to his understanding of the hegemonic regime that this 'freedom' is attenuated by various forms of state provision including welfare benefits and labour rights legislation. When briefly discussing Japan, Burawoy draws attention to the same issue from the other way round and argues that the unusually low level of state-provided social insurance compounds employees' subordination, making them dependent on the enterprise welfare system for housing, pensions, sickness benefits, and so on (1985: 145). It may be said, then, that there are a whole number of facets of material support, which merit consideration in understanding factory regimes, all of which broaden the scope beyond concern with ideological control. Burawoy's work is an excellent starting point from which to become sensitised to such issues. Needless to say their variability is such that the above examples are very far from being exhaustive. There is one respect, though, in which Burawoy's account lacks an important dimension. This concerns contract.

Contract

Included here may be employment by means of full time or part time work, by permanent or temporary work or fixed contract and agency work etc. There is now a voluminous literature on this area in the West with considerable debate about what in some accounts is referred to as 'fragmentation of labour' and in others as 'flexible' or 'contingent work' (Castells 1996; Harvey 1999; Beck 2000; Booth et al 2000; Cam et al 2003). It is quite possible that Burawoy did not say much about this (Burawoy 1985: 264) because such issues were less prominent at the time he wrote than they are today. By contrast, later writers have placed very considerable emphasis on them. Standing, for example, points to a long term trend toward more flexible labour markets, which he sees to have been accentuated by pressures of globalisation, privatisation of production and social policy, new technologies and the competitive pressures on managements (Standing 1997): He argues:

> There has been a trend toward more insecure, irregular forms of employment, typically also involving lower social wages, less representation security and fewer social entitlements. More companies have been turning away from reliance wholly or largely on full-time workers to use of temporary workers, part-time workers, contract labour and out-workers, and have been sub-contracting or using other forms of 'outsourcing'.

He continues:

> This pattern has been prevalent in South East Asian economies for many years, and was one reason for their low social wage, and thus a contributing factor to their economic dynamism. In recent years, as many studies have shown, a trend in that direction has become widespread in Europe and other industrialised labour markets (1997: 19).

We are fully convinced that the analysis of factory regimes should include not only labour control but material support and contract issues (and the latter two are clearly brought together in Standing's own account).[6] But there are some features of his account that need to be treated with caution.

With respect to contract, Standing presents data from ILO and OECD sources for selected industrialised countries 1973–1993 that show non-regular work to have increased as a percentage of total employment among the

18 countries for which he has information. However it needs to be appreciated that in two out of three of Standing's countries the largest component in non-regular work is part time work. In the case of the UK for example non regular work accounts for 40 per cent of total employment and over half of this (23 per cent) is accounted for by part time employment (1997: 20: Table 3). More pertinently for a sector study such as this one, the situation often differs according to sector within the same country. In the case of UK manufacturing, for example, less than 10 per cent of employees are part time (LFS 2002). In other words, what applies for one type of non-regular employment does not necessarily hold for another and aggregate figures can mislead about what is happening in a particular sector. The lack of attention to particular sectors has been a common deficiency in much popular discussion of 'flexibility' and comparative research into factory regimes in the same sector is thin on the ground.

In what follows, a brief restatement is attempted of the context in which the three East Asian factories in the white goods sector operate and on labour control and the use of new management methods in these companies. Consideration then turns to changes that have recently taken place within them in material support and contract.

The three East Asian companies in context

ChinaCo

In Europe, much that forms the impression of foreign companies in China is based on reports and hearsay about a numerically dominant, though still particular sector, represented by often foot-loose Chinese capital from Hong Kong or Taiwan. Such operations, predominately in the low-skill, labour-intensive sectors of industry are infamous for their treatment of labour and in particular rural migrants (Chan 1997a; Zhang 2000; Choi 2003). ChinaCo, by contrast, is currently owned by a major European white goods company. It started life in the state sector, then became a joint venture company in 1996 and since 1999 it has been 100 per cent foreign owned. It produces for the quality end of the refrigerator market in China, though its management is proud that it operates at such a standard as to be able to export some units to Europe. In January 2002 it had a labour force of circa 1,100.

TaiwanCo

TaiwanCo is a joint venture company, which is largely owned by the Japanese partner. TaiwanCo's highest level managers have been Japanese and it has been necessary for all top managers to speak the language. The company produces predominantly for the home refrigerator market with the 20 per cent of production that is exported, going mainly to hot countries where its design is at a technical advantage. In January 2002 the company had a labour force of circa 2,860. Although Taiwan is often depicted as a Newly Industrialising Country (NIC), it is relevant to the company's specific situation that it has been making refrigerators since the mid-1960s and has a considerable number of long service employees. Also relevant is that the company has come increasingly under pressure from the cheap refrigerator imports from China.

SKoreaCo

SKoreaCo is a Korean company that is substantially export oriented. Its refrigerator plant had a labour force of circa 1,110 in 2002. It has largely avoided the adverse consequences of the 1997 Asian crisis. A decisive change in its recent history can be readily understood in the context of the 'authoritarian, patriarchal, and despotic authority' that permeated both small and large industrial enterprises prior to the more favourable labour market of the mid-1980s (Koo 2001) and the coming to an end of three decades of military rule in 1987. The country's rapid industrialisation in the Park Chung-hee era (1961–79) had combined a relentless focus on exports and neglect of the domestic market, widespread corruption, the imposition of low wages and ruthless domination of the labour movement. All this and in particular the extreme abuse of workers, had bred a deeply resentful labour force and SKoreaCo workers were themselves resentful at the way they had been treated. They struck in 1989. They occupied the factory and took company managers hostage. Workers report that the then Head of the company was in fear of his life and shaking uncontrollably. This, for the workers, was – and still is – something to savour. For management, it was a traumatic event.

As a result of the strike, and fearful of where such resentment might lead, SKoreaCo management increased wages one hundred per cent. But both managers and workers agree that the strike brought about a major change of attitude on the part of the management. After the strike managers went to the length of bowing to workers when they entered the factory. At first workers regarded this with some cynicism but managers continued to do this every day for so long that many workers came to see it as evidence of managers' new-found good intentions. Managers also started to come to work early and to clean the car park, cafeteria and other areas. They still do. Workers have also often come to take this as a sign of real change. Some go as far as to arrive early to help the managers. They say that after the strike, managers started to treat them like human beings.

A further sign of the ending of the previously despotic labour regime has been that managers now chose to eat with workers in the same dining room. Eating in the same dining room is a small sign (though a not insignificant one, given the traditional rigidities of Korean society). However, for managers to bow to workers and to volunteer to do menial tasks was, from the workers' point of view, extraordinary. (A lot is heard nowadays about 'high performance workplaces' and often in the same breath, 'high commitment work practices'. Unremarkably, the retailers of high commitment remedies never seem to exhort *managers* to engage in practices like these.)

Labour control

The attempt by management to elicit commitment to a common goal on the basis that all interests demand this, and the use of 'modern' management techniques to this end, is well advanced in all three companies.

In ChinaCo modern management methods are imported from the European parent company which conducts benchmarking exercises. The MNC's own quality management system is used. The managing director sums up the gist of it in a way that echoes the ideas behind lean production – 'Reduce! Reduce!' A variety of modern quality and statistical control programmes are used. There are no Quality Circles as such but a special department is charged with passing information down and with attracting suggestions up. Teams of 12 to 24 people are asked to solve a problem each month and team leaders, appointed by management, hold short meetings before work starts each day. Neither teams nor requests to make suggestions are novel for Chinese workers. But the stress on performance measurement and the relation of this to reward is. Team performance is assessed every month, individual performance every six months.

In TaiwanCo the import of goods from China, where they can be produced more cheaply, makes workers fully aware that the company is under pressure. A full blown ideological offensive reinforces the view that everyone's fate is tied to the company and the importance of meeting the needs of customers, a term that is used with reference to 'customers' outside and inside the company. Promotional materials make much of the ideas of peace, happiness and prosperity and the need for harmonious industrial relations.

TaiwanCo has always put a strong emphasis on workers making suggestions. In 1988–89 about 70 suggestions per worker were recorded. But management did not always find these very useful, as a consequence of which the making of suggestions was made integral to the operation of teamworking the following year. The team idea came from Japan and there are about 12 workers plus supervisors and managers per team. The teams meet once a month to discuss productivity and quality and now contribute the equivalent of over 20 (according to management, more useful) suggestions per worker. There is an extensive training programme which plays an important role in promotion and also includes courses in self development and Japanese.

The Japanese parent company provides some technical and marketing experience and is the source of most management techniques. Information on new techniques is provided through its overseas training system. The company has its own version of lean production with the usual emphasis on using half the resources and half the cost. A JIT system is in place though its operation is frustrated by traffic problems.

There is resistance to accepting ideas from other companies more than necessary and Japanese methods are preferred to American ones. Six Sigma is an exception to this. It came into the factory via work performed elsewhere in the company on a sub contract basis for Ford, with Ford initially providing the training in order to secure good quality materials from the company. The actual defect rate attained is currently 64 per million rather than the ultimate Six Sigma standard of 3.4 but the stress on the reduction of defects is manifest throughout the factory. Workers provide lists of problems for consideration at daily meetings of managers.

In South Korea, like to a lesser extent Taiwan, the effects of the 1997 Asian crisis are well known to workers, even though their own company was not badly affected because of the cheapened price of its exports. Benchmarking is conducted against all major competitors world-wide and the results of such exercises are prominently displayed inside the factory. The company draws on its knowledge of management methods world-wide, especially from Japan and the USA. The company was influenced by Toyota until the late 1980s and early 1990s and it began to implement Six Sigma, obtained via GE later in the decade. Six Sigma was introduced along with a programme which fed information about the firm's objectives and performance to workers through a system of terminals, which also enabled workers to make suggestions. Managers report that the flow of suggestions is so great and so continuous that they have passed the stage of bothering to count them. A Digital Manufacturing System is being introduced.

The company emphasises the importance of joint endeavour. Workers are organised in teams of 5–7 people. Joint problem solving projects are undertaken – not least in the so-called Tear Down (Crying) Room where managers, workers and R & D specialists stay together as long as necessary to hammer out solutions to production problems. About 30 per cent of workers go through this process a year. The sharp contrast between the lack of dignity accorded to workers in the past and the approach followed today is acknowledged by managers and workers alike.

Material support and contract

Features that in the West are commonly associated with the ideological apparatus of hegemonic despotism are well in place in all three companies – the HRM emphasis on teams, suggestions, information about the company's position and the attempt to forge a company identity. But to review the three companies historically with respect to workers' means of material support and contract is to see something else – that the dismantling of established labour is also well underway. To anticipate: the term 'established labour' rather than for example 'corporate labour' is used in an attempt to encompass some broadly similar dimensions of employment in (pre capitalist) China as well as in the recent past in Taiwan and South Korea. The dismantling of such labour is seen to take two major although not mutually exclusive forms. In one of these, the proportion of workers who are relatively privileged is reduced whether by sacking, natural wastage, induced retirement or other means. In the other, the material support extended to such workers is reduced.

ChinaCo

ChinaCo has lived through the so-called 'smashing of the iron rice bowl' – the reforms introduced in the early 1990s which had major effects on the means of material support and employment. Before the reforms the state sector industrial worker had typically been assigned to a work unit (*danwei*) which was also the basis for the registration of *hukou*, the residential status of citizens. This has meant for example that many of the workers at ChinaCo, who had worked for the SOE, had urban, not rural, origins. The *danwei* supplied among other things, housing, education, medical care, pensions and ration cards for basic foods and other essentials. The list of 'social services' provided by large industrial enterprises could be extensive. A list of 'social services' provided by large industrial enterprises in 1985 included the provision of enterprise-owned housing, care personnel and hospital beds, the support of nursery school children and of students in elementary and secondary education, also the support of workers' vocational and post-secondary study and the provision of library books and recreational facilities (Naughton 1997).

At ChinaCo there are still a few workers who live in the houses that the SOE had provided for them. There are also a few employees, mostly single clerical and administrative staff who come from another city, who live in a company dormitory, but in keeping with state policy the company has now instituted a housing accumulation fund. What has happened on the housing front has also been happening with medical provision. A free medical system has been replaced by a medical insurance system which started in 1991. The kindergarten no longer exists.

At the same time that non-wage material benefits have become less workplace-dependent the actual wages received by ChinaCo's workers have improved. These had fallen in the early 1990s when the SOE lacked profitability but they are now considerably higher than those offered in all but one of the city's other factories. It is not just the size of the wage but the wage system that has undergone considerable transformation over the past decade however. Under the SOE, the wage system was based on different grades, each of which was decided by the state, and which made some allowance for seniority. In the mid-1990s a new structure was implemented, the so-called 'post-skill system' which excluded seniority and gave more scope to the recognition of performance criteria. ChinaCo's private management has carried the link to performance yet further. Today, the company operates with a series of wage grades. There is no seniority pay and wages themselves consist of three parts. The first part, the basic wage, accounts for only 40 per cent. There is a further element of 30 per cent for team achievement (based on the workshop level and with emphasis placed on the idea that each section is the customer of the other). Then there is another 30 per cent element which relates to individual performance, assessed at six month intervals. In other words, 60 per cent of the wage is determined by management's assessment of performance. Managers claim that in 90 per cent of cases workers will receive around the full 60 per cent performance related pay elements. But this is not guaranteed. In fact, it might be said that this is the whole idea.

The change represented by the new payment system is nothing as compared to the change that has taken place in contract. The *danwei* system had not only formed the basis for various welfare benefits but for a distinctive form of employment – in effect, lifetime employment. By 1992, following a period of experimentation, about one in six workers in China was employed on the basis of contract (National Bureau of Statistics 1996: 107). The new system has been unevenly implemented in the SOE sector and it is claimed that there is a much higher rate of implementation by foreign owned companies with the consequence that, in so far as state workers are absorbed into this system, their contracts will shorten and their insecurity increase (Gallagher 2001: 31–32). At ChinaCo such effects are evident already.

A striking feature of the implementation of the new labour contract system at ChinaCo, following the 1995 Labour Law, is that there is a standard two year contract for workers. The Labour Law provides that those workers who have worked in the same company for more than ten years have the right to seek to negotiate an open-ended contract – but there are still workers at ChinaCo who have worked much longer than this and remain on fixed contracts. In a few cases, too, management has smiled on workers with considerably less service and made them permanent.

Fixed contract workers make up about 60 per cent of the labour force, the remainder largely consists of workers made permanent, with a smaller proportion hired on the basis of three month contracts, largely to cover seasonal fluctuations. These temporary workers began to be recruited in 1997. They are paid on the bottom grade, less than the two-year contract workers, and they can be re-employed.

During the planned economy period, the managers of SOEs had little right to select workers and workers were allocated to jobs from which they could not be fired. At ChinaCo, the new labour contract system made it possible for the number of workers to be cut by half during the joint venture period. But the proportionate change in the types of contract is no less striking and has generally drawn less attention outside China (Figure 8.4).

Managers at ChinaCo are alive to the possibility of shortening the assembly line and contracting out work. Indeed they say 'This is the future'. For the present, they are not convinced of the cost advantages of this, nor are there sub-contractors available in the area to which they could reliably entrust the work. As for agency workers, agents who would be able to reliably supply agency (or 'dispatched') labour are again not yet available in the area.

Generally, though, the shift from jobs for life to contract worker status, from a situation in which managers could not sack workers to one in which they can, and the shift to a wage system that is 60 per cent performance-related, all mean a definite weakening of the worker's position. In addition, the extensive array of work-based benefits that applied to established workers has diminished in relation to those employed in other ways. The labour flexibility that the two year contract system gives ChinaCo management is a long way removed from the European social democratic ideal of 'Rhineland capitalism' and as the current Managing Director comments wistfully: 'This we have not got in Europe'.

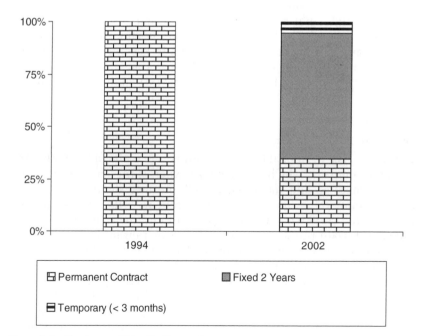

Figure 8.4   Contract – ChinaCo Proportions

The role of the trade union has also diminished. The union had never been confrontational but in a system in which social and welfare provision had been directly attached to the enterprise the trade union had played a major role in administering this. It played a role in allocating housing and in workers' welfare. It had also played some role in recruitment, which is no longer the case. It had also encouraged labour discipline, run productivity campaigns and mediated between workers and managers (and workers and workers) in individual disputes. These functions continue, albeit in relation to private profit rather than as in earlier times the fulfilment of a plan but even here the union is undermined by the activities of a separate company department dedicated to 'direct communication' between workers and managers. Since 1998, workers have elected representatives to 'communication teams' in order to take various problems and suggestions to the company through this separate department, these teams also operating as downward channels of communication from the company.

Whereas the Party reigns supreme at the level of the society as a whole, both the union and the party are marginalised at enterprise level. The formal status of the trade union Chairman (a former manager in the previous joint venture, who is also the party secretary) has fallen in relation to that of the enterprise director. The Chairman (who like two other union officials is paid by the company) has petitioned for collective bargaining rights but to no avail. The Chairman also wants the fixed proportion of wages to be higher. Even so, he clings to the idea that the company is 'a big family', a view more in keeping with the *danwei* system to which people did indeed belong as they did to a family, for life (Chan 1997b; Feng 1989) than the new system, based on contract and profit, and indeed, the fixed contract worker.

TaiwanCo

TaiwanCo has been making refrigerators since the mid-1960s. The Japanese company, which is the major owner, is the source of its management methods and managers are well informed about developments in that country to which they make frequent visits. They point out that lifetime employment has come to an end in Japan and that the pressures toward this are now no different in Taiwan. In keeping with this, seniority pay is being decreased. The attempt is also being made to reduce the core of permanent employees.[7]

The company faces particular problems with permanent workers both because their pay is seniority-based, which makes them costly, and because those with long service have every incentive to hang on to their employment in order to qualify for a pension. To be eligible for a retirement payment requires 26 years continuous service with the same employer and almost 45 per cent of the workers in the refrigerator plant already have 21 years service or more.

Demand for the company's products has been falling and part of the management's solution to this problem has been to reduce the permanent workforce by natural wastage to almost half since 1996. Recently however a new tactic has been adopted, which develops further a policy first introduced at the end of 2001 – the use of agency labour. The policy is to offer permanent workers a financial incentive to retire early. Workers near to retirement are being told that if they go they can save the factory for another 20 years – and be re-employed as agency labour (at reduced wages). All agency labour is currently taken on through one agent. Such is management's commitment to the further development of this type of labour that it was attempting to drum up some competition by bringing other agents into play and reducing the size of his fee. Meanwhile, workers offered an agency deal are told that if they don't accept, everyone will suffer.

At TaiwanCo two developments are taking place at the same time. There is an overall fall in the number of permanent workers and there is also a reorganisation within the ranks of non-permanent labour. In the past, male foreign workers were employed from Thailand. However, managers claim they behaved badly and drank too much. They have now been replaced by Filipino workers, usually female, who are better educated and, as reported by management, better behaved. They are employed on three year contracts. The share of such workers in the labour force is not scheduled to increase significantly however. Company policy is now to fill any vacancies with, first, retired workers in the guise of agency labour, second, young Filipino women, third temporary workers and fourth school leavers. On a straight pay comparison, agency workers cost more than Filipinos but they are only half the price of permanent workers and of course they have the same – or even greater – experience of doing the job, which is helpful for the maintenance of quality. Moreover, compared to temporary workers, who can only work for less than a year, they face no such legal restriction.

TaiwanCo is making moves to contract out more of the labour process. Panel cutting is being put out, also various wiring work. All cleaning and catering is contracted out already. Compressors are now imported (partly to help conform to NCFC requirements). Generally, though, agency labour is the preferred policy. The rise of agency work is the big change and it has occurred rapidly and is planned to continue (Figure 8.5).

The company union was established in 1965 and has collective bargaining rights. It occupies a salubrious office with lots of government awards displayed on its walls but no sign of campaigning posters, let alone of past historic struggles. Union officials talk of its purpose as to protect employees and increase productivity and they look favourably on

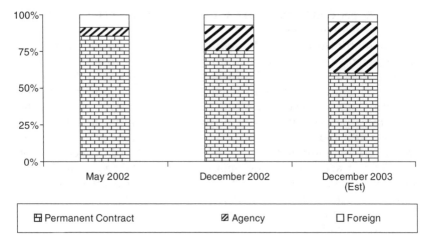

Figure 8.5   Contract – TaiwanCo Proportions

management practice toward retired agency workers, though stating
that they would like them to be paid more. Not being 'employees' of
TaiwanCo, agency workers are not organised by the union.

SKoreaCo

In the 1990s large firms or *chaebols* in South Korea implemented new management strategies. These often entailed the introduction of Personnel and
HRM Departments. Moves were made toward a reduction of authoritarian-
ism, the personal abuse and denigration of workers and the ending of such
personal interference as regulating the length of workers' hair and subject-
ing them to regular exercise. Status distinctions between blue- and white-
collar workers – which had been marked – were reduced with respect to
such matters as access to cafeterias, provision of bus transport and styles of
dress. At the same time, as part of a 'company culture movement', familial
language was deployed and educational programmes, clubs and festivals
were provided. It was in line with such developments that Hyundai Heavy
Industries is reported to have provided its employees with apartments,
college tuition fees for children, health insurance, a gymnasium, theatre
and other recreational facilities for their families (Koo 2001: 211). Such
benefits are relatively well in evidence at SKoreaCo. For instance, there is a
'families' scheme' which includes regular three day seminars during which
families are encouraged to discuss and share their problems. Amongst the
non-wage material benefits provided by the company are high school and
university fees for workers' children (university fees are about £4,000 per
year); free accommodation for unmarried workers; two free meals per day;
free transport to and from work; free work uniforms (though wearing them
is no longer compulsory).

The above and other company-related benefits have to be seen against the fact that the proportion of state government expenditure devoted to health, housing, social security and welfare has been extremely low (You 1995). However, some material benefits (like the payment of education fees for workers' children) are reserved for permanent workers. The same preferential treatment of permanent workers is evident when it comes to wages. Basic wages are low in relation to take-home pay, which, for the permanent workers, is good for South Korea generally, even if not as good as that obtained from employers in some nearby heavy industry. Basic wages are supplemented, amongst other things, by additional pay for gaining extra qualifications; by two per cent per year annual increments for seniority and by an annual profit-share payment at the end of each year (company profit is divided equally between re-investment, shareholder dividend, and employees). Profit sharing is only for permanent employees however. Moreover, whereas permanent employees get a bonus of eight hundred per cent of basic annual salary (divided into 8 equal amounts and paid every other month plus New Year and Harvest Festival), non-permanent workers get bonus at half this rate, four hundred per cent.

The distinctions made above between permanent and other workers are necessary because, as at ChinaCo where a drastic shift has occurred from life-time employment to contract labour, and as at TaiwanCo, where a less drastic change is being made to introduce agency labour, so at SKoreaCo a change is taking place in contract. The change means a decline in the permanent proportion of the work force and a pronounced increase in agency labour – paid at about half the permanent rate.

A major event in recent South Korean political economy is clearly the 1997 Asian crisis. Under pressure from the IMF, banks were forced to wipe extensive bad loans from their balance sheets and about half the 30 *chaebols*, which dominated the economy, were shut down. It is tempting therefore to attribute changes in contract directly to this. Although the IMF rescue package meant the pursuit of increased labour market flexibility to permit extensive corporate restructuring, the timing was a little more complicated (Kim 2002). The attempt to reform the labour law was first made in 1996 via a tripartite Commission for Reform of Industrial Relations. However, the law that resulted did little to appease trade unions, who wanted an improved legal position in exchange for increased labour flexibilities. This led to the first nation-wide general strike since 1948, following which amendments were made which inter alia postponed the legalisation of flexible working hours and redundancies for two years. After the 1997 crisis, and the threat of economic collapse, the newly established Kim Dae-jung Government then over-rode the moratorium on the implementation of these provisions in the name of national unity. It is the outcome of this legislation, which legalised layoffs and temporary work agencies that has had profound consequences for many hitherto established workers (Chang 2003).

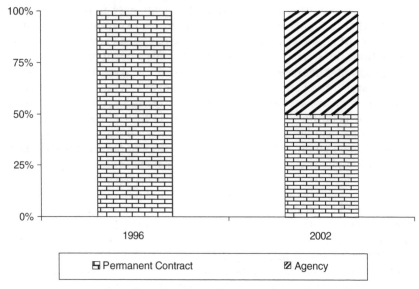

Figure 8.6   Contract – SKoreaCo Proportions

At SKoreaCo about 50 per cent of those who work in the fridge plant are now agency workers (Figure 8.6). Managers are very careful to refer to them as 'co-operating company workers' and not as 'employees' in an attempt to escape legal problems about continued employment (there are no such legal problems in Taiwan and China). But de facto these agency workers are employed by the company. They are managed by the same managers as are permanent employees and the agents themselves are former SKoreaCo managers. Agency workers are simply treated worse in term of pay and they miss out on other non-wage material benefits. They are also not permitted – since they are not 'employees' – to join the company trade union.[8]

In this particular company, the increased proportion of agency workers has not meant redundancies in the total number of permanent workers partly because of natural wastage but more importantly because production has increased. However, such casualisation of employment has meant that SKoreaCo has made significant reductions in wages per unit of output – by employing agency labour, paying it less, and making further savings with respect to seniority pay and other costly benefits. Moreover, another change in contract, allied to increased mechanisation, has meant a clear reduction in the number of SKoreaCo employees required to produce given products. This entails increased resort to sub contractors. More and more work has been 'exported' from the factory to sub contractors, whose labour costs are lower than those of SKoreaCo.

Such is the change that within a few years the length of the assembly line has been cut from 150 metres to 50 metres. Sub contractors are being encouraged to supply ever more extensive sub-assemblies.

The union, like the one at TaiwanCo, is a company union. It is affiliated to the Federation of Korean Trade Unions (FKTU), which was a direct extension of the state under Park Chung-hee and is still widely identified as the home of yellow unionism. The SKoreaCo union has very well appointed offices which are part of the management's own office accommodation, where they were deliberately re-located after the 1989 strike. Union officers are well disposed to modern management methods, which are seen to increase production and to be good for employment. They argue that the growth of agency labour has meant that redundant workers from other companies could be given jobs and they hope that in the long term 'the best' agency workers may come to be employed on a permanent basis.

In general terms the political transition to democracy in South Korea after 1987 led the state to assume a more neutral stance toward trade unionism and at the same time the despotic company management style gradually gave way to a more subtle form of control. Using Burawoy's terms, Koo (2001) describes the process as a change from 'despotic factory regime' to 'hegemonic regime', since the former was based on coercion, the latter primarily on consent and the institutional separation of state and factory apparatuses. But the point to note is that any such hegemonic regime is of relatively recent origin and it has also proved short-lived. For here, too, the dismantling of the established worker is now well advanced.

In short, in all three cases, a major reduction has occurred, over a short number of years, in the proportion of the labour force that is employed on a permanent basis and in TaiwanCo and ChinaCo there has been an absolute reduction as well. In TaiwanCo and ChinaCo the provision of work-based non-wage material means of support to more privileged workers (who are now clearly aware that they are on open-ended contracts rather than life-time ones) has also been reduced.

Within Europe, the British market is often regarded as a model of flexibility. However, the contrast between each of these cases and the situation of the domestic appliance industry in Britain, and with British manufacturing in general, is marked – much more marked than general talk about globalisation and flexibility would suggest. As was reported in Chapter 2, according to official data for 2002, 96 per cent of contracts in domestic appliances in Britain were permanent, under 4 per cent were fixed term or agency or casual or otherwise temporary and this was very much in line with British

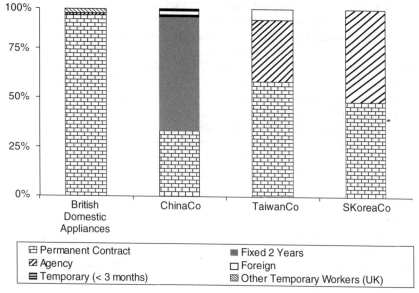

Figure 8.7   Contract – British Domestic Appliances, ChinaCo, TaiwanCo and SKoreaCo (2002/2003) Proportions
Source: Data for British domestic appliances from LFS, November 2002.

manufacturing as a whole (Figure 8.7). So sharp is this difference that it is difficult to exaggerate its importance. And despite the comments cited earlier from Standing, about patterns of irregular employment having been prevalent in South East Asia for many years, in these three East Asian companies in the big company white goods sector the changes, in all cases, are recent.

Final reflections

All three of the East Asian companies might be said to fit a general category of hegemonic despotism as far as the means of labour control are concerned. Workers in all these factories are urged to identify with their enterprise and there are mechanisms in all of them – teams, flows of information, QCs and their equivalents – to involve workers and to elicit their identification with the enterprise. In SKoreaCo, in particular, workers are bombarded by verbal, pictorial and electronic information about the company's relative position world wide. In other words, as far as labour control is concerned there is little here to surprise when judged against what passes as best international HRM practice. Much the same applies to the technology used in these firms. Although there are differences in the particular production functions that are performed in each factory, modern technology is generally utilised. Again, managers in all the companies are knowledgeable about modern management methods. Similar methods of management are used in all three companies.

As judged from Europe, the key difference concerns contract. The need for increased flexibility has been frequently claimed by governments in Europe over the last two decades and is now to be heard loud and clear in Germany, the home of 'Rhineland capitalism'. In Germany there are problems in laying- off people. Any business with more than five people must set up a works council if employees request it and it must submit all redundancy decisions to this. Unfair dismissal legislation means that there must be evidence that redundancies are unavoidable (Benoit 2003). What needs to be remembered is that this also used to be the case, again in companies with five or more employees, in Korea (Kim and Kim 2003: 347). Labour is by no means so well protected in 'Anglo-Saxon' capitalism. In the UK, for example, the highest compensation for redundancy required by law for any worker in 2003 was less than £8,000, no matter how many years service and no matter how high their earnings had been. But the degree of contract flexibility is still considerably greater in contemporary ChinaCo, TaiwanCo and SKoreaCo.

A major transformation has taken place in contract in these companies – and this has happened recently. The dismantling process followed different routes in each case. In ChinaCo the replacement of permanent labour with contract labour was made possible by a deliberate decision at the level of the state to introduce labour law which superseded the benefits to labour (and potential costs to capital) of a work unit-based system of welfare. In TaiwanCo, the increase in agency labour was resorted to by management who cited increased international competition in the context of constraints imposed by pension eligibility rules. In SKoreaCo the introduction of agency labour was again made possible by a deliberate decision at the level of the state (prompted by the IMF) to open a way for employers to circumvent pension and other obligations to those employed for more than a year.

The implications of the change in contract for gender balance vary between firms. At ChinaCo and TaiwanCo for example there are no sharp differences in the distribution of men and women across different means of employment other than in the small number of foreign workers at TaiwanCo who are exclusively Filipino women. At SKoreaCo by contrast the proportion of men in the permanent labour force increased from 60 to 85 per cent between 1996 and 2003 and the new temporary agency workers are 60 per cent women. The implications of these changes for job loss are also variable. In ChinaCo half the labour force went following the 1995 Labour Law. In TaiwanCo there has again been reduction. At SKoreaCo on the other hand the fact that the restructuring of contract has taken place in the context of the company's (far from typical) expanded production after 1997 has not had severe consequences for the net number of established workers (as opposed to the proportion of all such workers in the workforce).

All these developments have the effect of dismantling established labour as a proportion of the workforce however and it seems unlikely that the focus on these particular companies exaggerates what is happening. In China for example one year contracts are more common in the private sector than the two year contract at ChinaCo (Gallagher 2001). In South Korea, more than half of all employed workers (approximately 54 per cent) are now either temporary (about two thirds of them) or daily workers (OECD 2002). In TaiwanCo, management felt that they had held back longer than other companies in engaging agency labour.

Whichever route has been taken to change the contract composition of the workforce this is being pursued to an extent that deserves note in its own right. It represents an important structural change which is not necessarily apparent if the focus is on labour control issues and which is especially striking when considered in the manufacturing sector.

On reflection, it is the extent and rapidity of the change in contract in the East Asian companies that has struck us as the most significant development in factory regimes. In seeking to reinforce this point we drew attention to the different contract relations that characterise white goods industry in Britain and indeed British manufacturing more generally. In doing so, it might appear that we have provided chapter and verse for those who would see it to be only a matter of time before market pressures led to such contractual relations as fixed term contracts and agency labour everywhere. Such economism neatly overlooks the power of the state and the fact that in most societies such an outcome would require the state to intervene, to re-regulate the economy and in particular the rights of labour. In the present context, however, such a conclusion would overlook another relevant finding: that all three of the Turkish white goods factories, and the Brazilian factory in this study, had a contract profile like the one presented for Britain in Figure 8.7.

In Turkey, all the production workers were permanent with the exception of seasonal temporary workers. Sub-contracted 'tacheron' workers are confined, by the nature of the labour law, to non-production functions. In Brazil, the story is much the same: at BrazilCo, labour legislation, and the power of the trade union, keep the labour force predominately permanent. Of course labour law is not enough by itself. It needs to be enforced (as the law on agency labour in South Korea remains to be). Of course, too, the situation is not static. Recently, the Turkish state has passed legislation that may alter the situation in that country. In particular, in an attempt to make the Turkish labour market attractive for international capital and pave the way for EU entry, a new labour law was passed in 2003 which, among other things, legalised private employment agencies, made it legal for employers to vary working hours unilaterally and, following Japan's lead, to lend their employees to other companies (Nichols and Sugur 2004: 204–6). In Brazil, a tripartite National Labour Forum currently deliberates on trade union reform, the long term results of which for trade unions remain to be seen.

Meanwhile, in the factories reviewed in this book – in China, Taiwan, South Korea, Brazil and Turkey – and , from what we have seen, in the UK too – workers in the industry are working in similar working conditions and subject to similar modern management methods. They are however subject to very different contracts. This does not fit an interpretation of globalisation as a universalising process. Privileged as these workers may have been in the past, on the basis of local comparison, their desire that their children should not follow in their footsteps should also remind us that, for them, to labour in a global world has been a mixed blessing.

Notes

1 A standard question on what workers thought of foreign companies was omitted in Korea, our colleague taking the view that the lack of knowledge of foreign workers at SKoreaCo was such that they would be unable to answer it.

2 As reported in the Preface, the research in South Africa was not strictly based on the standard questionnaire used in China, Taiwan, South Korea, Brazil and Turkey, and is therefore excluded from most comparisons in this chapter.

3 Tables in this chapter are for single companies in the case of ChinaCo (n = 50), Taiwan Co (n = 51), SKoreaCo (n = 50) and BrazilCo (n = 51). In the case of Turkey, we have data available on three white goods factories. It seemed arbitrary to choose any one of these for comparison and data in this chapter are based on an average of all three companies (n = 53, n = 50 and n = 50), hence, in tables and elsewhere, 'Turkey3Co'. The Turkish data are disaggregated by company at various points in Chapter 6 and in Nichols, Sugur and Demir 2002; and Nichols and Sugur 2004.

4 The results for Taiwan reflect the moves being made at the time of the fieldwork to reduce the labour force against the backcloth of a long established paternalist tradition.

5 WERS 98 consisted of a survey of over 28,000 employees (Cully et al 1999: 9). Because we have sometimes used identical questions, we have drawn both upon data for employees in British manufacturing as a whole and upon information on workers in one particular white goods establishment, which we refer to as the 'UK comparator'. In WERS 98 self-completion questionnaires were distributed to 25 employees per establishment. There were two establishments that operated in the domestic appliance industry. Figures cited here are for a WERS 98 manufacturer of electric domestic appliances, which had 24 respondents out of 25. This establishment had over 1,000 employees and was one of 16 such establishments in a foreign owned multinational (further information is not available for reasons of confidentiality). The other establishment, results for which are not reported here, was a manufacturer of non-electrical domestic appliances and its employees provided only 11 responses. Data reported here that apply to manufacturing as a whole are weighted. Data that refer to the comparator establishment are unweighted.

6 Standing's view of the 'social wage' provides another route to the *material support* issues that feature in Figure 1, which of course derive from Burawoy's

account. Standing sees the 'social wage (or income)' to comprise the money wage; fringe benefits paid by the employer; firm-level or employment-related 'occupational welfare', including, entitlements to cover contingency risks (ill health, short term involuntary unemployment, etc); social transfers from the state; and kinship-community transfers (1997: 19).

7   The three pillars of Japanese management have often been said to be lifetime employment, the seniority system and the company union. The decline in the first two of these in Japan is now widely acknowledged and in various ways there are parallels with developments in the three companies reviewed here. For example one report of developments in Toyota in Japan refers to a 'trend toward diversification of types of employment' (Fujita 1997). The tendency for non-permanent workers to play both a larger and more stable role in production at Toyota and other large companies in Japan is certainly evident in all three companies. The related shift from seniority- to performance-based factors in the wages system is equally evident, as, in the case of SKoreaCo, is increased sub-contracting. Another account of what has happened in large firms in Japan concludes that most of them still maintain a core of regular employees 'and some (diminished) benefits, but the proportion of the work-force with a regular status has diminished' (Bernier 2000: 36). This again resonates with the situations described in the East Asian cases.

8   A recent study of a large car company in Korea (Byoung-Hoon and Frenkel 2004) confirms several of the features reported above – increased employment of agency workers, in this case from 12 to 23 per cent of the total production workforce over a period of three years; the exclusion of these workers from the company union; and the pretence that they are not managed by the client company when, in fact, they are. In addition, these authors explore an aspect not investigated here, the relation between these workers and those with permanent status.

References

Babson, S. (1995) 'Lean Production and Labour: Empowerment and Exploitation' in S. Babson (ed.), *Lean Work, Employment and Exploitation in the Global Auto Industry*, Detroit: Wayne State University Press.

Beck, U. (2000) *The Brave New World of Work*, Cambridge: Polity Press.

Bendix, R. (1956) *Work and Authority in Industry: Ideologies of Management in the Course of Industrialisation*, New York: John Wiley & Sons.

Benoit, B. (2003) 'German Business Hindered by Labour Laws', *Financial Times*, 17 January.

Berggren, C. (1993) 'Lean Production – The End of History?', *Work, Employment and Society*, 7 (2).

Bernier, B. (2000) 'Flexibility, Rigidity and Reactions to Globalisation of the Japanese Labour Regime', *Capital and Society*, 33 (91).

Booth, A., Francesconi, M. and Frank, J. (2000) *Contingent Jobs: Who Gets Them, What Are They Worth and Do They Lead Anywhere?* Brighton: Institute for Social and Economic Research.

Burawoy, M. (1976) 'The Functions and Reproduction of Migrant Labour: Comparative Material from Southern Africa and the United States', *American Journal of Sociology*, 81 (5).

Burawoy, M. (1979) *Manufacturing Consent*, London: University of Chicago Press.

Burawoy, M. (1985) *The Politics of Production*, London: Verso.

Burawoy, M., Krotov, P. and Lytkina, T. (2000) 'Involution and Destitution in Capitalist Russia', *Ethnography*, 1 (1).

Byoung-Hoon, L. and Frenkel, S. (2004) 'Divided Workers: Social relations Between Contract and Regular Workers in a Korean Auto Company', *Work, Employment and Society*, 18 (3).

Cam, S., Purcell, J. and Tailby, S. (2003) 'Contingent Employment in the UK', in E. Bass and E. Ola (eds) *Contingent Employment in Europe*, Cheltenham: Edward Elgar.

Castells, M. (1996) *The Rise of the Network Society*, Volume 1, Oxford: Blackwell Publishers.

Chan, A. (1997a) 'Labor Relations in Foreign Funded Ventures' in G. O'Leary (ed.), *Adjusting to Capitalism: Chinese Workers and the State*, Armonk, New York: M. E. Sharpe.

Chan, A. (1997b) 'Chinese Danwei Reforms' in L. Lu Xiaobo & E. Perry (eds), *Danwei: The Changing Chinese Workplace in Historical and Comparative Perspective*, Armonk, New York: M. E. Sharpe.

Chang, D. (2003) 'Korean Labour Relations in transition: Authoritarian Flexibility', *Labour, Capital and Society*, 35 (1).

Choi, Y-J. (2003) 'Managerial Styles, Workforce Composition and Labor Unrest: East Asian-Invested Enterprises in China', *Comparative Sociology*, 2 (2).

Cole, R. E. (1979) *Work, Mobility, and Participation: A Comparative Study of American and Japanese Industry*, Berkeley: University of California Press.

Cully, M., Woodland, S., O'Reilly, A., and Dix, G. (1999) *Britain at Work: As Depicted by the 1998 Workplace Employee Relations Survey*, London: Routledge.

Danford, A. (1999) *Japanese Management Techniques and British Workers*, London: Mansell.

Elger, T. and Smith, C. (1994) 'Global Japanisation?' in T. Elger and C. Smith (eds) *Global Japanisation?: The Transitional Transformation Of The Labour Process*, London: Routledge.

Feng, L. (1989) 'DAN WEI – A Special Form of Social Organisation', *Social Sciences in China*, 3 (September).

Fujita, E. (1997) 'Changes in Employment Practices, Personnel Management and the Wage System at Toyota in an Era of Globalisation', *Journal of Humanities and Social Sciences* 3 (November).

Gallagher, M. (2001) *'Grafted Capitalism: Ownership Change and Labor Relations in the PRC'*. Paper presented at the Conference on Uneven Transition in China: Reform and Inequality, University of Michigan, 7 April.

Harvey, M. (1999) 'Economies of Time: A Framework for Analysing the Restructuring of Employment Relations' in A. Felstead and N. Jewson (eds) *Global Trends in Flexible Labour*, London: Macmillan Business.

Kim, D-O. and Kim, S. (2003) 'Globalisation, Financial Crisis, and Industrial Relations: The Case of South Korea', *Industrial Relations*, 42 (3).

Kim, Y. C. (2002) 'The Politics of Labour Reform under the Kim Dae-jung Government' in C.-i. Moon and D. I. Steinberg (eds), *Korea in Transition: Three Years under the Kim Dae-jung Government*, Seoul: Yonsei University Press.

Koo, H. (2001) *Korean Workers: The Culture and Politics of Class Formation*, Ithaca: Cornell University Press.

LFS (2002) *Labour Force Survey*, Autumn LFS data sets (accessed November 2003) http://www.data-archive.ac.uk/findingData/lfsAbstract.asp

Lincoln, J. and Kallenberg, A. (1990) *Culture, Control and Commitment: A Study of Work Organisation and Work Artefacts in the United States and Japan*, Cambridge: Cambridge University Press.

National Bureau of Statistics (1996) *Chinese Statistics Year Book*, Beijing: Chinese Statistics Press.

Naughton, B. (1997) *Danwei:* 'The Economic Foundations of a Unique Institution' in L. Lu Xiaobo and E. Perry (eds), *Danwei: The Changing Chinese Workplace in Historical and Comparative Perspective*, Armonk, New York: M. E. Sharpe.

Nichols, T. and Sugur, N. (2004) *Global Management, Local Labour: Turkish Workers and Modern Industry*, London: Palgrave-Macmillan.

Nichols, T., Sugur, N. and Demir, E. (2002) 'Globalised Management and Local Labour: The Case of the White Goods Industry in Turkey', *Industrial Relations Journal*, 33 (1).

OECD (2002) *Economic Surveys – South Korea*, Paris: OECD.

Standing, G. (1997) 'Globalisation, Labour Flexibility and Insecurity: The Era of Market Regulation', *European Journal of Industrial Relations*, 3 (1).

Stewart, P., Lewchuk, W., Yates, C., Saruta, M. and Danford, A. (2004) 'Patterns of Labour Control and the Erosion of Labour Standards' in Charron, E. and Stewart, P. (eds) *Work and Employment Relations in the Automobile Industry*, Palgrave Macmillan.

Womack, J. P., Jones, D. T. and Roos, D. (1990) *The Machine That Changed the World*, New York: Maxwell Macmillan International.

You, J.-I. (1995) 'Changing Capital-Labour Relations in South Korea' in J. Schor and J.-I. You (eds), *Capital, the State and Labour: A Global Perspective*, Cheltenham: Edward Elgar.

Zhang, Y. (2000) 'State Power and Labor-Capital Relations in Foreign-Invested Enterprises in China: The Case of Shandong Province', *Issues & Studies*, 36 (3).

Index